AF572381

AMERICA'S HIVE of HONEY,

or

Foreign influences on American fiction through Henry James:

Essays & Bibliographies

By DAVID KIRBY

The Scarecrow Press, Inc.
Metuchen, N.J., & London 1980

BOOKS BY DAVID KIRBY

Individual and Community: Variations on a Theme in American Fiction (coedited with Kennedy H. Baldwin)

Grace King

American Fiction to 1900: A Guide to Information Sources

The Opera Lover

Excerpts from the following copyrighted works are reprinted by permission: Herman Melville: The Tragedy of Mind by William Ellery Sedgwick, copyright © 1945, Harvard University Press. The Road to Xanadu by John Livingston Lowes, copyright © 1927, Houghton Mifflin.

Library of Congress Cataloging in Publication Data

Kirby, David K
America's hive of honey.

Includes index.
1. American Fiction--Foreign influences--Addresses, essays, lectures. 2. American fiction--Foreign influences--Bibliogrpahy. I. Title.
PS374.F64K57 813'.009'3 80-20672
ISBN 0-8108-1349-1

Manufactured in the United States of America

This book is dedicated to

Douglas Fowler,

encyclopédiste sans encyclopédie,

who, if modesty allowed, could say truthfully,

in the words of Goethe's Faust,

"Of course, I am smarter than all the shysters,

The doctors, and teachers, and Scribes, and Christers."

"At present we can only get along with the old English writers, and we find that they are the hive from which all modern honey is stolen."

-- Sophia Hawthorne, in a letter to Mrs. Caleb Foote, December, 1942

"All great writers have robbed the hives of diligent bees and, paradoxically, genius might be said to be the faculty for clever theft."

-- Enid Starkie, Arthur Rimbaud

TABLE OF CONTENTS

EXTRACTS

Not even the famous comparison of lovers to compasses is necessarily original: we find it embedded in a madrigal by the Italian poet G. B. Guarini, published in 1598. Donne's poem is said to have been written thirteen years later.

-- Hugh Kenner, on "A Valediction Forbidding Mourning"

Italian literature provided him with an education and, in keeping with the habits of the time, a storehouse from which to borrow plots, situations, even characters. Such petty thievery was not only commonplace but recommended in the interests of artistic continuity --provided the jewels were then artfully recut.

-- William Byron, Cervantes: A Biography

Don Quixote is perhaps the most seminal novel ever written. We know for a certainty that Flaubert and Dostoevsky owe to the one-armed hero of Lepanto the germinal ideas of their Madame Bovary and The Idiot.

-- Angel Flores and M. J. Benardete, Cervantes Across the Century

[There is a tradition that] is marked by lines that radiate from heroes of Western culture on the order of Dante, Cervantes, Shakespeare. Such lines have shown little respect for centuries or national frontiers. One remembers that Fielding, though he represented a new age in England, placed himself in one of the lines when he formally stated that his Joseph Andrews was "writ in the manner of Cervantes." Another line is best represented in American fiction by Moby Dick and Absalom, Absalom! Different as these are from each other, they are both Shakespearean not only by virtue of their intention and their obsessed heroes but also partly in their language, which sometimes lapses or soars into blank verse.

-- Malcolm Cowley

A stanza of [Abraham] Cowley's, a poem of Catullus, a Greek epigram, possibly a neo-Latin one--we can see how they all played an essential part in the genesis of Marvell's poem, and yet, at the same time, we can also see that he has transmuted them into something unmistakably his own.

-- J. B. Leishman, on "To His Coy Mistress"

To follow Coleridge through his reading is to retrace the obliterated vestiges of creation.

-- John Livingstone Lowes, The Road to Xanadu

Byron knew his Bible as well as many of his most pious readers and had a skill in turning its phrases to good account in verses of haunting melancholy.

-- Leslie A. Marchand, Byron: A Portrait

Sir Walter Scott claimed Froissart as his master and acknowledged that in him he found the germ of the historical novel.

-- Charles W. Dunn

Discussions of The History [of New York] invariably mention echoes of Cervantes, Swift, and Fielding, but these youthful borrowings of Irving's are so often regarded in an apologetic or indulgent light that there can be no corresponding insight into why an author might positively choose to weave his art out of threads spun by earlier comic writers. This is a curious aversion in a century when so much vital literature, from Eliot and Joyce to Borges and Nabokov, demands that we regard quotation as a form of artistic reality superior to the outworn myth of actual experience.

-- Martin Roth, Comedy and America: The Lost World of Washington Irving

We find thoughts in all great writers (and even in small ones) that strike their roots far beneath the surface, and intertwine themselves with the roots of other writers' thoughts; so that when we pull up one, we stir the whole, and yet those writers have had no conscious society with one another.

-- Nathaniel Hawthorne, in a letter to Delia Bacon

If I stole this thought from Montaigne, as is very likely, I don't care. I should have said the same myself.

-- Emerson

It is interesting to see what unexpected material becomes a great poem--a trivial vaudeville by Scribe; odd scraps from books of magic or alchemy; passages from fellow-poets. Ignorance of these ingredients does not diminish the pleasure in the poems--the greatness lies elsewhere--but knowledge of them teaches us something concerning the poet's mind.

-- Enid Starkie, Arthur Rimbaud

If a work of imagination, of fiction, interests me at all ... I always want to write it over in my own way, handle the subject from my own sense of it.

-- Henry James

Conrad expressed dislike of Dostoevsky's works, but what is camouflaged thereby is his debt to them.

-- R. W. Stallman

Without those forerunners [the largely anonymous female intellectuals of the late eighteenth century], Jane Austen and the Brontës and George Eliot could no more have written than Shakespeare could have written without Marlowe, or Marlowe without Chaucer, or Chaucer without those forgotten poets who paved the ways and tamed the natural savagery of the tongue. For masterpieces are not single and solitary.... Jane Austen should have laid a wreath upon the grave of Fanny Burney, and George Eliot done homage to the robust shade of Eliza Carter--the valiant old woman who tied a bell to her bedstead in order that she might wake early and learn Greek. All women together ought to let flowers fall upon the tomb of Aphra Behn.

-- Virginia Woolf

All one can say is that literature has a double source: one in life, the other in literature itself, and if one is going in for the influence game, Goncharov's admiration for Tristram Shandy--the corresponding English comedy of domestic lethargy--may have helped to awaken his dilatory and very literary mind. From Sterne he learned to follow a half-forgotten tune in his head.

-- V. S. Pritchett on Oblomov

I read him, not to read him, but to lie upon his breast. He holds me like a child in his left arm. I sit there like a man on a statue.

-- Kafka on Strindberg

In the same way that Eliot began reading and commenting on the English metaphysical poets or the Greek and Elizabethan playwrights at the time he was experimenting with a new form of verse play, Borges studied and discussed Kafka when he was about to begin a new career as a storyteller.

-- Emir Rodríguez Monegal, Jorge Luis Borges: A Literary Biography

If anyone selects at random a dozen books from the copious literature on contemporary poetry, he will probably find that most if not all of them deal with this poetry virtually as a thing quite unrooted in the past. If, on the contrary, a reader at all familiar with the history of English poetry reads carefully a dozen leading modern poets, he will presumably find that most if not all of them stand greatly indebted in their own art and thought to poetry of earlier periods.

-- Henry W. Wells, New Poets from Old: A Study in Literary Genetics

I will mention one last check on fiction's honesty: tradition. No writer imagines he exists in a literary void. Though writers rarely read as widely as do critics, partly because writers can afford to be critical, throwing out books because of annoying little flaws of conception or execution, it is nevertheless true that writers would not be what they are if they didn't have a liking for books. A particular writer may read no one but George Gissing, or, perhaps, Aristophanes; but he knows full well that one of the things he's doing when he writes is laboring to achieve an effect at least somewhat similar to effects he has gotten out of other people's books.

-- John Gardner, "Moral Fiction"

Montesquieu says that "an original work almost always brings into being five or six hundred others which make use of the first approximately the way geometers make use of their formulas." I do not know whether Candide has served as a formula for five or six hundred other books. I believe it has not, unfortunately, because in that case we should have been less bored by so much literature. In any event, whether this story of mine is the first or the six hundredth, I have tried to make use of that formula.

-- Leonardo Sciascia, "Author's Note" to Candido, or A Dream Dreamed in Sicily

PREFACE

This book is an outgrowth of my research guide American Fiction to 1900: A Guide to Information Sources. In compiling the latter I unearthed instance after instance of external literary influence (not mere parallels) on early American fiction, and I began to wonder if it would not be a service to others if I were to review the scholarship and then offer both summaries and evaluations of it in compact form. To do an adequate job of this I had to reread the source works as well as the fiction, and inevitably my own insights creep in here and there, particularly in the essays that introduce each chapter; for the most part, however, I have tried simply to reduce a vast field of study to the point where it can be contained between two covers, so that scholars from this point forward can begin with this one book instead of an entire library of works, many of which are not in English or are out of print.

I discovered in my reading that there are sixteen main influences on American fiction, and I have devoted a chapter to each of these. The principles whereby chapter divisions were made were three: first, some chapters are devoted entirely to a body of literature (e. g., "The Classics") or an age (e. g., "The Victorians") in which no single figure dominates; second, other chapters deal with an age that has at its center a single representative figure (e. g., "Shakespeare and the Renaissance"); third, the remaining chapters treat isolated figures (e. g., "Sir Walter Scott") who are important in their own right yet do not sum up an age as might, say, a Milton or a Dante. To some extent these divisions are arbitrary, as is the placement of certain writers in certain chapters--an author who is a Victorian by dint of chronology might be treated in the chapter entitled "The Realists" because of his or her style, for instance. No doubt certain chapters will seem to give undue emphasis to a certain influence--the one on Jane Austen comes to mind, and in my own defense I can only say that I have spotlighted Austen because her impact on subsequent letters is undervalued; perhaps someone else will take a cue from this and explore her influence further.

Though minor American authors are mentioned throughout, I have attempted to give this survey both focus and substance by concentrating on the effect that foreign influences have had on the works of the following major writers: Charles Brockden Brown, Washington Irving, James Fenimore Cooper, Edgar Allan Poe, Nathaniel Hawthorne, Herman Melville, Mark Twain, Henry James, William Dean Howells, Frank Norris, and Stephen Crane.

Each chapter begins with a short essay in which I try to do

several things: assess the general influence of a person or group, guess at the reasons for the affinities between our authors and those who influenced them, and argue how in each case our authors used the person or group in question. Many readers will find the individual essays too general; in rereading them I often find them so myself. It is for that reason that I have made the bibliographies as specific as space will permit.

As for selecting the secondary works to be covered, it should be noted that save for one or two exceptions I have omitted coverage of scholarship dealing with traditions when they do not specify particular influences; for instance, I do not include in Chapter 11 an excellent article by Joseph A. Soldati entitled "The Americanization of Faust: A Study of Charles Brockden Brown's Wieland," ESQ, no. 74 (1974), 1-14, because it places Brown's novel within a Faustian tradition of Gothicism without citing specific possible sources. And in general I have limited coverage of studies that appropriate source-study terms without detailing direct borrowings. Richard Chase's Herman Melville: A Critical Study, for example, deals with two hero types in Melville, Ishmael and Prometheus. Chase's arguments are provocative and revealing; they carry with them the implicit notion of Melville's having derived his hero types from his reading. Yet since Chase does not discuss the Old Testament, Aeschylus, and Shelley to any significant extent, and since other scholars do, it is their work rather than his that is covered within these pages.

A small group of studies has been done on the influence of Emanuel Swedenborg on various authors, but I have not included him here. Part of the problem with Swedenborg is that his teachings, often vague and mystical in themselves, were usually transmuted in America into systems that were not only rather different from the original but also, in Quentin Anderson's words, "at once inclusive and parochial, quirky and cosmic." (Interested readers may nonetheless wish to consult Quentin Anderson, The American Henry James, New Brunswick: Rutgers University Press, 1957; William S. Gleim, The Meaning of Moby-Dick, New York: Brick Row Book Shop, 1938; Ernest Tuveson, "The Turn of the Screw: A Palimpsest," Studies in English [University of Texas], no. 12 [1972], 783-800; and Edward Wagenknecht, William Dean Howells: The Friendly Eye, New York: Oxford University Press, 1969; among others.) A larger group of studies discusses the relation between such writers as Melville and Crane and the Existentialists, but no clear agreement is reached as to influence: for instance, Betty C. Anderson, in "The Melville-Kierkegaard Syndrome," Rendezvous, 3, no. 2 (1968), 41-53, teases the reader with the possibility that Melville may have read Kierkegaard, while J. J. Boies, in "Existential Nihilism and Herman Melville," TWA, 50 (1961), 307-20, speculates that Melville "had probably never heard of Kierkegaard."

In annotating the books and articles covered herein I have for the most part discussed single studies singly, but where one critic has taken on one or more of his or her fellows I have usually integrated into my analysis of the pivotal study my comments on the others. Some dissertations have been covered, although in general I have preferred to allow the Darwinian process to select the worthiest dissertations--the ones that have become books--and winnow out those written merely "in partial fulfillment of the requirements," etc. It should be observed that the annotations are not necessarily to scale: many a book can be summed up in a brief sentence, and many a short article merits a page. In quoting from the studies covered I have reproduced the texts verbatim except for footnote numbers, which I have cheerfully excluded. I have translated items appearing in the foreign languages I am able to read (French, German, Italian, and Spanish). My apologies to the authors of these studies if I have not done justice to the full subtlety of their arguments; my sympathies also to the readers of this book who have no access to items appearing in languages that neither they nor I have mastered. This survey covers studies included in the 1976 PMLA bibliography, so readers who wish to follow current developments in this field should start with the 1977 number. Finally I have done my best to get authors' names right, although a peculiar academic schizophrenia sometimes prompts Professor J. Worthington Somebody to become Joseph W. Somebody in midcareer.

I have organized the book so that it can be read "in both directions." That is, a student of Shakespeare might want to read Chapter 7 to discover the extent and nature of Shakespeare's influence on early American fiction. Conversely, a student of Henry James who wanted to know what earlier writers influenced his work could read the relevant portions of each chapter. Thus it is my hope that this book will prove of benefit to both the comparative-literature scholar and the American-fiction specialist.

A project of this size could easily occasion a list of acknowledgments as big as the book itself. My calls for help brought answers from as nearby as the office next to mine and as far away as India. The first to aid me materially was Paula Barbour, who not only shared her research on the sources of Melville's fiction but also gave me the box I kept my note cards in. Adeline R. Tintner brought to my attention a number of studies that I would not have known about otherwise. Bobbie Christie, a library-science student at the time, ran a computer search that yielded a number of valuable items. The staffs of the Robert Manning Strozier Library of the Florida State University as well as those of the Bibliothèque Publique d'Information in the Centre Georges Pompidou, the Centre de Documentation Benjamin Franklin, and the American Library in Paris all facilitated my research, or at least they did not hinder it greatly. The students of English 6937, a graduate seminar in literary influence that I taught in the fall of 1979, contributed insights and helped me focus my thinking. (Since graduate students are often used as slave labor by their professors, I should point out that mine were not, at least in this instance--I reserve the right to think better of a practice that seems contemptible to me now as I grow older, and energy and inspiration wane.) Others who helped are Lawrence J. Berkove, Eugene Crook, Leon Golden, Bibhu Padhi, Donna Casella Kern, and the late T. Harry Williams. Judy, William, and Ian did their part, largely by keeping up my spirits without knowing it. Finally I should acknowledge my masters, the authors who remind us that writers of every time and place and genre, as well as of every degree of merit, are reliant on the works of others. Many of these I have cited in the pages that follow. Others are included in the "Extracts" with which I (taking a leaf from Moby-Dick) begin this book. Still others I have forgotten or never knew. But the world of the intellect is not mechanistic and fragmented; it is organic and interrelated, and even without knowing the names of this third group of authors, I am sure that they are there.

ABBREVIATIONS OF PERIODICAL AND SERIAL TITLES

AL	American Literature
ALR	American Literary Realism
ATQ	American Transcendental Quarterly
BNYPL	Bulletin of the New York Public Library
CE	College English
CL	Comparative Literature
CLQ	Colby Library Quarterly
CLS	Comparative Literature Studies
DAI	Dissertation Abstracts International
EA	Etudes Anglaises
ELH	Journal of English Literary History
ELN	English Language Notes
ES	English Studies
ESQ	Journal of the American Renaissance (formerly Emerson Society Quarterly)
MFS	Modern Fiction Studies
MLN	Modern Language Notes
MLQ	Modern Language Quarterly
MP	Modern Philology
MTJ	Mark Twain Journal
MTQ	Mark Twain Quarterly
NCF	Nineteenth Century Fiction
NEQ	New England Quarterly
NHJ	Nathaniel Hawthorne Journal
N&Q	Notes and Queries
PBSA	Papers of the Bibliographical Society of America
PLL	Papers on Language and Literature
PMLA	Publications of the Modern Language Society of America
POE S	Poe Studies

POE N	Poe Newsletter
PQ	Philological Quarterly
RLC	Revue de Littérature Comparée
SA	Studi Americani
SEL	Studies in English Literature
SSF	Studies in Short Fiction
TSLL	Texas Studies in Literature and Language
TWA	Transactions of the Wisconsin Academy of Sciences, Arts, and Letters

Other abbreviations

comp(s).	compiler(s), compiled by
ed(s).	editor(s), edition, edited by
enl.	enlarged
no.	number
n. s.	new series
p(p).	page(s)
[pseud.]	pseudonym
rev.	revised
trans.	translated by, translator
vol(s).	volume(s)

LIST OF WORKS FREQUENTLY CONSULTED

While I have allowed this book to range and sprawl as it must, I have given it a flexible thematic spine that runs through the introduction and the short essays that begin each chapter. As the reader will see, there is a general idea regarding the peculiar nature of the reading and writing habits of American authors; this idea is set forth in part B of the introduction and it is treated as necessary in the individual chapters. In addition, I have tried to attain a certain consistency by referring regularly to the following sixteen books, although I have incorporated my own insights as well as those from other, less frequently used, sources. In order to avoid a proliferation of footnotes in a work already brimming with bibliographic information, I list at the end of each short essay the authors and relevant page numbers of the books used (in the order of their use) in that essay.

Buell, Lawrence. Literary Transcendentalism: Style and Vision in the American Renaissance. Ithaca: Cornell University Press, 1973.

Cunliffe, Marcus. The Literature of the United States. Harmondsworth: Penguin, 1971.

Falk, Robert P. The Victorian Mode in American Fiction 1865-1885. East Lansing: Michigan State University Press, 1965.

Fiedler, Leslie. A Fiedler Reader. New York: Stein and Day, 1977.

Lynn, Kenneth. William Dean Howells: An American Life. New York: Harcourt Brace Jovanovich, 1971.

Matthiessen, F. O. American Renaissance: Art and Expression in the Age of Emerson and Whitman. New York: Oxford University Press, 1941.

Normand, Jean. Nathaniel Hawthorne: Esquisse d'une Analyse de la Création Artistique. Paris: Presses Universitaires de France, 1964.

Priestley, J. B. Literature and Western Man. New York: Harper, 1960.

Spiller, Robert E., et al., eds. Literary History of the United States. 4th ed., rev. New York: Macmillan, 1974.

Wagenknecht, Edward. Edgar Allan Poe: The Man Behind the Legend. New York: Oxford University Press, 1963.

________. Mark Twain: The Man and His Work. Norman: University of Oklahoma Press, 1971.

________. Washington Irving: Moderation Displayed. New York: Oxford University Press, 1962.

________. William Dean Howells: The Friendly Eye. New York: Oxford University Press, 1969.

Wager, Willis. American Literature: A World View. New York: New York University Press, 1968.

Walker, Franklin. Frank Norris: A Biography. Garden City: Doubleday, Doran, 1932.

Zipes, Jack D. The Great Refusal: Studies of the Romantic Hero in German and American Literature. Bad Homburg: Athenäum Verlag, 1970.

INTRODUCTION

A. On the Matter of Literary Influence in General

The hive metaphor, as represented in the epigraphs to this book, is a popular one among source hunters. Equally popular is the suggestion that literary influence works like fertilizer. In the ninth century Ermenrich of Ellwagen wrote: "Since even as dung spread upon the field enriches it to good harvest, so the filthy writings of the pagan poets are a mighty aid to divine eloquence." And nearly a thousand years later, in his "Oration on the Utility of Literary Establishments" (1814), the American John Bristed noted that "the most powerful mind is, in itself, but a barren soil, soon exhausted, if left to repeat often the periodical growth of its own native vegetation; a soil which will produce only a few scanty crops, unless continually fertilized with the abundant addition of foreign manure."

But what hives are robbed, and how much fertilizer is actually used? The beginning student of literary influence will be surprised to discover how many scholars, usually out of good-natured ignorance, decry the possibility of much significant literary influence at all. The most impressive evidence in refutation of that idea, of course, is the accumulated testimony of authors from all countries and periods of time. Goethe, for instance, writing to Eckermann (December 16, 1828), says that the attempt to find his influences "would know no boundaries." Melville, writing about Emerson to Evert A. Duyckinck (March 3, 1849), says "Lay it down that had not Sir Thomas Browne lived, Emerson would not have mystified--I will answer that had not old Zack's father begot him, Old Zack would never have been the hero of Palo Alto. The truth is that we are all sons, grandsons, or nephews or great nephews of those who go before us. No man is his own sire." Melville's own sire was legion ("he is at the mercy of the last book he has read," wrote Van Wyck Brooks), though if his own words are to be believed, Shakespeare was of preeminent importance: "Dolt and ass that I am, I have lived more than twenty-nine years, and until a few days ago never made acquaintance with the divine William. Ah, he's full of sermons-on-the-mount, and gentle ages, almost as Jesus. I take such men to be inspired. If another Messiah ever comes, he will be in the likeness of Shakespeare." Now here is Henry James, in the preface to The Princess Casamassima: "I may add moreover that the resuscitation of Christina (and, on the minor scale, of Madame Grandoni) put in a strong light for me the whole question, for the romancer, of 'going on with a character': as Balzac first of all systematically went on, as Thackeray, as Trollope, as Zola all more or less ingeniously went on." And James Joyce: "I love Dante almost as much as the Bible. He is my spiritual food, the rest is ballast." And H. L. Mencken (to Edward Stone, acknowledging receipt of Stone's H. L. Mencken's Debt to F. W. Nietzsche): "I was under the impression that my debt to Nietzsche was very slight. I must say now that your argument rather shakes me. Such influences are exerted, it appears, very insidiously. I was picking up Nietzscheisms without being aware of them, and they undoubtedly got into my own stuff." And Fitzgerald, who admitted the influence of Thackeray: "So far as I am concerned," he wrote an admirer, "you guessed right." And Jorge Luis Borges (writing on his "Hymn to the Sea"): "In the poem, I tried my hardest to be Walt Whitman." And William Burroughs, on Nova Express: "Joyce is in there. Shakespeare, Rimbaud, some writers that people haven't heard about, someone named Jack Stern. There's Kerouac. I don't know, when you start making these fold-ins and cut-ups you lose track." And so on--the "Extracts" that begin this book provide ample additional testimony in support of the idea that writers are absolutely reliant for their literary nourishment on the works of their contemporaries and forebears.

Indeed, once one begins to believe the authors themselves, one runs the risk of believing that art is largely plagiarism--of believing that, as Mencken says with characteristically hyperbolic acuity, "... the doctrine that art is an imitation of nature is full of folly. Nine-tenths of all the art that one encounters in this world is actually an imitation of other art. Fully a half of it is an imitation twice, thrice or ten times removed." These, then, are the extremes--that art, including literary art, is largely original, that it is mainly derivative. The truth is found, as it usually is, somewhere in the middle, and it is not long before the student of source study begins to see that all writers steal, yet great writers not only steal but also transform the stolen goods into something nearly unrecognizable, something clearly and uniquely their own. Thus thievery and transformation are the twin concerns of the source hunters who know what they are about. "Nothing is more original," wrote Paul Valéry, "nothing more personal than to nourish oneself from others. But one must digest them. The lion is made of the sheep he has eaten."

By looking at a novel like Cooper's The Spy, one can see evidence of the most obvious kinds of literary influence, in this case the influence of Shakespeare. First there are the Shakespearian epigraphs that hint at the plot or theme (or both) of individual chapters. Then there are borrowed characters, such as the surgeon Sitgreaves and Katy Haynes the housekeeper, who recall the second-rank yet essential characters in Shakespeare who entertain as they illustrate basic truths about the human situation (Sitgreaves's mordant drollery brings to mind the Fool in Lear, for instance). Finally there is borrowed dialogue--when Fanny Wharton and Katy discuss heavenly portents of coming evil in Chapter 25, one cannot but think of the similar conversation between Cicero and Casca in Act I, Scene iii, of Julius Caesar.

Yet what becomes evident after even the most basic research in the field is that there seem to be nearly as many kinds of literary influence as there are writers to be influenced. One might suggest the scope of possibilities by listing just a few examples and illustrating them with references taken from the text of the present volume. For instance:

(1) one writer influences a second who influences a third (see the Niess article on James in Chapter 15, the Vidan article on James in the same chapter, and the second Allott article on James in Chapter 14);
(2) one writer influences a second writer's use of a third (see the Hoben article on Twain in Chapter 14);
(3) one writer borrows a second writer's technique but expresses ideas completely opposed to those of the second writer (see the Lundy article on Norris in Chapter 16);
(4) one writer influences a second in different ways at different stages of the second writer's career (see the Vande Kieft article on Melville in Chapter 8, the second article by Jones on Hawthorne in Chapter 5);
(5) two styles combine in a single writer's work to produce an ostensibly anomalous tone that is actually ideal for the subject and the author's treatment of it (see the Hirsch article on Poe in Chapter 3);
(6) a writer is influenced by one culture's notion of a central figure in a second culture (see Cargill's article on James in Chapter 7);
(7) a writer speculates in fiction about a second writer's genius (see the Stafford article on James in Chapter 7);
(8) a writer evidences in fiction a fascination with the life as well as the works of a second writer (see the Tintner article on James in Chapter 12);
(9) a character in one writer's novel becomes the basis for a second writer's entire career (see the Colvert article on Crane in Chapter 14);
(10) a writer leads a second writer astray, causing inconsistencies in the latter's work (see the Gates article on Cooper in Chapter 9);
(11) a writer not only uses but revitalizes stock literary conventions (see the Wheeler article on Hawthorne in Chapter 9, the Jeffrey article on Poe in the same chapter);
(12) an American writer borrows from a foreign writer materials that originated in America for a kind of "round trip" influence (see the Haynes article on Cooper in Chapter 12, the first Orians article on Hawthorne in Chapter 13);
(13) a writer chooses from among several versions of a literary archetype, such as Satan, Prometheus, or Faust (see the Schwarz article on Hawthorne in Chapter 12, the D'Avanzo article on Melville in Chapter 2);
(14) a writer uses one, several, or perhaps all the possible sources of a single well-known line (see the Mathews article on Howells in Chapter 12);
(15) a writer draws a plot from life but supports it with a literarary correlate (see the first Tintner article on James in Chapter 14);

(16) a writer works within another's "climate" or "stream" of influence without experiencing the latter author directly (see the Noone article on Melville in Chapter 12).

But regardless of the type of influence studied the source scholar's joy comes not merely upon the apprehension of one writer's effect on another; rather it lies in his or her participation, at whatever remove, in the actual moment of creation. John Livingston Lowes discusses the discovery of such a moment in The Road to Xanadu:

> Chaucer (than whose mental processes there are none more normal) is imitating, in the "Parlement of Fowles," a stanza of Boccaccio which contains a list of famous lovers of antiquity. They are Semiramis, Pyramis and Thisbe, Hercules, and Biblis. And Semiramis is referred to, not by name, but by a phrase: "the spouse of Ninus" ("sposa di Nin"). But Dante, in the great fifth canto of the Inferno, has a list of lovers too, which likewise begins with Semiramis, and runs through Dido, Cleopatra, Achilles, and Paris, to Tristan. And Dante also refers to Semiramis by a phrase: she is one of whom we read that she succeeded Ninus, and was his spouse ("che succedette a Nino, e fu sua sposa"). In Boccaccio's list, then, which Chaucer was translating, occurs the phrase "sposa di Nin." In Dante's list appear almost identically the same words: "Nino, e fu sua sposa." Chaucer knew his Dante thoroughly. What happened? Boccaccio's phrase, as he read it, called up Dante's, and Dante's phrase, once recollected, carried along with it its accompanying list. And as a result Chaucer's bead-roll of ladies dead and lovely knights included not only every lover in Boccaccio's list, but every one of Dante's lovers too! Through a flash of association by way of a common phrase, two objects have telescoped into a third. And at moments of high imaginative tension associations, not merely in pairs but in battalions, are apt in similar fashion to stream together and coalesce.

B. On the Matter of Literary Influence in America

The television critic Michael Arlen posits what he calls the Moby-Dick theory, which says that readers are unable to ask their culture to produce the best work of which it is capable and that therefore great works like Moby-Dick must come from great solitary artists like Melville. Arlen uses his theory to naysay the notion that the producers of television shows should cater to popular demand, but to me it reinforces the idea of geniuses being radically and sometimes disturbingly different from their contemporaries, more so than the contemporaries know and certainly more so than they would want them to be if they did know. The measure of this difference in perception is seen in the difference in the public images of figures like Lincoln and Melville (to give a nonliterary example as well as a literary one) and their true natures. H. L. Mencken speculates that when Lincoln went to Gettysburg he found an audience too cold to hear a long speech and too stupid to hear a good one, so what he gave them was the Gettysburg Address, a document Mencken viewed with less than the conventional piety. Later, pondering his success, says Mencken, Lincoln must have "vacillated often between laughing at it sourly and hanging himself." Moby-Dick may be a fish story to some, and no doubt Melville realized that it would be safer if his neighbors thought so. But he described it privately as "a wicked book," one "roasted in hellfire."

How did Melville become so terrible, at least in his own mind? All serious artists are, of course. In his biography of Harry Crosby, Geoffrey Woolf notes that "subversion and rebellion are the first principles of invention, since invention seeks to replace what has been given with another something apprehended as ideal by its inventor." But American writers are unique, I believe, in the degree to which they searched for the tools of subversion in the thought and literature of older, more practiced cultures. Mrs. Hawthorne said that "the old English writers" are "the hive from which all modern honey is stolen," but the fact is that American writers have pillaged virtually everyone, from the Oriental philosophers to Darwin. Does that mean that the American writer is imitative and weak and unoriginal? Not if one agrees with Dr. Johnson, who believed that a system built on the discoveries of many minds is better than one produced by the workings of a single mind, which can do little on its own.

Ironically, Americans are predisposed to a certain blindness toward the workings of the many minds that constitute the source of their own culture. America was founded in a pragmatic, utilitarian context, which is to say a necessarily anti-intellectual one. Americans tend to look on cultural inventions as they do technological ones and take for granted an inherent originality; surely The Adventures of Huckleberry Finn sprang full blown from the mind of Mark Twain, say, just as the idea for the light bulb came from the mind of Edison. Or if there were external sources for such a novel, continues our hypothetical American, no doubt they were principally or entirely native ones. Indeed, the Norton Critical Edition of Huckleberry Finn lists eight sources for the novel, all domestic; yet we know that the Bible as well as the writings of Shakespeare, Cervantes, and a host of minor authors were all instrumental in the novel's composition.

In large part this insistence on the homegrown quality of American literature is a reaction to a contrary assumption that held sway during the lives of all the authors covered in this book. As recently as the early decades of this century it was assumed that American literature was merely a branch, and almost certainly an inferior one, of English literature. Naturally the native literature that was most highly praised was that which seemed least native. Thus the writings of Irving, Longfellow, and James Russell Lowell were within the canon of American literature while those of Melville, Whitman, and Twain were not. In 1920 the Modern Language Association committed a major act of heresy by including an American-literature study group in the program of its annual convention. Then as now, of course, the workings of the literary marketplace had as much or more to do with the value of a particular author's reputation as did the opinion of academics, and no doubt the MLA's change of heart simply reflected a financial reality. For before 1891 American publishers could pirate the works of English authors for nothing, a practice they much preferred to that of paying royalties to native authors, however deserving. But in that year the International Copyright Law was passed, and the publishers turned to their countrymen and women with open arms; if they had to pay the writers whose works thay published, at least the publishers could comfort themselves with the idea that they could save time and at least a little money by dealing with a New York or Boston novelist rather than one who lived in London.

Thanks to this unique and, no doubt, unrealized complicity between academe and business the movement for independence has never faltered, and the understanding of American literature as a discrete entity, separate from European and especially English literature, is an assumption so widely held as to be impossible to challenge. This emphasis on the independent nature of American literature, a correct assumption yet a misleading one in that it blinds one to that literature's foreign sources, received a major boost in 1927 with the appearance of V. L. Parrington's *Main Currents in American Thought*, an attempt to see native literature as a direct product of American economic and social realities rather than a long-distance imitation of English writing. Parrington helped make it possible to see the American qualities of writers who had been thought of as merely bumptious before; he showed how such authors as Henry James and Emily Dickinson could be understood as "native" in their peculiar ways; and he fostered the trend of examining minor authors' works, folk ballads, and legends that has culminated in recent years in the realization that American literature also includes the works of the original Americans, the Indians. But as Everett Carter writes in *The American Idea: The Literary Response to American Optimism*, Parrington "was wrong in failing to see that great art not only comes from the expression of a dominant social certainty but as often comes out of the anguish of a society's central beliefs and the attempt to create an order to fill the void left by the withdrawal of the sustaining faith." One might improve upon Carter and speculate that most great art is born of anguish rather than adherence to a "dominant social certainty" (or "hegemony," to borrow a fashionable phrase from Gramsci), especially in America, where the prevailing belief in material success is not leavened, as it is in other and older countries, by a long-lived cultural tradition.

After Parrington such classic studies as Alfred Kazin's *On Native Grounds*, R. W. B. Lewis's *The American Adam*, and F. O. Matthiessen's *American Renaissance* (as well as such worthwhile if less-heralded works as V. F. Calverton's *The Liberation of American Literature* and Benjamin T. Spencer's *The Quest for Nationality*) have chronicled the development of a native American literature. While each of these works deals in some way with the foreign models that American writers adhered to, each also emphasizes the novelty and originality of American literature. The purpose of the present study is not to deny that novelty and originality; rather it is to underscore and celebrate these qualities by making more evident than before the context of tradition in which American literature developed. No author of any country or period is wholly derivative, but none is completely original. All writers steal--part A of this essay and the "Extracts" that introduce this study make that clear. What matters is what the authors do with that which they glean from others, a proposition consistently emphasized in the pages that follow.

At this point it would be useful to speculate on the American authors' attitudes toward the hive of honey that older and alien cultures represented to them. To do so one must return to the circumstances of America's founding, the laudable attempt to create a nation free from Old World rigidity, intolerance, and supersition. America was founded in the spirit of the Enlightenment; in his essay "The Enlightenment and the American Dream" (in Margaret Denny and William H. Gilman, eds., _The American Writer and the European Tradition_) Theodore Hornberger defines that period in cultural history as

> the sum of the ideas of such men as Bacon, Hobbes, Locke, Newton, Descartes, Montesquieu, Voltaire, and Rousseau. It is the period of the New Science, of deism, of natural rights and natural philosophy, of primitivism and the idea of progress. Its distinguishing mark, perhaps, is a new emphasis upon the good in man, of which the corollary is that man has the power, through his intelligence and his industry, to improve his lot by ever-greater control of his environment.

These are lofty sentiments, but they are not wholly adequate ones. In the first place, all ideals are subject to debasement once they are widely diffused, and thus the substantive optimism of the Enlightenment became the facile optimism of the boosters and hucksters who became the targets of Mark Twain's satire and, in a later day, Sinclair Lewis's. Secondly, a theory of human nature founded almost solely on the notions of rationalism and optimism is of necessity incomplete; referring to the inadequacy of such a theory, F. O. Matthiessen says this in his _American Renaissance_: "Notwithstanding the humaneness and toleration that make Franklin and Jefferson among the strongest bulwarks in our social heritage, it is forced inescapably upon us that their rationalism was too shallow to encompass the full complexity of man's nature." The point is not that Jefferson and the Founding Fathers were wrong--the point is that they did not tell it all. It is equally important to observe that our major authors are not pessimists, as they are often called. It would be more accurate, I believe, to call them anoptimists; what they are saying is that "you can't know that all will be well, and you certainly can't guarantee it by being facilely optimistic."

It is this fundamental disjunction between the viewpoint of America's cultural leaders, its authors, and that of the representatives of America's "dominant social certainty" or hegemony--its religious, military, governmental, and business leaders, for the most part--that lies behind Richard Chase's statement (in _The Amer-_

ican Novel and Its Tradition) that "the imagination that produced much of the best and most characteristic American fiction has been shaped by the contradictions and not by the unities and harmonies of our culture." The American novel, says Chase, can be distinguished from the English novel, which

> has followed a middle way. It is notable for its great practical sanity, its powerful engrossing composition of wide ranges of experience into a moral centrality and equability of judgment.... The profound poetry of disorder we find in the American novel is missing, with rare exceptions, from the English.

Instead, the American novel "has been stirred ... by the aesthetic possibilities of alientation, contradiction, and disorder." And in his excellent Three Bags Full: Essays in American Fiction Philip Young notes:

> Serious fiction in America has generally operated, at least since Hawthorne, Melville, and Poe, as a reaction against the facile optimisms our country periodically produces. These important writers all are saying, as Melville said that Hawthorne did, "No! in thunder" to the cheerful, affirmative, and often commercial popular views of their times.... However obvious, it is too often forgotten that our writers live in a society where a kind of idiot optimism is popularly and commercially insisted on. Surrounded as they are by magazine fiction and movies, "family" television, Madison Avenue, and all the rest, they are incessantly driven to try to right the balance--driven by a completely human perversity that reacts in disgust from the piety and cant of an inescapable diet of fake satisfactions and sentimental sorrows. This is an important and often ignored partial accounting for all the misery and sickness you find in our best writers.... How can they do other?

In their struggle against the "idiot optimism" that is peculiarly American our writers found no better allies than their counterparts in older and alien cultures. Their reliance on these writers was crucial for their enterprise--after all, the Idiot Optimists had each other to rely on, whereas (to hearken once more to the Moby-Dick theory) virtually all great artists are solitary. It was the foreign writers, then, who provided the first American authors with the support and often the ammunition they needed in their war against facile piety and smugness. The examples of literary influence discussed in this book are as varied as one might imagine, and certainly there are numerous instances of mere borrowing, sheer appropriation of other writers' materials with no naysaying intent whatsoever. Yet one must believe that our writers read with the same purpose all serious readers have--to remind themselves that the obvious and the easy are neither true nor necessarily preferable. It is in this that the sedition of the American authors lies, and it is in their seditious desire that they were aided by allies from other cultures. A book of this sort needs no thematic backbone. That it has one, however, is inescapable. According to Stephen Spender, American writers are self-creating, in contrast to their self-actualizing English counterparts. They create a self that challenges and questions, and they form that self from materials that include the works of writers from other times and places. Our better understanding of this benign hive-robbing will lead to a better understanding of our culture, which is to say of ourselves.

1. THE ORIENTAL HERITAGE

The influence of Oriental literature, religion, and philosophy on American literature is markedly recurrent--it waxes and wanes, unlike the influence of other, more constant, sources, such as the Bible and the plays of Shakespeare. The first phase of influence derives largely from the work of the British and European comparative mythologists and philosophers who were contemporaries of the early nineteenth-century New England Transcendentalists and Romantics and culminates in the poems of Whitman. The second and fin de siècle phase is seen in the art of Whistler, the prose of Lafcadio Hearn, and the translations of Ernest Fenollosa. And the third phase stems from the impact of Zen Buddhism on the mid-twentieth-century Beat movement in American letters.

Clearly there is an element of fashion in the attractiveness of the East. There is a consistent tendency in American literature to naysay the self-righteous optimist whose slogan is "God and Country," and one of the most irritating forms of denial is the embrace of that which is alien to the enemy--in this case, another culture and someone else's gods. Thus, while the young Stephen Crane thought American religion "mildewed," he was interested in Buddhism. That he was also speaking out against bathing suits at this same time in his life, however, suggests that his flirtation with Buddhism may have been but one way of expressing a general desire to affront the orthodox.

But the faddishness of Eastern exoticism is seen mainly in the extraliterary milieus of the second and third phases of influence, in which the partisans of the literary, as well as those of a merely antiestablishmentarian bent, affected the dress and attitudes of their idols in order to express publicly their disdain for Victorian or Cold War ideas and institutions that seemed oppressive to them. No such widespread and, at least in part, politically motivated phenomena are noted in the first phase, the one in which the effects of Oriental influence are most profound. It is certain that the Transcendentalists and Romantics must have been attracted to the sheer otherness of the Orient, but of far greater interest is the fact that one often finds in the unfamiliar that which is so obvious in the familiar as to be invisible. The Zoroastrian account of the world, in which there is perpetual conflict between the creator, Ormazd, and his evil twin, Ahriman, is analogous to the Christian story of God and Satan. That Melville was strongly impressed by the Oriental account is a reminder that the shock of recognition often takes place in unfamiliar territory.

The impact of the Orient during the first phase of influence is also attributable to the eclecticism of the American authors (most of whom, as Thomas Jefferson said of himself, had a "canine appetite" for reading) in combination with their pragmatism. When reviewers of Melville's early novels compared them to the *Arabian Nights* they were confirming his ability to discover, assimilate, and use materials that, unlikely though they might have seemed to his readers, were precisely suited to his purpose.

This preface draws on the following sources (see "List of Works Frequently Consulted" for full bibliographic information): Matthiessen, p. 439; R. W. Stallman, *Stephen Crane: A Biography*, New York: George Braziller, 1968, p. 36; Watson G. Branch, ed., *Melville: The Critical Heritage*, London: Routledge & Kegan Paul, 1974, passim. Two general studies that are tangentially related to Oriental influence on American letters are Arthur Christy, *The Orient in American Transcendentalism*, New York: Columbia University Press, 1932, and Earl Miner, *The Japanese Tradition in British and American Literature*, Princeton: Princeton University Press, 1958.

The following studies (after the "General" section) are grouped under the names, listed alphabetically, of major American fiction writers through James who were influenced by Oriental sources.

General

Sharma, Mohan Lal. "The 'Oriental Estate,' Especially, *The Bhagavad-Gita* in American Literature." *Forum* (Houston), 7, i (1969), 4-11.

Deals with the influence of this Hindu classic and its message of "progressive self-exfoliation" on American authors from the Transcendentalists through J. D. Salinger.

Hawthorne

Tharpe, Jac. "Hawthorne and Hindu Literature." *Southern Quarterly*, 10 (1972), 107-15.

This essay argues that Hawthorne may have been influenced by the *Shakuntala* (a seven-act drama by the Hindu playwright Kalidasa) in writing "Rappaccini's Daughter" and by Book II of *The Ramayana* while composing "Roger Malvin's Burial." The first comparison depends largely on details common to both works, such as the identification of the heroine with a particular plant; the second depends on a basic plot similarity: the mistaken killing of a young man who is thought to be an animal. Neither argument overwhelms; together, however, they do suggest that "Hawthorne was familiar with some of the faddish reading of the Transcendentalists." (The *Shakuntala* was the first Sanskrit work to be translated and published in the United States; it appeared in 1805 in *The Monthly Anthology and Boston Review*.)

James

Gale, Robert L. "Blest Images and Sanctified Relics." In *The Caught Image: Figurative Language in the Fiction of Henry James.* Chapel Hill: University of North Carolina Press, 1964.

See the annotation of this item in Chapter 3, "The Bible."

Melville

Cohen, Hennig. "Melville's Copy of Thomas Duer Broughton's 'Popular Poetry of the Hindoos.'" *PBSA,* 61 (1967), 266-67.

Although it is not mentioned in Merton M. Sealts, Jr.'s authoritative *Melville's Reading: A Check-List of Books Owned and Borrowed,* this anthology was part of Melville's library. A signed copy now belongs to the Butler Library of Columbia University; there are some annotations of the introduction and notes but none of the poems themselves.

Finkelstein, Dorothee. *Melville's Orienda.* New Haven and London: Yale University Press, 1961.

As traveler in fact as well as in his fiction, Melville is best known for his visits to Polynesia. But this book concentrates on his use of what Finkelstein calls the nineteenth-century "Gesta Arabum and Persarum." Melville's reading on the Near East was encyclopedic; it included not only classical sources (Herodotus), travel books, histories, Oriental poems and romances by English authors (Thomas Moore's *Lalla Rookh,* William Beckford's *Vathek*) but also translations of the *Arabian Nights,* the *Rubaiyat,* and the medieval Persian poet Saadi's *Gulistan.* And in 1856-57 he visited Greece, Turkey, Egypt, and Palestine, a trip that yielded the long poem *Clarel* and the *Journal of a Visit to Europe and the Levant.*

Like Emerson and Hawthorne as well as the European writers of the day, Melville was intensely interested in such developments as Sufism, the Moslem mystical movement that flourished in medieval Persia and that left its mark on the Persian poets (themselves often mystics and dervishes) who were avidly read by nineteenth-century literati. Melville's interest in the Near East significantly influenced his choice of characters and symbols in *Mardi, Moby-Dick,* and other works. There is a double importance to Melville's Near Eastern allusions: they reflect the progress of contemporary discovery through archaeology and scholarship; more importantly, "the Near East, ... with its load of history, oppressed him in both spirit and body. Its very picturesqueness indicated decay; it was the phosphorescence of decomposition." Thus in *Mardi* Melville lamented: "Oh, Orienda! thou wert our East, where first dawned up song and science, with Mardi's primal mornings! But now, how changed! the dawn of light becomes a darkness."

Franklin, H. Bruce. *The Wake of the Gods: Melville's Mythology.* Stanford: Stanford University Press, 1963.

Melville's reading of the comparative mythologists of his era and his immersion in ancient and modern travel literature ("his favorite reading") yielded a knowledge of Eastern and other myths, which he used in his fiction and then transcended in order to make myths of his own. In *Typee* and *Omoo* he weighs both pagan and Christian religions against "a persistently assumed [ideal] religion which might be called anything from deism to a primitive Christianity." This ideal religion is not assumed in *Mardi*, which nonetheless "quests for it and questions all that quest discovers." *Mardi* is actually "a textbook of comparative mythology" that deals with the myths of the Hindus, Polynesians, Incas, Hebrews, Greeks, Christians, Romans, and the Norse, and the lesson of the text is that "any theology may or may not be mythology and any myth may or may not be divine."

In *Moby-Dick* Melville is even more destructive of religious and mythological orthodoxy, yet he creates a myth of his own. He draws on Herodotus, Diodorus, and Plutarch for the Egyptian myth of Osiris, the priest-king-god who hunts and is periodically dismembered by the aquatic monster Typhon, only to return and restore a world that has lain barren since his disappearance. But Ahab is mortal; his mistaken attempt to play God not only costs him his life but also those of humankind ("embodied by the polyglot crew of the *Pequod*"), save Ishmael, who lives to tell the tale and sound the warning. (Note: Gerard M. Sweeney questions the Ahab-Osiris equation in *Melville's Use of Classical Mythology*, Amsterdam: Rodopi N. V., 1975, p. 52n, pointing out that two of Ahab's four "dismemberments" [the loss of the original leg and the three fracturings of its replacement] are self-inflicted, thus suggesting that Ahab was at least partly responsible for his own suffering. Perhaps the two viewpoints can be reconciled in the observation that Ahab's deific status is self-conferred, even to the point of certain "dismemberments" being stage-managed in a way that might fool all but the observant reader.)

So far, so good. Franklin's argument reaches its peak in the chapter on *Moby-Dick*, but thereafter it becomes overambitious, repetitive, and bullyingly zealous. ("I say to anybody who thinks he finds a wasted or a misplaced word [in *The Confidence-Man*], 'Read the book again.' ") Sea captains ought not to play God, but neither should literary critics.

Isani, Mukhtar Ali. "The Naming of Fedallah in *Moby-Dick.*" *AL*, 40 (1968-69), 380-85.

See the annotation of this item in Chapter 12, "The Romantics."

________. "Zoroastrianism and the Fire Symbolism in *Moby-Dick.*" *AL*, 44 (1972-73), 385-97.

Both Melville's knowledge of and his use of Zoroastrian concepts in *Moby-Dick* are documented convincingly in this essay. If one compares and contrasts the attitudes toward fire of Ahab and the Parsee (that is, Indian Zoroastrian) harpooner Fedallah, one notes that Ahab defies fire and light while Fedallah venerates them. Thus "Ahab is the rationalistic rebel devoid of faith" while Fedallah is "the highly orthodox believer, relying on faith to the exclusion of reason and reducing it to ritual." They make an ironic pair, for neither "the rebel quester" nor "the orthodox quester ... can unveil the metaphysical mysteries."

Kulkarni, H. B. *Moby-Dick: A Hindu Avatar. A Study of Hindu Myth and Thought in Moby-Dick.* Logan: Utah State University Press, 1970.

Kulkarni briefly acknowledges Melville's thorough familiarity with Oriental matters (see the annotation of Finkelstein's *Melville's Orienda* for a partial list of major sources) and goes on to interpret *Moby-Dick* from a Hindu viewpoint. In an attempt to explain why Melville described his masterpiece as "a wicked book" Kulkarni speculates that its supposed wickedness might lie in its "departure from Christian theology and Western tradition, which may be described as a philosophy of either/or, where good and evil are regarded as exclusive entities," whereas "the special claim to distinction of Hindu thought is the reconciliation of good and evil, love and hate into the highest experience of the spirit. It is on the foundation of this mystic harmony and truth of unity that *Moby-Dick* firmly stands." While it may boggle Western minds, then, it is still possible to identify the whale with both Vishnu the Preserver and Siva the Destroyer. And when Moby-Dick sinks the *Pequod* he functions simply as a tool of the divine purpose, which periodically destroys the wicked and preserves the just.

Mansfield, Luther S., and Howard P. Vincent. "Explanatory Notes" to *Moby-Dick.* New York: Hendricks House, 1952.

Space will not allow that justice be done these indispensable notes, but it should at least be noted that commentary is offered on (among other things) Melville's handling of the following Oriental topics: Mohammed and Mohammedanism, Siva, Zoroaster, the Parsees, fire worship, and "Fadlallah," a character from Persian literature who may have lent his name to Ahab's harpooner.

Newbery, I. " 'The Encantadas': Melville's *Inferno.*" *AL*, 38 (1966-67), 49-68.

See the annotation of this item in Chapter 4, "Dante and the Middle Ages."

Sutton, Walter. "Melville and the Great God *Billy Budd.*" *Prairie Schooner*, 34 (1960), 128-33.

The epigraph of Melville's poem "Buddha" reads, "For what is your life? It is even as a vapor that appeareth for a little time and then vanisheth away." This poem appears in Timoleon, a volume of poetry completed, like Billy Budd, in the last months of Melville's life, a time during which he was affected by Schopenhauer's Buddhist-supported disillusionment as opposed to Emerson's Hindu-supported Transcendentalism. Billy Budd is conventionally read according to either a Christian-redemptive or a naturalistic interpretation, but this essay makes it possible to see Billy's happy acceptance of death as a Buddhist renunciation of a world of illusion in which both frames of reference are meaningless. Captain Vere recognizes this as he utters Billy's name prayerfully at the time of his own death. (Note: Thanks to such interpreters as Thomas Merton, Buddhism is often understood today as a religion abounding in joy and vitality. Therefore it should be observed that the translations of Buddhist texts that reached the West in the nineteenth century tended to emphasize Buddhism's world-denying and negative aspects.)

Poe

Cecil, L. Moffitt. "Poe's 'Arabesque.' " CL, 18 (1966), 55-70.
When Poe calls certain of his tales "Arabesques" he may use "Arabesque" to mean both "a carefully wrought design, which is colorful, intricate, symmetrical, and therefore pleasing, often fascinating in its effect" as well as "in the manner of the Arabians." Certainly he was familiar with George Sale's translation of the Koran, Moore's Lalla Rookh, and the Arabian Nights. Poe's "Arabesques" (a term he may have used to counter the charge of " 'Germanism' and gloom" that he refutes in the preface to his Tales of the Grotesque and Arabesque) have in common with the tales in the Arabian Nights three characteristics: (1) the primary purpose of entertainment: "The center of interest is always upon the event itself, not upon the narrator or a possible moral. The effect of the story is the thing. It must excite wonder, or terror, or laughter. It might transport one beyond the bounds of the known world as in the story of Sinbad.... By whatever means it achieves its effect, during the time of the telling, the story must captivate the reader's attention and stir his emotions"; (2) "a characteristic narrative point of view ... most [tales] ... are in the first person, told by casually identified narrators," i.e., narrators who turn up more or less by coincidence; and (3) a marvelous and "omniferous" or all-bearing universe in which anything can happen.

Murtuza, Athar. "An Arabian Source for Poe's 'The Pit and the Pendulum.' " Poe S, 5, ii (1972), 52.
Poe's familiarity with George Sale's translation of the Koran has been thoroughly documented in studies of other works, and here Murtuza speculates that he may have taken from a passage in the Muslim scripture both the idea of a torture pit as well as that of the Day of Judgment with its concomitant theme of retribution overtaking the torturers.

Twain

Campbell, Killis. "From Aesop to Mark Twain." Sewanee Review, 19 (1911), 43-49.
See the annotation of this item in Chapter 2, "The Classics."

2. THE CLASSICS

Descriptive and factual works had appeared earlier, but the first strictly literary work produced in the American colonies was George Sandys's translation of Ovid's Metamorphoses. The better-educated members of the colonial ruling class fostered an interest in the classics that lasted many generations, although their own writings continued to reflect the exterior world more than the workings of the imagination. It remained for the imaginative writers of post-Revolutionary times not only to absorb but also to use in their own idiosyncratic ways the poems, plays, and fables of the Greek and Roman authors.

In the last half of the fifth century B.C. a growing individualism led many away from the recognized religion with its remote and unresponsive Olympian gods. Just as some American writers and intellectuals in the nineteenth and twentieth centuries turned East partly in order to show their disdain for the dominant ethic of the middle class, so many Greeks took to the new mystery religions with their often exotic rites. But alongside the conservatism of the accepted outlook and liberality of the newer one, a third alternative existed, both in ancient Greece and in America: a rationalism and humanism that is expressed in the philosophical and literary works of the day rather than in religious ceremonies. There is in the fiction of nineteenth-century America a strong rationalist-humanist bent that exists either independently, in such novels as Howells's A Modern Instance, or interwoven with transcendental and exotic elements, in such works as Moby-Dick. And there is sound historical precedent for such a development: Homer made the gods responsible for the acts of mortals, while Euripides, a much later writer, made each individual responsible not only for the exercise of his or her rational and humane qualities but also for the consequence of such exercise.

And while it would be wrong to underestimate the influence of Homer in general and the importance of the Homeric simile in particular to such writers as Melville and Crane, it is nonetheless the Greek playwrights--like their literary descendant, Shakespeare--who most profoundly affected the American novel with their ethnocentric and tragic view of the world. More generally it is the storytellers rather than the philosophers who spoke most clearly to our authors: the Melville who admired Homer and Aeschylus cared not at all for "this Plato who talks thro' his nose."

This preface draws on the following sources (see "List of Works Frequently Consulted" for full bibliographic information):

Matthiessen, p. 186, 448, 379; Spiller et al., p. 40-41. For more on the rationalist-humanist bent in Greek tragedy see Charles Alexander Robinson's introduction to An Anthology of Greek Drama: First Series, San Francisco: Rinehart, 1949, p. viii-ix.

The following studies (after the "General" section) are grouped under the names, listed alphabetically, of major American fiction writers through James who were influenced by Classical authors.

General

Jacobson, D. L. "Thomas Gordon's Works of Tacitus in Pre-Revolutionary America." BNYPL, 69 (1965), 58-64.

"Americans of the revolutionary generation did not read just any Tacitus; most of those who became familiar with that author did so through the translation of Gordon and at the same time were exposed to his variety of radical Whiggery.... Measuring the full impact of Gordon's Tacitus would, of course, be impossible. But the popularity of that work was great enough and the reputation of Gordon himself high enough so that it ought to be remembered by anyone attempting to analyze the intellectual climate of late colonial America."

Cooper

Porte, Joel. "Romance as New World Epic." In The Romance in America: Studies in Cooper, Poe, Hawthorne, Melville, and James. Middletown: Wesleyan University Press, 1969.

The Last of the Mohicans and The Prairie are Cooper's Iliad and Odyssey. The world of the former "is divided between wily Greeks and noble Trojans (Mingoes and Delawares), and the action concerns itself with a coveted woman (Cora). Magua is specifically associated by Cooper, through epigraphs taken from Pope's Iliad, with the Greek leaders (both Achilles and Agamemnon); and the last chapter of the book, in which Chingachgook/Priam, along with the remaining members of his tribe, celebrates and mourns the death of Uncas/Hector, is obviously patterned after the twenty-fourth book of Homer's epic, the funeral of Hector." In The Prairie Cooper, like Homer, moves from a story of fragmentation to one of reintegration. (Porte observes that Cooper's hero, like Odysseus, is something of an anachronism in the world that is being born around him.)

Crane

Anderson, Warren D. "Homer and Stephen Crane." NCF, 19 (1964), 77-86.

Though Henry Fleming is no Achilles, he, like the hero of the Iliad, "retires from battle, is profoundly affected by the death of a comrade, and returns to overwhelm the enemy with a furious attack." The Red Badge of Courage enjoys other Homeric parallels, most notably in its reliance on similes--more than 160--which compare men in war to animals and suggest humanity's oneness with all creation. Importantly, Anderson notes that this sense of oneness disappears with the development of civilization and that it is not until the naturalists that the gap between humanity and nature is closed once more.

There are other similarities between Crane's novel and Homer's works; for instance, the odd endings of the twenty-four chapters of The Red Badge of Courage, which come with disconcerting frequency and often at no break in the action, may be based on the division of the Iliad and the Odyssey into twenty-four books each. Is there evidence of Crane's having read Homer during his brief flirtation with higher education at Lafayette College and Syracuse University? Following his 1897 visit to Greece he drawled to a friend: "When I planted these hoofs of mine on Greek soil I felt like the hull of Greek literature, like one gone over to the goldarned majority. I'd a great deal of Greece. One catches these fleas at Syracuse, N'York." As Anderson observes, "... it would be interesting to know just what truth lies concealed in that jest."

Dusenberry, Robert. "The Homeric Mood in The Red Badge of Courage." Pacific Coast Philology, 3 (1968), 31-37.

One feels certain that this is a first draft and that it was sent to the editors of Pacific Coast Philology by mistake. There is an unfinished quality to this essay, both in the formal elements (the odd punctuation, the lack of transition between paragraphs) and in the tone; a writer may begin by reducing a complex and challenging novel like The Red Badge to "a study in triumph, in heroism" that is "more Homeric" than anything else, but in the course of revision ordinarily modifies some of the earlier stridency and absolutism in the understanding that the point can be made more effectively by adoption of a more reasonable and dispassionate viewpoint. There are, of course, echoes of the Iliad in The Red Badge. A number of these echoes are discussed in this article, and sometimes the connection is made convincingly, which is why readers will find this essay of at least limited interest: even a stopped clock is right twice a day. It is true, for instance, that Crane was fond of the Homeric simile that linked the worlds of war and peace ("he hopped like a schoolboy" and "he was like a babe") and the Homeric epithet (Conklin becomes "the tall soldier" and Wilson "the loud soldier"). But don't these and other Homeric echoes remind us of the difference rather than the similarity between the majesty of the epic and the ugliness of actual war? Do they not confirm that Crane's hero was correct when he " 'despaired of witnessing a Greek-like struggle' "?

Hawthorne

Boswell, Jackson Campbell. "Bosom Serpents Before Hawthorne; Origins of a Symbol." ELN, 12 (1975), 279-87.

"The simple fact is that literary bosom snakes have been with us since Aesop and Virgil; indeed English literature is fairly crawling with them, as is evidenced by twenty-three new citations--all possible inspirations for Hawthorne--noted hereinafter. This paper will rehearse the provenance and distribution of bosom snakes and show that Hawthorne's usage of the symbol is, though original and typically American, deeply rooted in a rich literary tradition."

Among Boswell's twenty-three snakes are ones found in Spenser, Shakespeare, and the other Elizabethans, and in Milton, in addition to those taken from Classical sources.

Cowley, Malcolm. "Five Acts of The Scarlet Letter." In Twelve Original Essays on Great American Novels, ed. Charles Shapiro. Detroit: Wayne State University Press, 1958.

See the annotation of this item in Chapter 9, "The Eighteenth Century."

McCullen, J. T., Jr. "Ancient Rites for the Dead and 'Roger Malvin's Burial.' " Southern Folklore Quarterly, 30 (1966), 313-22.

The idea for Roger Malvin's delayed burial may have been taken from accounts of the Lemuria ceremonies of the ancient Romans, who propitiated the angry spirits of the unburied dead each year between the ninth and the thirteenth of May (the crucial action of Hawthorne's story takes place on the twelfth of May). No attempt is made in this essay to establish a specific source, although Ovid's description of the Lemuria rites in his Fasti is cited several times.

McPherson, Hugo. Hawthorne as Myth-Maker: A Study in Imagination. Toronto: University of Toronto Press, 1969.

"Three themes dominate in Hawthorne's recreation of the materials that he found in Charles Anthon's Classical Dictionary. The first, as revealed in the legends of Perseus, Cadmus, Bellerophon, Jason, Theseus, and Hercules, is the narrative of the hero: a young man undertakes a dangerous quest; he undertakes it at the prompting, or command, of a jealous king, an uncle or father; its fulfilment involves the killing of a monster; and the hero's reward (with the exception of Hercules and Bellerophon, the rider of Pegasus) is kingship. A related narrative, the stories of Pandora, Circe, and Proserpina, deals with an attractive female who, like Eve, appears to be responsible in one way or another for mankind's fallen state. And the third situation, treated in the tales of Baucis and Philemon, Midas, and the Pygmies, underlines the ideas that man's happiness is inextricably involved with the happiness of his fellows; men must learn to be brothers. The pattern of a quest, however, is central, though it is not, finally, separable from the related themes of the Dark Lady and the Brotherhood of man." Which is to say

(1) the quest hero usually has dealings with a Dark Lady (a blameless creature who is "dark" only in Calvinist eyes) and (2) the quest hero's goal is the brotherhood of man.

An example of Hawthorne's fusion of the three themes is "Young Goodman Brown": in his quest Brown mistakes his wife for a Dark Lady; his quest fails and he ends in isolation. This story is an embodiment of the "New England Myth" rather than the "ideal myth"; it shows the way things usually work out in the historical world. McPherson deals in detail with _A Wonder-Book_, _Tanglewood Tales_, and the romances.

Peterich, Werner. "Hawthorne and the 'Gesta Romanorum.' The Genesis of 'Rappaccini's Daughter' and 'Ethan Brand.' " In _Kleine Beträge zur Amerikanischen Literaturgeschichte_, ed. Hans Galinsky and Hans-Joachim Lang. Heidelberg: Carl Winter-Universitätsverlag, 1961.

See the annotation of this item in Chapter 4, "Dante and the Middle Ages."

Pritchard, John Paul. "Nathaniel Hawthorne." In _Return to the Fountains: Some Classical Sources of American Criticism_. Durham: Duke University Press, 1942.

"No critic himself, Hawthorne has nevertheless so deeply impressed his image upon American literature that his way of writing has molded the literature more than if, like Poe, he had left a large body of critical essays." Hawthorne's writings, many of which are stories of art and artists, betray a strong Horatian influence insofar as they embrace the following precepts: the artist is born as well as made; should study both books and life; should mingle profit with pleasure (_utile et dulce_); should write when inspired and refrain from writing when not inspired; should practice "file-work" (_limae labor_) on his or her prose; should not be concerned with originality (or lack of it); should accept criticism gracefully. Hawthorne did not obey all of Horace's rules, of course, and he flagrantly violated some of Aristotle's: he thought that a subject could be treated in any space instead of seeking a "proper size"; he overused the supernatural; he had scant regard for the precise organization of a given work; he did not strive for (or succeed at) universality; with the exception of _The Scarlet Letter_, he did not create characters who were true to life, true to type, and consistent. So much the worse for Hawthorne, says Pritchard: "Where he succeeded, he was often in accord with classical theory and practice; some of his failure is traceable to the disregard of classical guidance."

Rose, Marilyn Gaddis. "Theseus Motif in 'My Kinsman, Major Molineux.' " _ESQ_, no. 47 (1967), 21-23.

Readers must struggle against the ungainly style of this essay before they agree that Robin in "My Kinsman, Major Molineux" is like Theseus in "The Minotaur," Hawthorne's retelling of the

Classical story, which appeared in Tanglewood Tales. Both Robin and Theseus pass through a labyrinth, find at its center a creature in the worst of all possible states--that of alienation from its fellows--and affirm their own relation to human society.

Shroeder, John. "Miles Coverdale as Actaeon, as Faunus, and as October: With Some Consequences." PLL, 2 (1966), 126-39.
See the annotation of this item in Chapter 5, "Spenser."

Walsh, Thomas F., Jr. "Rappaccini's Literary Gardens." ESQ, no. 19 (1960), 9-13.
See the annotation of this item in Chapter 5, "Spenser."

Howells

Pritchard, John Paul. "William Dean Howells." In Return to the Fountains: Some Classical Sources of American Fiction. Durham: Duke University Press, 1942.
Pritchard's purpose is to show how Howells's literary criticism was influenced by Aristotle's Poetics and Horace's Ars Poetica through his reading of either the originals in translation or such later critical works as were affected by the theories of the two Classical authors, e.g., the critical writings of the Renaissance or the eighteenth century. Pritchard does not address the fiction directly, but his useful summary of Howells's critical principles should be interesting nonetheless to the student of his imaginative writing. Because of the numerous correspondences that are set forth, perhaps the best way to present Pritchard's argument is by means of a table that shows the ways in which Howells agreed with the critical tenets of Aristotle and Horace:

ARISTOTELIAN IDEAS WITH WHICH HOWELLS AGREED

A good play need only be read and not necessarily produced in order to be enjoyed.

The proper effect of tragedy is catharsis.

A play should not be merely episodic; it should be tightly knit into beginning, middle, and end (a novel may be more loosely constructed, however).

A work should be outlined in detail before pen is put to paper.

Characters should be individuals as well as representative types and should have well-defined physical, mental, and moral characteristics which they manifest consistently.

A work should not exceed a "proper size."

Improbable episodes are to be shunned.

HORATIAN IDEAS WITH WHICH HOWELLS AGREED

Excessive emotion should be avoided.

The writer is born but also made, and the ability to write well is acquired through years of arduous work.

The writer should study books and nature, including human nature.

There is such a thing as inspiration, and the writer must not force himself to create when inspiration is absent.
The writer must be sincere above all else.
It is difficult to impute plagiarism, since all writers work a common ground.
The writer should conscientiously practice "file-work" (limae labor) so that his productions are properly polished; his critics will show him where to file, and the writer should receive their suggestions gratefully.
The true work of art will be ethical as well as aesthetic.
The writer should not write to please himself.

IDEAS COMMON TO BOTH AUTHORS
WITH WHICH HOWELLS AGREED

The dramatic unities must be observed.
Comic and tragic elements should not be mingled.
Bloodshed should not be depicted on stage.
The writer should remain objective and not insert asides into the narrative.

Vanderbilt, Kermit. "A Modern Instance (1881-1882): Freedom and Fate in Modern America." In The Achievement of William Dean Howells: A Reinterpretation. Princeton: Princeton University Press, 1968.

Readers of A Modern Instance who have been influenced by the theories of Freud may not realize how deeply this study of jealousy and incest was affected by Howells's knowledge of Euripidean tragedy. Howells read much Greek drama in translation, and in 1875 he witnessed a Boston performance of Medea; a year later he wrote to Charles Eliot Norton that his "New Medea" was underway. "The drama of A Modern Instance reverberated with the domestic upheavals of Euripidean tragedy, particularly the violent passions generated in the Medea, though it would carry echoes also from the Electra and Orestes. In his new Medea [sic], Howells traced the stages of pathological jealousy, and related them to a destructive syndrome of incest within the house of Gaylord. At the same time, he deepened the tragedy by allowing his doomed Jason and Medea the illusion that they are free moral agents capable of circumventing their fate. Put another way, Howells had discovered in his Greek sources an esthetic analogue to a ... feature of postwar morality--the withering effects of scientific determinism on traditional religious sanctions in America, and especially on the vaunted freedom of the American individual.... In its anti-pastoral overtones, [A Modern Instance] becomes an American tragedy endowed with a depth and geographic sweep which few novels in our literature have equalled." In this book Vanderbilt also treats Howells's earlier novel The Undiscovered Country; he calls it "a sobering version of American pastoral" but does not treat in detail specific sources as he does in this chapter.

James

Berland, Alwyn. "Henry James and The Aesthetic Tradition." Journal of the History of Ideas, 23 (1962), 407-19.
See the annotation of this item in Chapter 14, "The Victorians."

Cox, C. B. "Henry James and Stoicism." Essays and Studies (London), 8 (1955), 76-88.

This important article goes a long way toward explaining the occasionally perverse-seeming behavior of James's characters. Early in his career (the year was 1866) James wrote an approving review of Thomas Wentworth Higginson's edition of The Works of Epictetus--a significant act, says Cox, because "James so rarely committed himself to direct statements of his own moral ideals." In the essay James endorses the stoical idea of satisfaction with things that are in our power and independence of things that are not; he agrees that human happiness is in our own hands, and that Paris was undone not by the Greek invasion of Troy in which his family died but by his own loss of "modesty, faith, honor, virtue."

Thus, while James believed in the liberal ideal of progress that was so popular in the latter half of the nineteenth century, "his stoical leanings lead him to conceive this progress in terms not of practical reform but of the development of human consciousness. The individual can do little to change this world of suffering and evil, but in active relationship with works of art, with nature, and, most important, with other people, his sense of what is noblest in life can be developed." In other words, James's "ideal of progress is concerned with the development of unique individuals, rather than with the general amelioration of the condition of all classes of society." In The Princess Casamassima, to mention but one of the works Cox discusses, Hyacinth Robinson could have avoided trouble if he had realized this instead of attempting what James saw clearly as an impossible effort to reconcile social reform with personal cultivation.

See also the Berland article in Chapter 14, "The Victorians."

Freedman, William A. "Universality in 'The Jolly Corner.' " TSLL, 4 (1962), 12-15.
This short but gracefully written and insightful note suggests that there is a universality to Spencer Brydon's experience, even though few readers have had the opportunity, like Brydon, to (a) turn down a million dollars and (b) receive a hint of what it might have been like to have accepted. The universality of the story lies in the idea of the appeal of knowledge concerning a fate that one might have suffered but did not, an idea bolstered by "terminology distinctly reminiscent of and metaphorical allusions to three of the greatest sources of symbolic and allegorical reference in all literature: The New Testament, Dante's Divina Commedia, and Plato's Republic, Book VII--'The allegory

of the Cave.' " Although Lazarus' return from death and Dante's from the Inferno are significant, the cave analogue is more so; indeed, "the house on the jolly corner is, mutatis mutandis, an analogue of the cave," just as Brydon's vision, while not a vision of the Good, is one that brings him to knowledge (as happens with Plato's Philosopher-King)--the knowledge that Alice Staverton is his "all," his "everything." "All," "everything," and other similar words are used so frequently ("all" occurs sixty-six times) in the story that it is difficult to underestimate the stakes for which Brydon gambles in his search for knowledge.

Gale, Robert L. "Blest Images and Sanctified Relics." In The Caught Image: Figurative Language in the Fiction of Henry James. Chapel Hill: University of North Carolina Press, 1964.

See the annotation of this item in Chapter 3, "The Bible."

Lerner, Daniel, and Oscar Cargill. "Henry James at the Grecian Urn." PMLA, 66 (1951), 316-31.

According to Lerner and Cargill, James's The Bostonians is influenced by Daudet's L'Evangéliste and Sophocles' Antigone; his The Other House is similarly affected by Ibsen's plays as well as by Euripides' Medea; and in both cases the Greek influence is the more important one. The thesis is interesting and at least partly convincing, and thus this article can be recommended honestly. The egotism and surliness of the authors are most objectionable, however. They do scholarship a disservice by sneering at those with whom they disagree, and they do James a disservice--and, unconsciously, sneer at him in the bargain--by suggesting that The Other House is the greater novel because it does a better job of incorporating the source material. Anyone who has taken literature courses knows and loathes the teachers who praise or damn an author, not on the author's merits or their absence, but because the author aids or hinders the teachers in the establishment of theses of their own device. The reader will find two such teachers here.

Tintner, Adeline R. "The Countess and Scholastica: James's 'L'Allegro' and 'Il Penseroso.' " SSF, 11 (1974), 267-76.

See the annotation of this item in Chapter 8, "Milton and His Age."

________. " 'High Melancholy and Sweet': James and the Arcadian Tradition." CLQ, 12 (1976), 109-21.

Tintner distinguishes the Arcadian tradition from the pastoral by emphasizing the former's inclusion of a "melancholy and sweet" note in the chord of happiness; the Arcadian time is evening, not noon, and Arcadians are aware of inevitable death. The tradition began with Vergil, lay dormant throughout the

Middle Ages, revived in the Renaissance in the paintings of Poussin and in other works, and reached James primarily through the paintings of Watteau (e.g., The Voyage to Cythera) and Balzac's Comêdie Humaine. The Arcadian strain can be seen in a number of James's works, including The Europeans, The Portrait of a Lady, The Ambassadors ("his most complete Arcadian novel"), and The Wings of the Dove. An informed, lucidly written, and pleasingly illustrated essay.

________. "The House of Atreus and Mme. de Bellegarde's Crime." N&Q 20 (1973), 98-99.
See the annotation of this item in Chapter 15, "The Realists."

Melville

Braswell, William. "Melville's Use of Seneca." AL, 12 (1940-41), 98-104.
Since its founding, what American Literature has lacked in readability and originality it has more than compensated for in the impeccable quality of its scholarship. The article in hand is ample proof of this: its author located Melville's copy of Seneca's Morals (in the Gansevoort-Lansing Collection of the New York Public Library) and by placing quotes from Seneca alongside ones from Mardi--the most telling way to establish a source and, perhaps for that reason, one that is too infrequently used--to show that "like Seneca, [the people of Serenia] advocate love of God and one's fellow men; they practice religious tolerance; they have no use for magnificent temples; they set good deeds above words; they maintain that the guide to virtuous living is within oneself. Their belief in immortality is scarcely mentioned; they live to be happy here. In short, except for their faith in Christ, or Alma, their religion is virtually Seneca's." This revelation will not shake the world of letters on its axis, but it is honestly reached and wholly convincing, and that is enough. Incidentally, Melville inscribed his copy of the Morals for his brother Thomas, calling it "a round-of-beef where all hands may cut & come again."

Dale, T. R. "Melville and Aristotle: The Conclusion of Moby-Dick as a Classical Tragedy." Boston University Studies in English, 3 (1957), 45-50.
The last four chapters of Moby-Dick "constitute a drama in narrative form which conforms in all but a few respects to Aristotle's principles as presented in the Poetics, and which exhibits marked similarities to features of Sophocles' tragedies." Dale finds no evidence of Melville's having read the Poetics but speculates that at least he may have studied some of Sophocles' plays in translation. Puzzlingly, Dale observes that the conclusion of Moby-Dick "bears a greater resemblance to ... Shakespeare's Macbeth than to any Greek tragedy," which makes one wonder why he didn't explore that relationship instead.

D'Avanzo, Mario L. "Ahab, the Grecian Pantheon and Shelley's Prometheus Unbound: The Dynamics of Myth in Moby-Dick." Books at Brown, 24 (1971), 1944.

"Ahab ... is a developing character (in terms of myth) and not a static entity. That is, his character is Protean; he is a shifting composite of gods in the Grecian pantheon. A close examination of Ahab's mythic character suggests that Melville's imagination is both a try-works in which old myths are melted and a forge on which new shapes and relationships are hammered.... While he may play the role of Zeus to the crew (most notably Perth, who is in turn identifiable with subordinate gods in the pantheon), he also plays Prometheus to Moby Dick, whom he regards as the tyrant Zeus. But Melville not only reworks the Greek myths but also a Romantic adaptation of those myths, specifically ... Shelley's Prometheus Unbound, which further informs us of the dynamism of mythmaking in the novel." Regarding the latter work, Avanzo argues again that to Ahab, the whale is Zeus, in relation to whom Ahab takes on both the character of the suffering Prometheus of Aeschylus and that of the defiant, unregenerate Prometheus of Shelley. A carefully argued, convincing essay.

Finkelstein, Dorothee. Melville's Orienda. New Haven and London: Yale University Press, 1961.

See the annotation of this item in Chapter 1, "The Oriental Heritage."

Franklin, H. Bruce. The Wake of the Gods: Melville's Mythology. Stanford: Stanford University Press, 1963.

See the annotation of this item in Chapter 1, "The Oriental Heritage."

Lewis, R. W. B. "Melville on Homer." AL, 22 (1950-51), 166-76.

Melville's markings in his copy of Chapman's Homer (in the Houghton Library at Harvard) suggest that the novelist's reading of the epics was a good deal darker than conventional interpretations. In the Iliad "the bustling intrusion of the gods on either side of the battle is largely forgotten, and we are left with a remote and hostile race [of gods], quick to anger, harshly indifferent to the fate of man, interfering only to blast his tenuous hopes. Human will and freedom count for little; an impression rises from the marked pages of men accomplishing their own destruction in the midst of forces they can neither identify nor control." Similarly, Melville "dims some of the brightness" of the Odyssey, and, in so doing, suggests a theme for the epic: education. Through suffering, Odysseus learns not only to distinguish between appearance and reality but also discovers that "evil" and "real" are virtually synonymous. This reading "brings the Odyssey effectively close to Moby-Dick," notes Lewis. Thus the wise artist, like Odysseus and Melville, will always "'[bestow] / A veil on truth'" (Odyssey, XIII, 370).

Mansfield, Luther S., and Howard P. Vincent. "Explanatory Notes" to Moby-Dick. New York: Hendricks House, 1952.
Among the classical allusions and references in the novel discussed in these indispensable notes are the following: Josephus, Diogenes Laertius, Pythagoras, Ovid, Plato, Pliny, Plutarch, and Prometheus.

Matthiessen, F. O. "The Levels Beyond." In American Renaissance: Art and Expression in the Age of Emerson and Whitman. New York: Oxford University Press, 1941.
In Moby-Dick Melville "did not let his Homeric similes remain mere ornaments.... The controlled accumulation of such similes was the prime source for both his volume and variety in the narrative of the final chase," as Matthiessen demonstrates. Although he states later in this section that "Melville's breadth and dignity are often more Biblical than Homeric," Matthiessen's ultimate point is that, by means of the ancient writings, Melville "had cut through the dead tissues of the culture of his day, and had rediscovered the primitive and enduring nature of Man."

McNamara, Anne. "Melville's Billy Budd." Explicator, 21 (1962), item 11.
This article addresses those who think that classical references in fiction are purely pedantic and decorative and informs them that, in this instance, "references to the Graces, Love, Apollo, Hyperion, Hercules, the Vestals, and the Fates" are actually "major functional elements" in Melville's presentation of his hero's physical and moral character.

Murray, Henry A. "Introduction" to Pierre. New York: Hendricks House, 1949.
See the annotation of this item in Chapter 7, "Shakespeare and the Renaissance."

Rose, Edward J. " 'The Queenly Personality': Walpole, Melville, and Mother." Literature and Psychology, 15 (1965), 216-29.
See the annotation of this item in Chapter 11, "The Gothic Novelists."

Satterfield, John. "Perth: An Organic Digression in Moby-Dick." MLN, 74 (1959), 106-07.
Like Hephaestus in the Iliad, Perth in Moby-Dick is a "crippled smith-god and sometimes victim of alcohol"--more reason, says the author, for reading the book as an epic rather than a tragedy.

Sealts, Merton M., Jr. "Melville's Neoplatonic Originals." MLN, 67 (1952), 86-92.

References in Mardi and The Confidence-Man make it clear that Melville was acquainted with Thomas Taylor's The Six Books of Proclus on the Theology of Plato. But Melville used Proclus' writings as a target for what he saw as gibberish pretending to be philosophy. Further, Melville may have been taking a poke at Emerson when he took one at Proclus. He knew of Emerson's fondness for the Neoplatonist, and perhaps it is no mere coincidence that Mark Winsome, the character in The Confidence-Man who is said to be modeled on Emerson, quotes Proclus. "Oracular gibberish" was one of Melville's true bêtes noires, and for him it was "best symbolized by Taylor's translation of Proclus, representing the sacred texts of the cult, and by Emerson as its modern prophet."

Singleton, Marvin. "Melville's 'Bartleby': Over the Republic, a Ciceronian Shadow." Canadian Review of American Studies, 6 (1975), 165-73.

"Bartleby, the shade of Cicero, exemplifies the highest reach of ideal kin/friendship within the aspiration of the stoic tradition. This spirit ('Like a very ghost') 'agreeably to the laws of magical invocation' is pulled into the office of a 'Mastery' of 'Chancery,' which office is decorated by a bust of Cicero. Once there, Bartleby prefers to assume a level of obligation which defies the commonsense expectancies and allodial rackrent proprieties of his patron. Bartleby selects the office in question, according to the logic of our myth, because it evokes the great tradition of Natural Law, a tradition at least vestigially administered as Equity in its Chancery context, and a tradition organically related to the original Roman chancery and the original decretal power in the unitary empire. Such a conception was possible for the Type-haunted Melville, especially a self-taught writer with strongly mixed feelings concerning Plato and republicanism." To some readers this kind of writing is strong or forceful; to others it is merely hard to read. Interesting argument, though.

Sweeney, Gerard M. Melville's Use of Classical Mythology. Amsterdam: Rodolpi N. V., 1975.

This study strikes me as a loose shuffling of several articles. Its main focus is on Melville's use of the Prometheus myth, mainly in Moby-Dick and Pierre. Possibly this facet alone of Melville's use of the classics should have been studied in a single long article and the others--his allusions to Sophocles, Ovid, and Plutarch--treated in several shorter pieces; at any rate it will be more profitable to read this book as the long article it might have been than in any other way.

Sweeney notes that Ahab is really two Promethei in one: he is "simultaneously the counterpart of the classical Prometheus, the criminally defiant Titan punished by an external force for his unregenerate rebellion, and the counterpart of the Renaissance Prometheus, the intense thinker and self-consumed melancholiac." Such an ambitious amalgam is possible only in a work of Moby-Dick's scope, whereas in Pierre "the domestic setting and the absence of a major symbol preclude both a defiance as grand as Ahab's and an external catastrophic punishment that is so uniquely classical. As a result, most of the book's Promethean mythology is rooted, as it must be, in the Renaissance versions of the myth, wherein the torment (or punishment for excess) is internal and the sufferer is at once both a host and a parasite of himself."

In later works Melville moves even farther away from the doubly-Promethean Ahab: his later characters are more Odyssean than Promethean. Instead of boldness and defiance they practice deceit (Babo, the Confidence-Man, Claggart) or silence (Bartleby, Benito Cereno, Billy Budd). Sweeney concedes that there is more to Ahab than Prometheus; in discussing Melville's "collage-making" use of allusions, he notes that "to say that Ahab is the counterpart of Prometheus, Oedipus, and Narcissus is not to deny that he is also the counterpart of Satan, Faust, or Lear. The fact that Ahab is related to all these characters (and to many others besides) attests Melville's indebtedness; the fact that Ahab is none of them--he is, after all, Ahab--attests Melville's originality and genius" [sic].

Thompson, Lawrance. Melville's Quarrel with God. Princeton: Princeton University Press, 1952, passim.

Throughout his works Melville sneers at what he saw as the "sickly sweet" and sophomoric nature of Platonism, which he saw as a malevolent element of Emerson's Transcendentalism and of Christian dogma in general.

Poe

Pritchard, John Paul. "Edgar Allan Poe." In Return to the Fountains: Some Classical Sources of American Criticism. Durham: Duke University Press, 1942.

A particularly headstrong and contentious person, even for a writer, Poe is notable in the way that he accepts, defies, and misapprehends the tenets of the classical literary theoreticians. He ultimately approximated Aristotle's position on imitation, writing that "the drama, while never losing sight of nature's general intention, should surpass nature." He was almost obsessional in his insistence on the dramatic unities, and he believed, like Aristotle, that the improbable and the supernatural were to be avoided. Also like Aristotle, Poe required writers to work out their entire plots before beginning. On the other hand, he did not attribute to plot the primacy that Aristotle did; he does not mention catharsis; and he follows Coleridge's lead in misrepresenting Aristotle by having him say that poetry is the most philosophical of all writing, whereas the Stagirite only said that poetry is more philosophical and serious than history.

Along with Horace, Poe believed that characters must be consistent; that *utile* and *dulce* are to be blended in art; that the true poet is a genius and one who has an almost priestly function; that the poet should choose a suitable theme; should be utterly sincere; should receive criticism gracefully. Poe was concerned with plagiarism in a way that Horace was not and apparently saw it everywhere. Where Horace and Aristotle agreed, Poe was likely to as well. Thus one ought to write nothing that is against nature, and violent death should not be depicted graphically.

If, on balance, there is more of Horace in Poe than Aristotle, it is because "Aristotle had been presented to Poe as an arbitrary lawgiver, and against such Poe always rebelled; but Horace, whom he knew at first hand, could not be misrepresented to him by any amount of 'neoclassical legislation.' "

Twain

Campbell, Killis. "From Aesop to Mark Twain." *Sewanee Review*, 19 (1911), 43-49.
Twain's "A Dog's Tale" has as predecessor the variously titled story of "The Dog and the Snake," which "had its origin in India some five hundred years before Christ" and "is preserved in upwards of twenty-five different versions [including Aesop's], representing every language of Europe and a good half of the languages of Asia." Campbell concedes the difficulty of ascertaining a precise source for Twain's story.

Laverty, Carroll D. "The Genesis of *The Mysterious Stranger*." *MTQ*, 8, iii and iv (1947), 15-19.
See the annotation of this item in Chapter 9, "The Eighteenth Century."

3. THE BIBLE

Each of our authors knew the Bible. Some of them may have tried to throw it away on occasion, but as Edgar Lee Masters said of Twain's Bible, "it seemed to be attached to a rubber band, and was likely to bounce back into his lap at any time." Of course these writers read the Bible more as Hellenists than as Hebraists, to use Matthew Arnold's distinction. To Hawthorne, for instance, the Bible was a basis for dreaming rather than spiritual exercise, and its theology meant less to him than its allegory.

Once again the evidence shows the propensity of our writers for appropriating public materials for private use. However, what is particularly striking about the effect of the Bible on American literature is that the Scripture that is the backbone of the dominant ethic is so often used by our authors to gainsay that ethic. Cotton Mather saw the American colonists as Jews and John Winthrop as the Moses who lead them into the wilderness, thus beginning a tradition that continues to this day: a tradition in which American religious and political leaders identify themselves and their followers with God's chosen people. In contrast, Emerson noted in the Divinity School Address (1838) that while "the Hebrew and Greek scriptures contain immortal sentences, that have been bread of life to millions ..., they have no epical integrity; are fragmentary; are not shown in their order to the intellect," and thus it remained for some "new Teacher" to make manifest the significance that the Bible concealed. Elsewhere, Emerson was even more forceful still when he wrote, "We too must write Bibles."

Scandalous in their day, Emerson's remarks seem rather mild in ours. Their importance lies in the fact that they helped make it feasible for writers in the decades that followed to depart from stifling orthodoxy and at the same time put to good use the themes and technical devices of the Bible, orthodoxy's unwitting legacy to the unorthodox. More than any other writer, Twain made this curious partnership obvious, for in burlesquing the Scripture he took for granted every reader's thorough knowledge of it.

This preface draws on the following sources (see "List of Works Frequently Consulted" for full bibliographic information): Buell, p. 31; Cunliffe, p. 28; Normand, p. 33; Wagenknecht, _Mark Twain_, p. 62; Edgar Lee Masters, _Mark Twain: A Portrait_, _New York_: Scribner's, 1938, p. 15. The second Emerson quotation is from _Representative Men_, cited in Roy Harvey Pearce, _The Continuity of American Poetry_, Princeton: Princeton University Press, 1961, p. 190.

The following studies (after the "General" section) are grouped under the names, listed alphabetically, of major American fiction writers through James who were influenced by the Bible.

General

Baker, Carlos. "The Place of the Bible in American Fiction." In Religious Perspectives in American Culture, ed. James Ward Smith and A. Leland Jamison. Princeton: Princeton University Press, 1961.
A necessarily general yet thoughtful survey of Biblical influence from Cooper's day to Faulkner's. Baker notes that the Bible's stylistic influence, once strong, has waned; still, he says, "our best novelists continue to make full use of the Bible as a source-book for ideas, images, and mythological frameworks."

Brumm, Ursula. "The Figure of Christ in American Literature." Partisan Review, 24 (1957), 403-13.
Serious novelists from Melville to Hemingway invoke (rather than literally depict) the image of Christ to bestow dignity on the sufferings of "the luckless American Adam" and give him "a benediction which he could never attain by himself." See Suderman, below.

McAleer, John J. "Biblical Symbols in American Literature: A Utilitarian Design." ES, 56 (1965), 310-22.
The story of the New England Puritans is the story of Moses, the Chosen People, and the Promised Land. McAleer ponders adaptations of the Mosaic myth and the eventual replacement of the Old Testament concept of a worldly kingdom with the New Testament promise of a heavenly one in the works of American authors from Hawthorne forward.

Suderman, Elmer F. "Jesus as a Character in the American Religious Novel: 1870-1900." Discourse, 9 (1966), 101-15.
The novelists Suderman considers, all of them decidedly second-rate, depicted an "impotent Jesus"; their novels "demanded as little intellectually as bad television demands of us today." See Brumm, above.

Cooper

McAleer, John J. "Biblical Analogy in the Leatherstocking Tales." NCF, 17 (1962), 217-35.
Cooper opposed the Puritans' belief that they were "neo-Israelites who had reached a promised land" because in his day that belief had become secularized and thus dangerous to much that

he loved. "In the eighteenth and nineteenth centuries enterprising Yankees, magnificently led by Benjamin Franklin, poured out of New England, domesticating Puritanism's business ethic throughout the young country and dispatching to the frontiers a steady stream of energetic prosperity seekers. Although they were convinced they had a natural right to the wealth of the wilderness and were at liberty to dispossess its inhabitants as they saw fit, a secularized concept of the promised land impelled them." Thus two characters in the Leatherstocking series who don conspicuously Biblical roles (David Gamut in The Last of the Mohicans and Judith Hutter in The Deerslayer) are portrayed unfavorably. In the last book of the series, The Prairie, Cooper has Natty Bumppo take on and then put aside the role of Moses; the Moses-Bumppo analogy might have been handled more skillfully by Cooper, but at least it shows how wrongheaded (from Cooper's viewpoint) is the materialism of the day.

Crane

Gargano, James M. "Crane's 'A Mystery of Heroism': A Possible Source." MLN, 74 (1959), 22-23.

In II Samuel 23:13-17, three men go behind enemy lines to bring David a drink of water from a distant well. In Crane's story a soldier performs essentially the same act. His deed is made to seem ludicrous and futile, however, in accordance with Crane's jaundiced view of battlefield heroes.

Knapp, Daniel. "Son of Thunder: Stephen Crane and the Fourth Evangelist." NCF, 24 (1969), 253-91.

Knapp points out correctly that Crane's writings pose major problems for the pigeonholers. Crane is not entirely a naturalist (he is too moral and "religious"); nor an impressionist (impressionism defines the surface of Crane's writing but not its structure); nor a Howellsian realist, even though he claimed that realism was his goal (in Howells, but not in Crane, the individual's fate is at bottom his or her own responsibility); nor an ironist (Crane debunks some forms of sentimentality, but he subscribes simultaneously to others). Question: What, then, is a, if not the, consistent model for his prose? Answer: Seven of Crane's most important works are probably "based directly and consciously on the New Testament." Four of these works--"The Monster," "The Blue Hotel," Maggie: A Girl of the Streets, and George's Mother--receive close readings, or perhaps over-readings. For instance, the Blue Hotel is actually named the Palace and is owned by the Scullys, making it the Palace of the Scullys or the Place of the Skull or Golgotha--just the right setting for a modern crucifixion allegory. There are many other correspondences, of course (here as well as in the other three cases), and Knapp says that "the pattern is fantastic, but it hangs together." Another reader might say that the pattern is fantastic and that it almost hangs together. But Knapp's writing is witty, his citations are learned, and he is much less overbearing than this redaction might make him seem. Too, there is much food for thought in his belief that "secretly [Crane] appears to have set out to write a still newer testament, for a world that had forgotten the doctrine of love."

Stein, William Bysshe. "New Testament Inversion in Crane's Maggie." MLN, 73 (1958), 268-72.
Maggie is the Magdalene, of whom it is written: " 'Wherefore I say unto Thee, Her sins which are many, are forgiven; for she loved much.' " That her innocent love does not gain forgiveness for her on earth, however, is evidence of the failure of Christianity.

Hawthorne

Brennan, Joseph X., and Seymour L. Gross. "The Origin of Hawthorne's Unpardonable Sin." Boston University Studies in English, 3 (1957), 123-29.
The idea of the unpardonable sin is not so paradoxical as it seems. The point is not that there is a sin so terrible that God refuses to pardon it; rather the unpardonable sin--opposition to God and His truth--by its nature precludes forgiveness, since the heart that is thus guilty is closed to all except its own error. At least this is the interpretation of Matthew 12:31-32 that Hawthorne had in mind when he wrote "The Man of Adamant" (1837). Later Hawthorne realized that the theme of the unpardonable sin was necessarily undramatic, for the sinner must realize the sin if there is to be dramatic movement. Thus in later stories Hawthorne focuses on the sinner rather than the sin.

Geraldi, Robert. "Biblical and Religious Sources and Parallels in The Scarlet Letter." Language Quarterly (University of South Florida), 15 (1975), 31-34.
The possible sources include the following: (1) the New Testament's treatment of sin as a source of grace (adultresses come off pretty well in the NT); (2) the 32nd Psalm, which extols the joys of confession; (3) the arguments against adultery in Proverbs (where it says "can a man rake together fire into his bosom and yet his very garments not be burned?" Apparently not, since Dimmesdale feels flames in his chest and the pain of the branding iron); (4) the Song of Songs (in the description of Hester); and (5) the description of the passion of Christ, which is parodied when Dimmesdale appears on the scaffold flanked by Hester and Pearl.

Magretta, Joan. "The Coverdale Translation: Blithedale and the Bible." NHJ, 1974, 250-55.
In reading The Blithedale Romance and noting Hawthorne's use of Biblical themes and techniques we are not inclined to turn

from the novel to the Bible so much as we are liable to see that the novel is _like_ the Bible, i.e., an explanation of things. "That there are no _new_ truths under the sun is the wisdom of Ecclesiastes. That the seasons come and go, that human endeavor is all vanity, that the generations pass but the earth abides forever--this is finally the wisdom which Coverdale has accumulated, albeit too late for his own salvation. This is ultimately what he has come to see and the vantage point from which his testament is issued."

Stock, Ely. "The Biblical Context of 'Ethan Brand.' " _AL_, 37 (1965-66), 115-34.

In creating the character of "Ethan Brand," Hawthorne used the Cain story as well as a variety of other Biblical materials to "enrich otherwise insignificant details with the fascination and power of myth and legend." Further, Hawthorne was indebted to Byron's Cain as portrayed in the verse drama _Cain: A Mystery_ (1821). This Cain is, like Ethan Brand, "a _Hamlet_-like prototype of the nineteenth-century intellectual."

________. "History and the Bible in Hawthorne's 'Roger Malvin's Burial.' " _Essex Institute Historical Collections_, 100 (1964), 279-96.

Hawthorne's tale begins with a reference to Lovell's Fight, a cowardly massacre of Indians by white mercenaries who were sentimentally made into folk heroes by balladeers and journalists. Hawthorne comments ironically on the historical event and then moves into the story of the two survivors of the struggle, Reuben Bourne and Roger Malvin. Their tale is enriched by Biblical references of various kinds; rather than merely sentimentalize the historical occasion, then, Hawthorne differed from his contemporaries in that he saw "the human situation ironically and the religious implications of the human situation meaningfully." Stock notes that earlier critics have studied both the historical and the Biblical basis of this tale (see Thompson's article, below, for an example of the latter type of study) but points out that his essay is the first to show how the two sources are linked as well as discuss the significance of their linking.

Thompson, W. R. "The Biblical Sources of Hawthorne's 'Roger Malvin's Burial.' " _PMLA_, 77 (1962), 92-96.

Whereas some readers _mistakenly_ think that Hawthorne's use of Biblical allusions "represent pure overflow and are not truly integral to the pieces in which they are embedded," Thompson finds that "the skilled superimposition of archetypal figures on fictional characters" is "the distinctive hallmark of Hawthorne's allegory at its best; and it serves in this particular case ["Roger Malvin's Burial"] to point up the nature of a highly complex method of composition."

________. "Patterns of Biblical Allusions in Hawthorne's 'The Gentle Boy.' " South Central Bulletin, 22, iv (1962), 3-10.
Whereas it is widely assumed that Hawthorne's Biblical allusions are merely "an unconsious by-product of his known familiarity with the Bible," Thompson maintains that this story is proof that Hawthorne knew what he was doing. In brief, Hawthorne has his characters "quote and paraphrase Scriptural passages in such a way as to justify their own peculiar angles of vision."

________. "Theme and Method in Hawthorne's 'The Great Carbuncle.'" South Central Bulletin, 21, iv (1961), 3-10.
Hawthorne's Hannah, says Thompson, has as prototype the Hannah of I Samuel; both set out on quests, both have specific, unselfish goals in mind. He argues less convincingly that the Great Carbuncle itself, which blazes like a star, has in its background the light-under-a-bushel injunction from Matthew 5:14-16.

Walsh, Thomas F., Jr. "Rappaccini's Literary Gardens." ESQ, no. 19 (1962), 9-13.
See the annotation of this item in Chapter 5, "Spenser."

James

Bellman, Samuel. "Henry James' 'The Tree of Knowledge': A Biblical Parallel." SSF, 1 (1964), 226-28.
James's tale of the inept sculptor whose failure is kept at a distance by a loyal family and a friend named Peter is an inversion of the story of Christianity, in which "a Great Movement ... is prevented from succeeding because of the limitations of its founder."

Freedman, William A. "Universality in 'The Jolly Corner.' " TSLL, 4 (1962), 12-15.
See the annotation of this item in Chapter 2, "The Classics."

Gale, Robert L. "Blest Images and Sanctified Relics." In The Caught Image: Figurative Language in the Fiction of Henry James. Chapel Hill: University of North Carolina Press, 1964.
Gale gives examples of James's numerous allusions to Biblical persons and concludes that "the Bible did almost nothing for James's style but provide it with an occasional ornamental allusion"--this, no doubt, because "the only religion to James seems to have been the adoration of art." (In addition to Biblical references this chapter takes into account altogether more than eight hundred figures of speech in James's writings that

allude to "Greek and Roman deities, pagans alone or in conflict with Christians, and ... many elements of Christianity.")

West, Muriel. A Stormy Night with "The Turn of the Screw." Phoenix: Frye & Smith, 1964, passim.
West is a nut but a learned one (see the main annotation of this item in Chapter 11, "The Gothic Novelists"). For example, when the governess of The Turn reports that Miles played for her as David played for Saul (I Samuel, 16:23), West recalls that Saul was mad when David played for him; this, she says, is James's way of telling us that the governess is insane.

Melville

Heflin, Wilson. "A Biblical Source for 'The Whale-Watch' in Moby-Dick." Extracts, 23 (1975), 13.
While acknowledging the influence of Macbeth on Fedallah's utterings in Chapter 117, "The Whale-Watch" (as pointed out in the "Explanatory Notes," p. 819, of the Hendricks House edition of Moby-Dick, ed. Luther S. Mansfield and Howard P. Vincent, New York, 1952), Heflin points also to Job, 8:12-15, which begins "Am I a sea, or a whale, that thou settest a watch over me?" and ends with what might be a prediction of Ahab's peculiar death: "So that my soul chooseth strangling, and death rather than life."

Hoffman, Daniel G. "Moby-Dick: Jonah's Whale or Job's?" Sewanee Review, 69 (1961), 205-24.
Hoffman is a skillful poet as well as a critic, and poets are often better at asking questions that answering them. If I understand this essay correctly, it says that Moby-Dick is, first of all, Jonah's whale, for the fate of the Pequod's crew is "to relive aspects of Job's rebellion against God's Word, his incarceration in the whale, his being cast forth, and his redemption. Only Ishmael can reenact the entire myth; for the others, to each is given his own portion of Jonah's suffering, wisdom, and glory." Yet Moby-Dick is Job's whale, too--not the whale that redeems but the whale that chastens and reminds us of our limitations. In my Bible the Lord asks an unrepentant Job: "Canst thou draw out leviathan with a hook?" When he realizes that he cannot, Job simultaneously realizes his own humble state and repents of his anger at the Lord's unknowable ways. According to Hoffman, Moby-Dick shows us that "we can come no nearer to the Source than to behold the greatest of His works."

Holman, C. Hugh. "The Reconciliation of Ishmael: Moby-Dick and the Book of Job." South Atlantic Quarterly, 57 (1958), 477-90.
Ordinarily a rapid writer, Melville slowed his pace during the

final months of Moby-Dick. This, says Holman, is because a rereading of the Book of Job resulted in a rewriting of what could have been a mere whaling adventure. There are two fused elements in Moby-Dick: the adventure plot is Ahab's, but the theme centers on the passive Ishmael. Ishmael observes that "there is a wisdom that is woe; but there is a woe that is madness." The woe of Ahab is madness; the wisdom of Ishmael is only woe. What Melville learned from Job and then wrote into his novel is the lesson "that, though in this darkly imperfect world wisdom is woe, still man must learn to avoid the woe that is madness. He knows that there is no sane alternative to shouldering the burden of this ambiguous and affrightening world."

Jeffrey, Lloyd N. "A Concordance to the Biblical Allusions in Moby Dick." Bulletin of Bibliography, 21 (1956), 223-29.
A supplement to Nathalia Wright's Melville's Use of the Bible (described below).

Joseph, Vasanth. "Some Biblical Nuances in Moby-Dick." Osmania Journal of English Studies, 8 (1971), 70-77.
"Because the Bible stresses the need for mending one's ways in the light of experience [see the story of Jonah, for instance], Melville appears to use Biblical ideas as a contrast to life as plunged into by most human beings. That is, he finds the message of the Bible to be relative, and therefore contrasts it with the cock-shure [sic] notions of the absolute which men and women everywhere hold." Take Ahab, whose notion of the absolute includes the assumption of the White Whale's evil nature. Ahab both questions his fate ("in Biblical terms, man is not in a position to question his fate") and attempts to redress it; hence his downfall.

Mansfield, Luther S., and Howard P. Vincent. "Explanatory Notes" to Moby-Dick. New York: Hendricks House, 1952.
"Far outranking all other books in its all-pervading influence was the King James version of the Bible, which Melville read and reread, annotated and marked in more than one edition." These indispensable notes detail and explicate the numerous Biblical references in Moby-Dick.

Matthiessen, F. O. "The Levels Beyond." In American Renaissance: Art and Expression in the Age of Emerson and Whitman. New York: Oxford University Press, 1941.
See the annotation of this item in Chapter 2, "The Classics."

Newbery, I. " 'The Encantadas': Melville's Inferno." AL, 38 (1966-67), 49-68.
See the annotation of this item in Chapter 4, "Dante and the Middle Ages."

Quirk, Tom. "Saint Paul's Types of the Faithful and Melville's Confidence Man." NCF, 28 (1974), 472-77.
When he comes aboard the Fidèle the confidence man writes on his slate some slogans from I Corinthians 13. A glance at the preceding chapter of the Biblical book reveals a passage that suggests a structure for Melville's novel: "And God hath set some in the church, first apostles, secondarily prophets, thirdly teachers, after that miracles, then gifts of healings, helps, governments, diversities of tongues" (I Corinthians 12:28; the italics are Quirk's). These types of the faithful are the various incarnations that the confidence man takes, in slightly different order, thus giving to what strikes most readers as a maddingly unstructured novel a "framework which would allow the author to be discursive, even anecdotal, and still remain faithful to an almost formulaic structural pattern."

Singleton, Gregory H. "Ishmael and the Covenant." Discourse, 12 (1969), 54-67.
The covenant of the Pequod is the covenant of death as opposed to the covenant of life of the Bible. This is Melville's "greatest inversion of the Christian-Calvinist cosmology," and it leads to the final irony of the novel--that Ishmael survives because he is excluded from the covenant. Thus it is in Genesis. Most scholars point to the fact that Ishmael (in the Bible) is a wild man, but they neglect the rest of his story, which includes the information that God established his covenant with Abraham and his legitimate children only. Ishmael is characterized as a wild man only in the opening chapter, where he tells us that when he is tempted to start knocking people's hats off, he goes to sea, whereupon he joins the crew of the Pequod and calms down. After that, the important connection between the Biblical Ishmael and his namesake is that each is excluded from a covenant, the one of life and the other of death. At this point a question arises: what kind of mother would name her son after a bastard and an outcast? None, of course. When he says, "Call me Ishmael," our narrator, whose true name we will never know, is adopting a name that is peculiarly appropriate in light of the experience he is about to relate.

Thompson, Lawrance. "Divine Depravity." In Melville's Quarrel with God. Princeton: Princeton University Press, 1952.
In a footnote to this chapter Thompson notes that "Melville's entire leaning toward an exceptional form of figurative and symbolic and allegorical narrative owes much to his having been saturated in Biblical modes of expression." Writing that is figurative, symbolic, and allegorical rather than merely expository insists upon interpretation and sometimes receives readings that are mutually exclusive yet equally convincing. Thus Billy Budd can sustain both a Christian frame of reference and one that is ironically anti-Christian, in which Billy's last words--"God bless Captain Vere!"--are thus "palpably at odds with the dark facts

of the situation; those last words [within the anti-Christian context] can even be used to hypnotize the crew, because the crew is also duped, doped, kept in ignorance as to the truth."

How is a reader to choose, then? From the standpoint of seeing Melville's work as a whole, says Thompson, for "Billy Budd is cut from the same piece of cloth ... which supplied the making of White-Jacket, Moby-Dick, Pierre, The Confidence-Man"; together these works reflect a "disillusionment, hate, skepticism, agnosticism, wistfulness" that amounted to an "obsession" that "remained quite constant" and "achieved an increasingly Schopenhauerish intensity of hate toward the end of his life." The less convincing pro-Christian interpretation is set forth in works as profound as Milton R. Stern's The Fine Hammered Steel of Herman Melville (Urbana: University of Illinois Press, 1957)--which notes that "in Billy Budd Melville tells his history of humanity in a reworking of the Adam-Christ story, placing prelapsarian Adam and the Christ (both represented by Billy) on a man-of-war, and demonstrating the inevitability of the Fall and the necessity of the Crucifixion"--and as silly as H. E. Hudson IV's "Billy Budd: Adam or Christ?" (Crane Review [Tufts University], 7 [1965], 62, 67)--which argues that, since it took Melville three years to write Billy Budd the work must be a straightforward presentation of the Christian viewpoint, because it takes longer to write "serious" (as opposed to ironic) fiction.

In quarreling with God, notes Thompson, Melville often disputed with His self-appointed spokesmen, and his anti-Calvinism is also discussed at length in this book.

________. "God's Stony Heart." In Melville's Quarrel with God. Princeton: Princeton University Press, 1952.

See the annotation of this item in Chapter 7, "Shakespeare and the Renaissance."

Wright, Nathalia. Melville's Use of the Bible. Durham: Duke University Press, 1949; reprinted (with an appendix), New York: Octagon, 1969.

First, the facts. (1) The Bible was "of all his sources ... the earliest and best known, the only one with which he was well acquainted before his late twenties.... It was also one to which he deliberately turned and returned with the years." (2) "Melville echoed the Bible in novels, stories and poems persistently from Typee in 1846 to Billy Budd in 1891--in every piece, in fact, of his collected work except five sketches and a few poems.... There are upwards of fourteen hundred allusions to it." (3) The number of allusions "mounted as Melville's career developed. By actual count they increase from a dozen in Typee to 100 in Mardi to 250 in Moby-Dick and then decrease, to rise again in Clarel to 600 and in Billy Budd to 100."

How did this single source create in Melville what might be called, without exaggeration, a dependence? To the novelist the significance of the Bible lay in its "mythology, or its allegorical representation of metaphysical truth." Thus Melville, skeptic that he was, took issue with the so-called Higher Critics, who wanted to reduce scripture to mere geography and history; and he anticipated "the Freudian theory that the myth is the record of the racial unconscious and as such possesses spiritual value far superior to that of history. [The Bible's] artistic value, in turn, can hardly be overestimated. For economy, for universality, for suspension of historical time, for depth and dignity of association the myth is not to be matched, as writers like Joyce and Mann have known."

Melville came to the Bible naturally (see Chapter 1 of William Braswell's Melville's Religious Thought: An Essay in Interpretation, New York: Pageant Books, 1959, for an account of the religious background of Melville's family), but no thinker as widely read and independent-minded as he would have stayed with a book over the years had there not been a particularly magnetic attraction. To Melville Christianity, and thus the Bible, commended itself to him because of "its belief in the dignity and possibility of the individual." This "possibility" is often amplified into "a sublime egotism, at least as much Satanic as theistic.... Hence all Melville's characters have something in common with the Renaissance and with the Byronic hero." Yet all of his characters belong to history--it "towers up everywhere"--and history belongs to the past, of which it is but a fraction. There is a known world and an unknown one, and man, as Sir Thomas Browne wrote, is the great amphibian who lives in both. The authors of the Bible recognized this; so did Melville; so does "every great imaginative writer: Job [?], Dante, Shakespeare, Rabelais, Goethe. The world which they all saw was neither exact nor final; it was the approach, not the end, which they described."

Wright's book is a model study, for it demonstrates brilliantly not only what Melville found in the Bible and how he used it but also why he used it and to what effect. The result is an enhanced understanding of the novelist, both in his own right and as part of a tradition, and a renewed respect for the literary scholar who explains patiently and lucidly what you never knew and are glad to know now.

________. "Moby Dick: Jonah's or Job's Whale?" AL, 37 (1965-66), 190-95.

The forty-two "cetological chapters" of Moby-Dick have been attacked as digressive, but "they are to Ahab's pursuit of Moby Dick what Jehovah's reply is to Job's complaints: an oblique denial that morality is inherent in creation. Like Jehovah, Ishmael bypasses the whole problem of evil in human experience, which obsesses both Job and Ahab, and describes a natural world which is neither good nor evil but sheerly marvellous, or in Job's words, 'too wonderful for me'.... The cetological chapters also represent a correction of Ishmael's own tendency to lose himself in abstract speculation about the nature of the universe and the identity of the self.... The knowledge of cetology which he acquires seems calculated to save him from a fate similar to Ahab's by persuading him of the purely physical nature albeit the endlessly marvellous complexity of the universe."

Poe

Hirsch, David H. "The Pit and the Apocalypse." Sewanee Review, 76 (1968), 632-52.
In "The Pit and the Pendulum" Poe uses "the language patterns of neo-classical rationalism" to describe a terrifying situation, which lends an air of twentieth-century alienation to the tale. But an undercurrent of apocalyptic Biblical imagery becomes a tide and turns "an account of alienation ... into a tale almost as eschatological as Revelation itself." This is not as paradoxical as it seems: in an absurd world there is nothing out of place about an absurd ending. As to the blending of detached neoclassicism and fiery apocalyptics, Hirsch notes that this was not only an invention but, "coming from a writer stranded in what was surely, at the time, a backwater of civilization, an astonishing invention. But then it may be that only a provincial could have invented it."

Pearce, Donald. " 'The Cask of Amontillado.' " N&Q, 1 (1954), 448-49.
"The tale has a strong flavour of a profane rite, a sort of Black Mass, or parody of archetypal events and themes in holy scripture." As one might expect from so wildly Romantic an author as Poe, "the elements of scriptural parody wind throughout the tale demoniacally, as the mottled striations in a slab of black marble, suggesting powerful but indeterminate patterns that have a mythic feel." For instance, Montresor's "intimate betrayal" of Fortunato recalls the kiss of Judas, yet Fortunato is clearly no Christ.

Twain

Brodwin, Stanley. "The Theology of Mark Twain: Banished Adam and the Bible." Mississippi Quarterly, 29 (1976), 167-89.
Despite Twain's "overt rejection of the Bible and its theology of a fall, repentance, sacrifice and redemption, it remained a dynamic force to which he responded on many levels.... He felt he had emancipated himself from 'traditional' Christianity, its uses and abuses, to become part of the progressive scientific thought of the nineteenth century. Yet the image of the banished Adam and man's innate sinfulness, of the Adamic myth as a whole, persists throughout his work." At the end of his career Twain tried to cast off the Adamic myth: in The Mysterious Stranger and Letters from the Earth "Twain was not only seeking release from the mortal conditions of the fall, but also from the very weight of the Bible itself with its call to repentance and

the acceptance of God's creation, regardless of how mysterious and unjust that creation may appear to be."

Budd, Louis J. "Mark Twain and Joseph the Patriarch." American Quarterly, 16 (1964), 577-86.

Twain had a career-long fascination with Joseph for two reasons. First, Joseph was a symbol for the Gilded Age: he triumphed over adversity and amassed a fortune, all with God's approbation and even His assistance. Second, he was Twain's kind of guy; he contrived "to stage an unveiling of his identity that must have stirred the exhibitionist side of Twain--who worked a scene along the same lines into almost every novel he wrote." Mostly, however, Twain treated Joseph with satire. He was skeptical of much that the masses embraced (Barnum regularly put on a Joseph spectacle for his customers), and Joseph comes off in his writings as a shrewd speculator who loves nothing more than to take the suckers for all they are worth.

In 1902 Twain obliged his financial mentor Henry H. Rogers by addressing an adult Bible class conducted by John D. Rockefeller, Jr. Twain was then made an honorary member of the class, a kudo that tarnished rather quickly as the Rockefellers' monopolistic practices came under closer journalistic scrutiny. In February 1906 Rockefeller defended Joseph to his class as a commendably thrifty and level-headed fellow, a description that "many orthodox Christians of a laissez-faire generation had approved" but which prompted Twain's final word on Joseph, who to him not only took the Egyptians' very freedom as well as their property but also managed to buy off the clergy, who had stayed bought ever since.

Ensor, Allison. Mark Twain & the Bible. Lexington: University of Kentucky Press, 1969.

The year before he died Mark Twain noted that the Bible is "full of interest. It has noble poetry in it; and some clever fables; and some blood-drenched history; and some good morals; and a wealth of obscenity; and upwards of a thousand lies" (Letters from the Earth). Given a choice between the mot juste and the bon mot, Twain always went for the latter, which is why his statement on the Bible is funnier than it is expressive of his true feelings. The fact is that Twain abominated the Bible, and his hatred of it was often irrational. He did not distinguish the Old Testament from the New, nor the God of Retribution from the God of Love, and he often treated the Bible as though it were synonymous with organized religion. His main complaint was that the Bible didn't live up to its promise; the virtues that Samuel Clemens learned about in Sunday school were discovered by Mark Twain to be flimsy covers for sham and hypocrisy. Of course nothing else from his youth ever lived up to its promise in adult life, and perhaps it is not surprising to find Twain using certain stories from the Bible that support that view. These stories--The Prodigal Son, Adam and Eve, Noah and the Flood--

contrast a better world and a worse one, as do most of Twain's writings. Thus the Bible that he hated confirmed Twain's suspicions about the transience of happiness; too, it was the one book that his audience was likely to know well, so he used it despite his misgivings. Twain was an autodidact, by and large, and it never seemed to have occurred to him that ideas that struck him as original might have been chewed over thoroughly by others in centuries past. Similarly, his most controversial self-teachings (e.g., that the Bible is a fraud) were expressed most trenchantly in letters to friends who were unlikely to disagree with him. Thus Twain's rantings against the Bible and the churches often read like third-rate Tom Paine. He never had the grasp on the Bible that Melville did, and while this book details Twain's relation with the Bible, it does not explore and explain him the way Nathalia Wright's book (above) does Melville. This isn't Ensor's fault, of course. It's just that Twain's relation with the Bible was different in nature from Melville's, and it is to Twain's credit as a professional writer that he exploited this fruitful source of character and anecdote as he did.

Rowlette, Robert. "Mark Twain's Barren Tree in The Mysterious Stranger: Two Biblical Parallels." MTJ, 16, i (1972), 19-20.

In The Mysterious Stranger Satan feeds multitudes with a miraculous fruit-bearing tree that he curses when it is claimed by a rapacious Portuguese on whose land it grows. Here Twain has combined two of Christ's miracles, the feeding of the multitudes and the blighting of the fig tree, into one of Satan's. "The examination of Twain's use of this source emphasizes anew his inobtrusive [sic] drawing upon the Bible for raw material and his versatile skill in shaping that material to his own purposes."

4. DANTE AND THE MIDDLE AGES

Of the several single authors (rather than groups) who influenced American fiction Dante seems the least likely. The appeal of Spenser, Milton, Shakespeare, Scott, and even Cervantes is more readily apparent than that of the Florentine poet, whose great work is informed primarily by references to partisan political struggles, an outmoded cosmology, and a faith that must have been alien, at best, to the majority of our writers.

Yet sound reasons for the respect and admiration with which Dante was viewed are equally evident. First, The Divine Comedy employs any number of mythic devices (e.g., the poet's crossing the River Styx) and allegorical-symbolic ones (e.g., the Dark Wood of Error) that would have been useful to the eclectic and pragmatic Americans. Second, these fiction writers, and especially those who wrote great sprawling epics, must have been struck, like T. S. Eliot in a later generation, by the near-perfect order and unity of the multilevel universe described in Dante's poem. Third, and like another writer of a later generation, Ezra Pound, the often self-consciously original Americans must have apprehended the freshness and spontaneity in Dante, the lack of which would have left his partisan references meaningless and obsolete. Fourth, the writers who, like Hawthorne, relied heavily on the Puritan heritage in their work, would have recognized that Dante, like the Puritans, numbered pride as the worst, most fundamental, and most pervasive of sins. Fifth, it is apparent from the writings of authors as diverse as Hawthorne, Melville, and Twain that they, like others, indulged the natural inclination of artists to revenge themselves on their enemies by immortalizing their villainy in the manner of Dryden, Michelangelo, and Dante, and of these the Florentine poet is the undisputed master of the rhetoric of retaliation. Sixth, the colloquial and frank character of Dante's language would have struck a democratic chord in the hearts of the American fiction writers, most of whom would have doubtless concurred with Emerson's verdict: "I find [Dante] full of the nobil volgare eloquenza; that he knows 'God damn,' and can be rowdy if he please, and he does please."

Finally, and in sum, Dante shares with the Americans that marked ability to subvert from within, to criticize subtly, and not so subtly, a world order to which he and they ostensibly belonged. In light of the richness and variety of Dante's appeal it is little wonder that Melville, brooding over Hawthorne's "Young Goodman Brown," invoked the Florentine, pronouncing it "deep as Dante."

None of the other medieval writers was nearly as significantly influential as Dante. (For structural purposes I use the standard and, no doubt, overly broad definition of the Middle Ages as the period that followed the disintegration of the Western Roman Empire in the fourth and fifth centuries and lasted until about 1500, the beginning of the Renaissance; Dante himself lived from 1265 to 1321.) The most striking absence of possible influence is seen in the case of Chaucer, whose profile seems surprisingly low. In a letter to me the Chaucer scholar T. A. Kirby observed that the "translations" of Chaucer available to nineteenth-century readers were largely inept; that Chaucer was thought to lack high seriousness, as Matthew Arnold said; and that great literature was generally (though not exclusively) thought of as tragic or allegorical in nature. Hence our writers' wider interest in Greek tragedy, the Bible, Shakespeare, Spenser, Milton--and Dante.

This preface draws on the following sources (see "List of Works Frequently Consulted" for full bibliographic information): Cunliffe, p. 337-38; Matthiessen, p. 33, 191, 342; Normand, p. 33. Studies that deal with the rise of interest in Dante in the United States include Werner P. Friedrich, "Dante in the United States," in _Dante's Fame Abroad, 1350-1850_, Chapel Hill: University of North Carolina Press, 1950; Theodore W. Kosh, _Dante in America_, Boston: Ginn, 1896; Angelina La Piana, _Dante's American Pilgrimage_, New Haven: Yale University Press, 1948; Gian A. Vergani, "Lo Studio di Dante negli Stati Uniti d'America," _Filologia e Letteratura_, 14 (1968), 225-32.

The following studies (after the "General" section) are grouped under the names, listed alphabetically, of major American fiction writers through James who were influenced by Dante or another medieval author.

General

Mathews, J. Chesley. "The Interest in Dante Shown by Nineteenth-Century American Men of Letters." _SA_, 11 (1965), 77-104.

Dante was almost entirely unknown in America until the end of the eighteenth century, but in the first three quarters of the nineteenth century every major American writer except Cooper showed an interest in his writings; more specifically, "the conception of Dante which was commonly held was based largely upon the _Inferno_. And it was the _Inferno_ that was most often spoken of and quoted from." Mathews attributes this rise in interest to the publication of Henry F. Cary's translation of Dante's works in 1822 and to the teaching of Dante at Harvard.

The American authors Mathews considers in this survey are Irving, Bryant, Emerson, Hawthorne, Whittier, Poe, Holmes, Thoreau, Melville, Whitman, Longfellow, and Lowell. For more detailed treatment of Dante's influence on specific authors see the individual studies by Mathews (below).

Hawthorne

Broes, Arthur T. "Journey into Moral Darkness: 'My Kinsman, Major Molineux' as Allegory." NCF, 19 (1964), 171-84.
See the annotation of this item in Chapter 8, "Milton and His Age."

Doubleday, Neal Frank. "Hawthorne's Inferno." CE, 1 (1939-40), 658-70.
Fundamental to understanding Hawthorne is the realization that he believed in the equality of all men and women based on our common status as sinners. Thus Hawthorne distinguished himself from his Calvinist ancestors, who presumed the election of some and the damnation of the rest. More importantly, he set himself apart from contemporaries like Emerson and the other Transcendentalists who, taking a leaf from Unitarianism, trumpeted the natural goodness of humanity so loudly that they committed the sin of pride, the worst of all sins since (according to Aquinas) it is the sin of which all others are born. The proud in Hawthorne end up like Dante's damned: "Just as the sinners in the Inferno find their punishment alone in spiritual solitude despite the presence there of legions of others--in contrast to the mutual love and community of the disciplined in Purgatory--so in Hawthorne the state of sin is a state of separation from both God and man.... Hawthorne's sinners are generally characterized by rebellion; like Dante's sinners, they are miserable, not repentant."

Kesterson, David B. "Journey to Perugia: Dantean Parallels in The Marble Faun." ESQ, no. 71 (1973), 94-104.
Numerous parallels as well as direct references establish Dante's influence on the twelve-chapter (14-35) Monte Beni-Tuscany portion of The Marble Faun: Donatello (Dante), prompted by Kenyon (Vergil), takes a journey that ends with his meeting Miriam (Beatrice) and realizes "a progress from unhappiness to the qualified happiness of the mature man cognizant of the redeeming powers of love." Coming at the center of the novel, these chapters are shown to be analogous to the central scaffold scene (Chapter 12) of The Scarlet Letter and the "Arched Window" midpoint (Chapter 11) of The House of the Seven Gables by Kesterson, who demonstrates authoritatively the transforming effect that an older writer can have on a newer one.

Mathews, J. Chesley. "Hawthorne's Knowledge of Dante." Studies in English (University of Texas), no. 20 (1940), 157-65.
This essay cites all the evidence available at the time of Hawthorne's knowledge of Dante as well as his specific uses of the Italian poet's writings in his own. It does not pretend to explicate specific works but notes that "the evidence ... shows that Hawthorne certainly read the Inferno, presumably all of it, by 1843--probably by 1835; and strongly suggests that he read the

Purgatorio and Paradiso too.... The evidence seems to indicate also that he appreciated the allegorical fitness of the different punishments of the Inferno to the different classes of sinners punished there, and Dante's symbolical use of light and darkness; and one may assume that, with his great interest in moral symbolism and the soul of man, he found much in Dante congenial to himself."

Peterich, Werner. "Hawthorne and the 'Gesta Romanorum.' The Genesis of 'Rappaccini's Daughter' and 'Ethan Brand.' " In Kleine Beiträge zur Amerikanischen Literaturgeschichte, ed. Hans Galinsky and Hans-Joachim Lang. Heidelberg: Carl Winter-Universitätsverlag, 1961.

Peterich finds in the Gesta Romanorum possible sources for two of Hawthorne's tales. Beyond that he notes that the source for "Ethan Brand" recapitulates an ancient myth (about an emperor's heart that could not be destroyed by fire) and the source for "Rappaccini's Daughter" refers to an attempt to kill Alexander via a desirable but envenomed maid. This allows us, says Peterich somewhat tendentiously, to "place Hawthorne into a great tradition and indicate once more that, in the Western World, there is no such thing as an exclusively National Literature."

Schoen, Carol. "The House of the Seven Deadly Sins." ESQ, no. 70 (1973), 26-33.

See the annotation of this item in Chapter 5, "Spenser."

Van Doren, Mark. "Tales and Sketches." In Nathaniel Hawthorne. [No city given]: William Sloane Associates, 1949.

See the annotation of this item in Chapter 5, "Spenser."

Howells

Woodress, James. "Italian Literature: Dante and Longfellow." In Howells & Italy. Durham: Duke University Press, 1952.

Woodress discusses in detail Howells's considerable admiration for Dante rather than the Italian poet's influence on the American man of letters, noting that "Dante became a literary passion" during Howells's term as consul in Venice (1861-65) and continued as one during Howells's attendance at the meetings of the Dante Club in Cambridge, Massachusetts (where Howells settled in 1866), as Longfellow read aloud his translation of the Divina Commedia, James Russell Lowell and Charles Eliot Norton offered suggestions for revision, and the twenty-nine-year-old Howells "followed faithfully in his Italian Dante, content to enjoy silently one of the great intellectual experiences of his life."

Irving

Mathews, J. Chesley. "Washington Irving's Knowledge of Dante." AL, 10 (1938-39), 480-83.
From letters and journal entries it is evident that Irving read all of the Inferno at least once and in Italian. He mentions Dante's work in "The Story of a Young Robber" as well as in his nonfiction prose.

James

Freedman, William A. "Universality in 'The Jolly Corner.' " TSLL, 4 (1962), 12-15.
See the annotation of this item in Chapter 2, "The Classics."

Melville

Giovannini, G. "Melville's Pierre and Dante's Inferno." PMLA, 64 (1949), 70-78.
Giovannini musters evidence to show that "references to the Inferno in the first half of the novel, from the time when Pierre first sees Isabel to his pretended marriage and departure with her for the city, are closely coordinated with Pierre's development toward a realization of the ubiquity and universality of evil." For further proof of Melville's reliance on Dante see J. Chesley Mathews's comment on this article in PMLA, 64 (1949), 1238, and Giovannini's acknowledgment in PMLA, 65 (1950), 329.

Gollin, Rita. "Pierre's Metamorphosis of Dante's Inferno." AL, 39 (1967-68), 542-45.
"Melville's departures in his use of Dantean material are at times more significant than the similarities, generating ironic force as well as thematic reinforcement.... Dante finally emerges from the inferno to see the light of the stars; but Pierre dies in darkness.... It is the ultimate mordant ambiguity of Pierre, or The Ambiguities that Pierre's idealistic quest should end with Pierre himself the chief sinner and central cause of suffering. This metamorphosis is Melville's major inversion of Dante's vision, intensifying the book's anguished pessimism."

Mansfield, Luther S., and Howard P. Vincent. "Explanatory Notes" to Moby-Dick. New York: Hendricks House, 1952.
Among the medieval allusions and references in Moby-Dick discussed in these indispensable notes are the following: St. Augustine, Chaucer, Dante, Rabelais, and Froissart.

Mathews, J. Chesley. "Melville's Reading of Dante." Furman Studies, 6 (1958), 1-8.

Consistent with the format of Mathews's article on Hawthorne and Dante (above), this one establishes Melville's familiarity with the Italian poet's work and concludes that "it appears ... that Melville began reading a copy of [the Reverend Henry Francis] Cary's translation of the Divine Comedy in 1848 or 1849.... if he ever read the Purgatory and Paradise, they seem to have made much less impression upon him than did the Inferno, for one finds no clear indication of his having read them. And indeed, his appreciation even of the Inferno was somewhat limited. Although he was strongly impressed by some of its qualities ... he seems to have been too much inclined to see in the Inferno the spirit of pessimism and revenge."

Newbery, I. " 'The Encantadas': Melville's Inferno." AL, 38 (1966-67), 49-68.
Melville borrowed not only from travel literature in writing "The Encantadas" but also relied on references to Milton, Spenser, Dante, the Bible, and Oriental myth (the "Hindoo tortoise" is an avatar of Vishnu the Preserver). Thus "the function of the allusions and factual borrowings in 'The Encantadas' is twofold: they re-create a real world by means of descriptions, geographical data, historical facts, references to other travelers, and a collection of legends connected with the islands; but they match these hard facts with metaphysical overtones [signifying] the omnipotence of evil."

Schless, Howard H. "Flaxman, Dante, and Melville's Pierre." BNYPL, 64 (1960), 65-82.
The author examines half a dozen representative passages in Pierre to show that "by direct quotation from or allusion to Dante at crucial moments of narrative and psychological crisis in Pierre, Melville foreshadows or resolves the action of the characters and brings into focus the background in which they move." Further, he establishes that Melville had in mind not only Dante's poem but John Flaxman's illustrations of it as he wrote Pierre; thus "the graphic and the literary versions of [The Divine Comedy] must both be consulted when determining [Melville's] use of Dante." Some readers will be interested in Schless's "Moby Dick and Dante: A Critique and Time Scheme," BNYPL, 65 (1961), 289-312; others may find that essay windy and self-indulgent in comparison with this one.

Sedgwick, William Ellery. "Moby Dick." In Herman Melville: The Tragedy of Mind. Cambridge: Harvard University Press, 1945.
In Moby-Dick "Melville aimed to strike a balance between Dante and Shakespeare. Certainly, there are two actions in the book which although they mesh are distinct from one another, one of which is Shakespearean, the other Dantesque. The Shakespearean or outward tragic action includes Ahab's conflict with forces outside himself and, also, the bitter, agonizing self-conflict which

follows on its heels. All the other characters are caught up in this action, but it centers in Ahab. The other action, the Dantesque, lies entirely with Ishmael.... In Dante each incident, each observation that adds to his comprehension gains from the next; each shares in the accruing interest of his unfolding vision, and each participates by undergoing a transfiguration in the completion of the whole. It is much the same in point of action with Ishmael. His every realization gains from the next and each is the more realized by the completion of his comprehension of things. But how appallingly different is the substance of his vision! Dante came at last to the beatific vision and beheld the divine love enfolding the orders of creation as a lordly rose enfolds its own petals. The long accumulation of Ishmael's comprehension of things rolls back along the dark interior windings of Moby Dick. From his last word of all Ishmael has seen into a sundered or cloven universe and he ends by calling himself another orphan. His vision takes a direction opposite to Dante's; it shows him at the core of creation, not love but destruction. His vision has bereft him of all sense of kinship either below among bodies terrestrial, or on high, among the celestial orders."

Thompson, Lawrance. "God's Stony Heart." In Melville's Quarrel With God. Princeton: Princeton University Press, 1952.
See the annotation of this item in Chapter 7, "Shakespeare and the Renaissance."

Wright, Nathalia. "Pierre: Herman Melville's Inferno." AL, 32 (1960-61), 167-81.
To compare the novel with the poem is to clarify a number of Melville's intentions, notably that "here he came close to writing an anatomy of sin, as in Moby-Dick he wrote an anatomy of cetology. His hero proceeds systematically through most of the categories of sin recognized by the ancient and medieval worlds, from the least to the most offensive. Of these sins, moreover, to Melville as to Dante, those of fraud ... were most widespread in society."

Poe

Mathews, Joseph Chesley. "Did Poe Read Dante?" Studies in English (University of Texas), no. 18 (1938), 123-36.
Probably so--at least "there are in Poe's writings a number of references to Dante and the Inferno, three quotations, and several instances of resemblance, some more striking than others," and all fully documented here. Yet "Poe certainly shows no depth of feeling for Dante, and ... he was not profoundly moved by him." (It should be observed that Poe was almost never "profoundly moved" by other authors the way, say, Melville was.)

Twain

Baetzhold, Howard G. "Postscript I." In Mark Twain and John Bull: The British Connection. Bloomington: Indiana University Press, 1970.

"Clemens knew the Canterbury Tales ... and liked them well enough to jot down some notes early in 1897 for an operetta or fantasy to be titled, 'The Pilgrimage to Canterbury,' with Chaucer himself in a featured role. Before that he had bestowed many of the characteristics of Chaucer's pilgrims on his own group in Chapter Twenty-one of A Connecticut Yankee, specifically citing their variety of occupations and attitudes. Though his greatest emphasis was on their slavery to superstition, he used the allusion to Chaucer chiefly to stress the coarseness and indelicacy of some of the 'merry tales' which they told."

________. "Thunder and the Storm (1885-1889)." In Mark Twain and John Bull: The British Connection. Bloomington: Indiana University Press, 1970.

"Clemens' initial inspiration for [A Connecticut Yankee] resulted primarily from his fascination with the archaic diction and the chivalric derring-do that he found in Malory. Some of the passages in Le Morte Darthur remained his favorites for life. The tale of Arthur's passing he considered 'one of the most beautiful things ever written in English,' and Sir Ector's lament for Launcelot no less than 'perfect.' But the knightly adventures appealed likewise to his sense of the ridiculous."

Hoben, John B. "Mark Twain's A Connecticut Yankee: A Genetic Study." AL, 18 (1946-47), 197-218.

See the annotation of this item in Chapter 14, "The Victorians."

Werge, Thomas. "The Sin of Hypocrisy in 'The Man That Corrupted Hadleyburg' and Inferno XXIII." MTJ, 18, i (1975-76), 17-18.

"Mark Twain's delineation of the nature and effects of the sin of hypocrisy in The Man That Corrupted Hadleyburg echoes Dante's delineation of the same sin in Inferno xxiii. For Twain as for Dante, of course, hypocrisy is preeminently a sin of stealing and fraudulence, whether such fraudulence assumes the form of a false reputation, or image, or both. The inhabitants of the sixth bolgia of the eighth circle of the Inferno and the town of Hadleyburg are identical in their morally perverted and grotesque forms.

Within this general and obvious similarity of treatment are two specific parallels; the use of a pervasive tone and imagery of weight, weariness, and oppressiveness to dramatize the external and inner life of the hypocrite."

Wilson, Robert H. "Malory in The Connecticut Yankee." Studies in English (University of Texas), no. 27 (1948), 185-206.

A detailed study of how Twain used the Morte Darthur "intensely and cleverly" in the composition of his own work. Wilson notes that Twain's affection for the book was genuine and that his ridiculing of it was merely part of a broader attack on the Middle Ages.

5. SPENSER

Spenser's chief contribution to American literature is that he, along with Bunyan, revealed Hawthorne to himself and provided him with an allegorical model that he could use to elucidate the moral and psychological themes that preoccupied him. Some critics go so far as to see a case of absolute dependency in the Hawthorne-Spenser relationship; they say that Melville would have written essentially the same Moby-Dick even had he not read the Bible, Shakespeare, and Milton, but that The Blithedale Romance would have been substantially different had Hawthorne not had the example of Spenser.

The obvious admiration that Hawthorne felt for Spenser's writings, however, was more than matched by the indifference of other authors. Howells thought Spenser's poetry duller than Presidential messages prior to the time of Teddy Roosevelt, and although there are exceptions (Melville is one), most of our writers seem to have agreed with this dictum. In addition to finding Spenser dull, perhaps they apprehended a certain formlessness in his writings, a failure to attain the tightness and clarity that mark Dante's work. Of course Hawthorne shares with Spenser this quality of diffuseness as well as an inclination--better realized in his writings than in those of the English author--toward spiritual probing. The difference is that Hawthorne often begins with Spenser's clearly distinguished extremes of good and evil and then blurs the distinction; in The Scarlet Letter, for instance, a heroine who is a rank sinner in Spenser's terms as well as those of New England society becomes, if not a saint, at least a human being.

This preface draws on the following sources (see "List of Works Frequently Consulted" for full bibliographic information): Matthiessen, p. 248; Normand, p. 249; Wagenknecht, Howells, p. 13.

The following studies are grouped under the names, listed alphabetically, of major American fiction writers through James who were influenced by the works of Spenser.

Hawthorne

Boswell, Jackson Campbell. "Bosom Serpents Before Hawthorne: Origin of a Symbol." ELN, 12 (1975), 279-87.

See the annotation of this item in Chapter 2, "The Classics."

Broes, Arthur T. "Journey into Moral Darkness: 'My Kinsman, Major Molineux' as Allegory." NCF, 19 (1964), 171-84.
See the annotation of this item in Chapter 8, "Milton and His Age."

Chambers, Jane. "Two Legends of Temperance: Spenser's and Hawthorne's." ESQ, no. 77 (1974), 175-79.
On "The Birthmark." Chambers speculates that "not only Hawthorne's chief symbol for this tale, but also the motivation of its chief character, Aylmer, as well as its basic conflict and central theme were suggested to the author, in part at least, by an episode in Book II of The Faerie Queene--the episode of Guyon and Ruddymane, the infant with blood-stained hands." That story, like Hawthorne's, is a tragedy of intemperance in which people die when reason is unseated.

Emry, Hazel Thornburg. "Two Houses of Pride: Spenser's and Hawthorne's." PQ, 33 (1954), 91-94.
In describing the ancestral home of the Pyncheons in The House of the Seven Gables Hawthorne relied on "a mass of realistic notebook jottings, family traditions, and familiar Salem background," but he also borrowed from Spenser's description of the House of Pride in The Faerie Queene.

Himelick, Raymond. "Hawthorne, Spenser, and Christian Humanism." ESQ, no. 78 (1975), 21-28.
This well-reasoned essay does not try to attribute to Spenser any of Hawthorne's characters, symbols, techniques, or stories. Rather it argues that Hawthorne's principle debt to Spenser is an intellectual one. Through Spenser Hawthorne reached the pre-Spenserian tradition of early Tudor humanism, which recognized "all moral effort as the uneasy equipoise of opposites," "the Protean nature of the human situation," and "the subtle metamorphoses of virtue and vice."

Jones, Buford. "The Faery Land of Hawthorne's Romances." ESQ, no. 48 (1967), 106-24.
In his early (and failed) romance Fanshawe Hawthorne used the conventional romantic landscape that he associated with the works of Sir Walter Scott and William Gilmore Simms. In contrast, the four completed romances of his late period take place in " 'a neutral territory ... where the Actual and the Imaginary meet, and each imbues itself with the nature of the other' " ("The Custom-House"). Hawthorne took the idea for this "neutral territory" from The Faerie Queene and even uses Spenserian terminology in the prefaces to three of the four romances. Jones examines these and other works in terms of Spenser's influence on Hawthorne's themes.

________. "Hawthorne and Spenser: From Allusion to Allegory." NHJ, 1975, 71-90.
Hawthorne not only referred to Spenser throughout his career but also reused the same Spenserian materials (e.g., Mammon's Cave, the Hall of Fantasy) until he was satisfied with their handling. Jones discusses the presence of certain Spenserian elements in some early sketches and again in The House of the Seven Gables and The Blithedale Romance; the difference between the two groups of writings is the difference between "contrived allegory and convincing allegory."

________. "Hawthorne's Coverdale and Spenser's Allegory of Mutability." AL, 39 (1967-68), 215-19.
The theme of mutability in The Blithedale Romance is taken from The Faerie Queene, but whereas Spenser's poem points beyond mutability to a time when immutability will reign, Coverdale can see only the change that is synonymous with decay.

________. " 'The Man of Adamant' and the Moral Picturesque." ATQ, 14 (1972), 33-41.
Sources include Sir Walter Scott's Old Mortality and the Legend of Holiness from Book I of The Faerie Queene.

Leibowitz, Herbert A. "Hawthorne and Spenser: Two Sources." AL, 30 (1958-59), 459-66.
The author points to two Hawthorne tales that have their origin in Spenser: "Rappaccini's Daughter" is set in a garden that is a "symbol of artificiality and death" like the Bower of Bliss in Book II of The Faerie Queene. Book I on the same poem provided Hawthorne with the material for "Young Goodman Brown," although he diverged from the original considerably in the use of it: whereas the "promise of Divine grace, of God's forgiveness and support of man ... makes possible a happy resolution of Redcross's dark night of the soul," Hawthorne's protagonist "turns away from the church. To him it symbolizes hypocrisy and cant. He has lost his faith in good and cannot accept evil; his is a spiritual no-man's land, in bleak isolation from man and God."

Mounts, Charles Eugene. "Hawthorne's Echoes of Spenser and Milton." NHJ, 1973, 162-71.
Mounts mentions briefly but specifically the various uses to which Hawthorne put the works of the English poets and concludes that "Hawthorne's work contains many echoes of Spenser, principally in the embellishment of his own allegorical manifestations. From Milton he appears to derive much less that can be precisely pinpointed, but what he does derive, as in 'Young Goodman Brown' and The Marble Faun [both Adam and Eve stories, according to

Mounts], is both better assimilated and directed into channels of speculation more distinctly his own."

Schoen, Carol. "The House of the Seven Deadly Sins." ESQ, no. 70 (1973), 26-33.
Beginning with his thorough knowledge of the seven deadly sins as treated by Spenser and Dante, Hawthorne constructed The House of the Seven Gables so that certain chapters deal with certain sins according to a complex and highly unified plan that--as described by Schoen--is marvelous to ponder, even if it is perhaps too good to be true.

Shroeder, John. "Alice Doane's Story: An Essay on Hawthorne and Spenser." NHJ, 1974, 129-34.
Based on the Archimago episode of The Faerie Queene, "the Alice Doane story is the first of many Spenserian paraphrases." Both tales may be summed up by this formula: "A young man is caused to disbelieve in the purity of a spotlessly pure maiden, the disbelief issuing from the machinations of a scheming wizard; the consequence is in the young man's jealous rage and murderous hatred, which rage and hatred eventuate in murder done. The characters match exactly, for Una, Alice; for Red Crosse, Leonard; for Archimago, the wizard; for the sprite in the form of the lusty squire, Walter Brome. Even Spenser's device of the deceptive simulacrum is preserved, though its sex is shifted and its origin rationalized, Spenser's False Una being paralleled by Walter Brome, Leonard Doane's twin and very counterpart."

Leaving "Alice Doane's Appeal" aside, Shroeder speculates that Hawthorne saw something in Spenser that his contemporaries would have missed, namely, the anallegorical insights into human nature (what triggers Red Crosse's homicidal rage, after all, is not "moral indignation" but "raw erotic envy").

________. "Hawthorne's 'Egotism; or, The Bosom Serpent' and Its Source." AL, 31 (1959-60), 150-62.
"Egotism" is one of two major Hawthorne tales that "paraphrase famous originals point by point, the other member of this pair being, of course, 'The Celestial Railroad.' Yet though 'Egotism' is indebted in no smaller measure to its source than is 'The Celestial Railroad' to Bunyan's The Pilgrims's Progress, the former tale, quite unlike the latter, does not parade this debt, makes no effort whatever to draw strength from its constant allusions to its original; but instead seems, if anything, intent to disguise the fact of indebtedness." Hawthorne's footnote to his title, in which he assures the reader that actual bosom serpents have been documented, is intended to divert the reader's attention from a source that, for whatever reason, the author wanted to hide. At any rate, "Spenser's Book One [of The Faerie Queene] and Hawthorne's 'Egotism' are reducible to a single plot-outline: The Hero's jealousy of his lady prompts his wilful separation

from her; he spends a period retired from the world, attended by a devoted servant. Re-entering the world, he encounters there a pageant of the Seven Deadly Sins. Subsequently, he is imprisoned, this imprisonment effecting a sad alteration in his health and appearance. But he is at last freed, reunited with his lady, and restored to himself. The characters correspond exactly...." See Shroeder's essay on "The Man of Adamant," described below (Note: Shroeder may or may not be correct about Hawthorne's using his footnote as a red herring, but one could offer two reasons why he might have done so: (1) Any author would be quick to disguise what detractors might take as evidence of a decline in the creative faculties; and (2) American authors of this period would be acutely sensitive to the charge that they had failed to do their part in cutting the ties that bound American literature to English.)

________. "Hawthorne's 'The Man of Adamant': A Spenserian Source-Study." PQ, 41 (1962), 744-56.
"The main source of 'The Man of Adamant' is the first half--stanzas one through twenty-eight--of the first canto of The Faerie Queene's first book, the episode of the Wandering Wood and Error's Den, some additional levy being made on later cantos of the same book." So complete is the correspondence, in fact, that Shroeder affirms that "The Man of Adamant" is as thorough a paraphrase of Spenser as "Egotism; or The Bosom Serpent," described by him previously as the most thoroughgoing of Hawthorne's Spenserian paraphrases (see the preceding article). Too, as with "Egotism," Hawthorne hides his source, and to ill effect. By impeding the reader's perception of the equivalences between elements in Spenser's poem and his own story, Hawthorne "deprives himself of a source of considerable allusive richness and, worse, causes his allegory to seem less firm, significant, and interesting than it in fact is. Further, his technique of concealment keeps us from seeing the really considerable ingenuity with which he bends his Spenserian materials into a form Spenser never gave them; and so we are robbed of what is doubtless a minor, but still a genuine, source of pleasure regarding his sheer virtuosity."

________. "Miles Coverdale as Actaeon, as Faunus, and as October: With Some Consequences." PLL, 2 (1966), 126-39.
Coverdale recalls the mythic protagonist Actaeon, the unlucky fellow who spied Diana at her bath, was changed into a stag, pursued by his own hounds, and slain. He recalls as well Spenser's comic version of Actaeon, Faunus, as well as the allegorical figure of October, who like Faunus is from The Mutabilitie cantos. Zenobia and the Blithedalers, like the female reformer Mutability, prove "the folly of man's trying to substitute for the established order of things some high-minded but idiosyncratic, privately cherished project of reform" as well as "the folly of ... attempting to divorce human reform from the great natural

cycle." It is ironic that Coverdale thinks of himself as " 'like an allegorical figure of rich October,' " since in truth he is Faunus, Spenser's "foolish god."

________. "Miles Coverdale's Calendar; or a Major Literary Source for The Blithedale Romance." Essex Institute Historical Collections, 103 (1967), 353-64.
"Hawthorne found himself at Brook Farm in something quite close to the artificial pastoral-world of Spenser; and he had not been long at the Farm before he found himself in Colin Clout's very situation; a writer unable to get any writing done." So Hawthorne took from The Shepheards Calendar much of what he needed for The Blithedale Romance: "the annual structure, with its wintry beginning; the continued conceit of the seasons and the weather as emblematic of human life; the psychological landscape; the dying Fall of the close." This article is important not only for what it reveals about The Blithedale Romance but also because it demonstrates how, when faced with relatively simple creative problems that he might have solved himself, Hawthorne turned to Spenser instead. Stewart (below) writes that Hawthorne was most probably not influenced by any Spenser work other than The Faerie Queene; this essay suggests otherwise.

Stewart, Randall. "Hawthorne and The Faerie Queene." PQ, 12 (1933), 196-206.
Stewart notes the various ways in which Spenser's poem influenced Hawthorne's works. For instance, "his typical villain, the bearded, vulnerable man of apparent guilelessness [e.g., Rappaccini, Chillingworth], seems to have been suggested by Spenser's arch-villain, Archimago." Too, one of Hawthorne's favorite devices of characterization, the association of a significant symbol with a character (as in the case of the minister's black veil or Hester's scarlet letter), was also one of Spenser's (cf. the Red Cross Knight's bloody cross). And Hawthorne borrowed settings and other elements as well from Spenser.

Van Doren, Mark. "Tales and Sketches." In Nathaniel Hawthorne. [No city given]: William Sloane Associates, 1949.
Van Doren argues that due to the influence of Spenser and Bunyan Hawthorne was too much the allegorist and too little the realist. "Among the labors Hawthorne could not or would not perform was the labor, which Dante never shirked, of keeping his significations always solid, always clear. Hawthorne knew Dante, but he knew Spenser and Bunyan better, and they are masters of the second class. Chillingworth is less a man than an Archimago, as Donatello is something of a Satyrane and as Lucifera returns to earth in the Lady Eleanore. Hawthorne's places--his chambers, his villages--are often Caves of Despayre and Sloughs of Despond which occupy no plausible areas on the map of human experience."

Walsh, Thomas F., Jr. "Rappaccini's Literary Gardens." ESQ, no. 19 (1960), 9-13.
Walsh acknowledges that the Bible and Ovid's Metamorphoses provided Hawthorne with gardens that he emulated in "Rappaccini's Daughter." These two sources suggest a melancholy contrast--prelapsarian innocence as opposed to man's present and fallen state. A third source, The Faerie Queene, provides another garden, the Bower of Bliss, that complements the others. For it is a place of "sexual intemperance," which is one aspect of postlapsarian life.

Wilson, Rod. "Further Spenserian Parallels in Hawthorne." NHJ, 1972, 195-201.
This article has three purposes: (1) to discuss heretofore-undiscovered but nonetheless "striking parallels between several of Hawthorne's characters in The Blithedale Romance and Spenser's Sir Calidore and Pastorella in Book Six of The Faerie Queene"; (2) to point out that Hawthorne "used the scene in front of Mercilla's palace in Book Five of The Faerie Queene as a prototype for the scene in his short story 'Endicott and the Red Cross'"; and (3) to show that Hawthorne, for whatever reasons, attempted to conceal his borrowings from Spenser.

I offer two reasons for Hawthorne's disguising his sources in my comment on Shroeder's discussion of "Egotism; or, The Bosom Serpent" (above). Anyway, Wilson takes the matter too far in assuming that any change that Hawthorne makes on a Spenser original is an attempt to conceal his borrowings. It may be that secondarily and even primarily in certain cases, but let us assume until shown otherwise that Hawthorne's first concern was to create something durable and aesthetically sound and that most of his decisions were made with that general principle in mind rather than the desire to cover his tracks.

Zivley, Sherry. "Hawthorne's 'The Artist of the Beautiful' and Spenser's 'Muiopotmos.'" PQ, 48 (1969), 134-37.
Hawthorne took the butterfly in this story from Spenser's "Muiopotmos: or The Fate of the Butterflye."

Melville

Howard, Leon. "Melville and Spenser--A Note on Criticism." MLN, 46 (1931), 291-92.
Howard identifies most of the verse quotations that precede each of the ten sketches in "The Encantadas." With one exception, the quotations identified are from Spenser, which implies "an interesting and unique criticism of the picturesque values of the Elizabethan poet's work. The selections are more than conventional chapter headings or captions: they are presentations in verse of the same pictures that are sketched in prose, and the

closeness of the parallel is emphasized by the fact that Melville changed several of them slightly in order that they might correspond exactly with the actual scenes.... When [Melville] chooses Spenser to illustrate the sketches drawn largely from his own observations in the South Seas, he is paying a high and sincere tribute to that poet's art."

In "Melville's Use of Some Sources in The Encantadas," AL, 3 (1931-32), 432-56, Russell Thomas identifies two more quotations, one from William Collins and the other from Thomas Chatterton.

Jones, Buford. "Spenser and Shakespeare in The Encantadas, Sketch VI." ESQ, no. 35 (1964), 68-73.
A verse epigraph from Mother Hubbard's Tale is only partly applicable to this sketch, since the story of the rascally Fox and Ape misrepresents Melville's buccaneers, who became philosophers. Thus a prose epigraph based on As You Like It prefigures the pastoral element that is also part of the sketch.

Mansfield, Luther S., and Howard P. Vincent. "Explanatory Notes" to Moby-Dick. New York: Hendricks House, 1952.
Melville's passing references to Spenser are identified in these indispensable notes.

Moses, Carole. "Melville's Use of Spenser in 'The Piazza.' " CLAJ, 20 (1976), 222-31.
Specific mentions of Spenser and The Faerie Queene "serve a dual function in the story; they define the narrator himself and and the world he inhabits, both lacking in spiritual values. In almost parodic inversion of the Renaissance concept of the microcosm-macrocosm hierarchy, we see the narrator's internal spiritual limitations matched by the absence of any spiritual values in the external world.... Instead of Spenser's morally ordered world, we see a sham knight questing after an empty ideal."

Newbery, I. " 'The Encantadas': Melville's Inferno." AL, 38 (1966-67), 49-68.
See the annotation of this item in Chapter 4, "Dante and the Middle Ages."

Rees, John O., Jr. "Spenserian Analogues in Moby-Dick." ESQ, no. 68 (1972), 174-78.
Canto 12 of The Faerie Queene, "in which Sir Guyon sails to and destroys the sorceress Acrasia's sinister island paradise, the Bower of Bliss," has been shown by other scholars to have influenced Mardi, "The Encantadas," and Pierre (see the studies by Howard, Thompson, and Wright covered in this chapter).

Rees shows how it influences the climactic chapters of *Moby-Dick*, especially Chapter 133, "The Chase--First Day."

Thompson, Lawrance. "God's Stony Heart." In *Melville's Quarrel with God*. Princeton: Princeton University Press, 1952.
See the annotation of this item in Chapter 7, "Shakespeare and the Renaissance."

________. "Quest for Atonement." In *Melville's Quarrel with God*. Princeton: Princeton University Press, 1952.
Like the heroes of the first two books of *The Faerie Queene*, "the mature and penitent Taji resists the devil, the world, the flesh, and in the final tableau he turns his back on all things temporal."

Travis, Mildred K. "Spenserian Analogues in *Mardi* and *The Confidence Man*." *ESQ*, no. 50 (1968, supplement), 55-58.
"Although Melville appears to modify sequence and ideas, three scenes in *Mardi* seem to have their models in Spenser's Bower of Bliss, Garden of Adonis, and Temple of Venus. And Melville's novel *The Confidence Man* seems to have its origin in Spenser's complaint 'Prosopopoia: or Mother Hubberds Tale.' "

Wright, Nathalia. "A Note on Melville's Use of Spenser: Hautia and the Bower of Bliss." *AL*, 24 (1952-53), 83-85.
"The last episode in Herman Melville's *Mardi*, the meeting of Taji and Hautia on the island of Flozella, contains several notable parallels with Canto xii of the second book of Spenser's *Faerie Queene*, wherein Sir Guyon visits Acrasia's Bower of Bliss."

6. CERVANTES

The fundamental tension in American life and letters is between the neoclassical façade of Reason and the Romantic dream that lurks behind it; it is the tension between the hopes of the Republic and those of the Revolution. This conflict between a culture's public wishes and its private ones is neither new nor peculiarly American, of course. In the sixteenth and early seventeenth centuries such writers as Cervantes, Calderôn, Shakespeare, and Tasso embodied in their works the conflict between the mythic hero, the apotheosis of any society's desires, and his Romantic counterpart. The mythic hero is a descendant of the gods, whereas the Romantic hero is unmistakably mortal; the mythic hero is an example to society, whereas the Romantic hero is to be pitied--or, if envied, then envied secretly.

Hence the appeal of a Don Quixote to Romantic authors, elsewhere and in America; versions of the addlepated knight and his squire recur in works of fiction by Hugh Henry Brackenridge, Tabitha Tenney, and Washington Irving, and later in those of Mark Twain, who once wrote in a letter to his brother Orion that Goldsmith's *The Citizen of the World* and *Don Quixote* were "my *beau ideals* of fine writing."

In the middle of *Moby-Dick*, in the first of two chapters fittingly entitled "Knights and Squires," the reader encounters a most unlikely linking of names; asking for divine sanction of his tendency to endow the common sailor with heroic tendencies, Melville writes: "Bear me out in it, thou great democratic God! who didst not refuse to the swart convict Bunyan, the pale, poetic pearl; Thou who didst clothe with doubly hammered leaves of finest gold, the stumped and paupered arm of Old Cervantes; Thou who didst pick up Andrew Jackson from the pebbles; who didst hurl him upon a war-horse; who didst thunder him higher than a throne! Thou who, in all Thy mighty, earthly marchings, ever cullest Thy selected champions from the kingly commons; bear me out in it, O God!" In the lives of Bunyan, Cervantes, and Andrew Jackson, Melville read the vindication of his own feelings about human dignity. And in general American literature bears out its makers' concurrence with Melville's notion of the admirable: not the descendant of the gods but the irredeemably human creature who prevails in spite of flaws; not the pious merchants of the Republic but the "meanest mariners, and renegades and castaways."

This preface draws on the following sources (see "List of Works Frequently Consulted" for full bibliographic information):

Fiedler, p. 145-46; Zipes, p. 29-30; Joseph H. Harkey, "Don Quixote and American Fiction Through Mark Twain," Dissertation Abstracts, 29 (1968), p. 229-A; Matthiessen, p. 444-45.

The following studies are grouped under the names, listed alphabetically, of major American fiction writers through James who were influenced by Cervantes.

Hawthorne

Cherry, Fannye N. "The Sources of Hawthorne's 'Young Goodman Brown.' " AL, 5 (1933-34), 342-48.
Hawthorne had "more than a passing knowledge of the works of Cervantes," and "Young Goodman Brown" may have been influenced by his reading "El Coloquio de los Perros" ("The Conversation of the Dogs").

Howells

Wagenknecht, Edward. William Dean Howells: The Friendly Eye. New York: Oxford University Press, 1969, p. 44.
Howells took as the model of his own books the loose design of Don Quixote rather than the tightly controlled standard plot of the Victorian novel, says Wagenknecht.

Williams, Stanley T. The Spanish Background of American Literature. 2 vols. New Haven: Yale University Press, 1955.
See the annotation of this item in Appendix A.

Irving

Roth, Martin. Comedy and America: The Lost World of Washington Irving. Port Washington: Kennikat Press, 1976, passim.
Roth attributes the self-conscious element and other distinctive features of The History of New York to the tradition of burlesque comedy, one work of which, Don Quixote, is a preeminent influence on Irving's writings. Other burlesque comedies include The Praise of Folly, The Anatomy of Melancholy, Gargantua and Pantagruel, Hudibras, "A Tale of a Tub," Tristram Shandy, and, in our time, Ulysses and Finnegans Wake.

In addition to literary self-consciousness burlesque comedies (including The History of New York) are characterized by their lack of moral reference and their use of a fanciful, whimsical, or mad narrator.

Melville

Levin, Harry. " 'Don Quixote' and 'Moby Dick.' " In Cervantes Across the Centuries, ed. Angel Flores and M. J. Benardete. New York: Dryden Press, 1947.

With his customary sweep and erudition Levin traces the spread of Quixotism throughout Western culture to America, where it is evidenced first in the writings of Hugh Henry Brackenridge, Tabitha Tenney, and Washington Irving, then in those of Melville, Twain, and Howells. While the relation between Don Quixote and Moby-Dick is "neither close nor similar" but "complementary and dialectical," the two works share a number of affinities and in particular a set of attitudes, namely, "a questioning of the nature of reality and an affirmation of the brotherhood of man." Levin bases much of his discussion on the annotations made by Melville in his personal copy of Don Quixote.

Mansfield, Luther S., and Howard P. Vincent. "Explanatory Notes" to Moby-Dick. New York: Hendricks House, 1952.

Melville's half a dozen allusions to Don Quixote as well as his references to Cervantes himself are identified and explicated in these indispensable notes.

Twain

Moore, Olin Harris. "Mark Twain and Don Quixote." PMLA, 37 (1922), 324-46.

Moore discusses Cervantes's influence throughout Twain's career, although the Spanish author's effect seems to be most important in the cases of Tom Sawyer and Huckleberry Finn. Refuting the conventional autobiographical identifications, Moore dissociates Tom Sawyer from the young Mark Twain, who had a hatred for reading as opposed to Tom's passion for it, and Huck Finn from Tom Blankenship, who was a visionary rather than a pragmatist like Huck. Instead, Tom is based on the romantic, book-addled Quixote, and Huck is a latter-day Sancho Panza, whose commonsensical counterings of Tom's nonsense provide the humorous contrast to the novels. Quixote's "this would have been made clear to thee, hadst thou read as many histories as I have" becomes Tom's "hain't you ever read any books at all?"

Roades, Sister Mary Teresa. "Don Quixote and A Connecticut Yankee in King Arthur's Court." MTQ, 2, 4 (1938), 8-9.

This article is superficial, illogical, and apparently written in ignorance of Moore's (above). I list it only because it does note numerous correspondences between the two works and may thus provide grist for the intelligent reader's mill.

Schönemann, Friedrich. Mark Twain als Literarische Persönlichkeit. Jena: Verlag der Frommanschen Buchhandlung, 1925.

Schönemann feels that Cervantes confirmed and encouraged Twain's native satirical bent and his proclivity for undermining that which is obsolete and outmoded. Both authors exploit the humorous juxtaposition of imaginative and unimaginative characters; both "utilize the specific humor which rests upon linguistic misunderstanding, even though it may be merely an accidental coincidence."

(This quotation is from Edgar H. Hemminghaus's commentary on Schönemann in Mark Twain in Germany, New York: AMS Press, 1966, p. 106).

Williams, Stanley T. The Spanish Background of American Literature. 2 vols. New Haven: Yale University Press, 1955. See the annotation of this item in Appendix A.

7. SHAKESPEARE AND THE RENAISSANCE

From time to time it is observed that we underestimate the talents of Francis Beaumont and John Fletcher, George Chapman, Thomas Dekker, John Ford, Thomas Heywood, Ben Jonson, Christopher Marlowe, John Marston, Philip Massinger, and John Webster. Whether we do or not, we read their works less than we do those of Shakespeare, and so did the authors with whom we are concerned. While the impact of the other English Renaissance dramatists is obvious in certain limited instances, the influence of Shakespeare is second only to that of the Bible in American letters. In the New World his plays were ubiquitous; Tocqueville noted that there was hardly a pioneer's cabin that did not contain some work of Shakespeare, and he recalls reading _Henry V_ for the first time in a log house. Too, the mid-nineteenth century was one of the great ages of Shakespearean dramatization; Shakespeare's genius was thus doubly accessible, and surely Howells was not the only writer of American fiction to feel that "when the curtain rises on the opening scene of _Hamlet_, or _Macbeth_, or _Romeo and Juliet_, a thrill goes through one as if at the behest of a supreme authority, and one marvels that while such plays still speak a living language, any other plays can be represented."

Like the Bible, the writings of Shakespeare are put to as many uses as are conceivable. In the fiction of Melville, for instance, a Shakespearean speech in the mouth of a sailor suggests a fundamental dignity in every person, a dignity perhaps not readily apparent to those who are equipped to hear only the coarseness in the speech of the sailor's real-life counterpart. Other writers use Shakespeare to achieve the opposite effect: as T. S. Eliot was to do in "The Love Song of J. Alfred Prufrock," they deliberately force a comparison between a Shakespearean character or setting and a contemporary one to the detriment of the latter. James's "Master Eustace," for example, describes a latter-day Hamlet who flies into a rage when his widowed mother remarries; though he is incapable of a Shakespearian monologue, his sputterings have their effect--his mother dies at the shock of hearing them. In another tale, "The Velvet Glove," James alludes to _The Winter's Tale_ as he freights with mythic and pastoral significance a romantic encounter between two authors. But it is an encounter deliberately engineered by one of the writers, an amateurish and unscrupulous romancer who only wants her better-known colleague to write a laudatory preface to her new novel.

This preface draws on the following sources (see "List of Works Frequently Consulted" for full bibliographic information):

Spiller, p. 491; Wagenknecht, Howells, p. 13; Priestley, p. 33-34; Leon Edel, Henry James: The Conquest of London, 1870-1883, London: Rupert Hart-Davis, 1962, p. 37, and Henry James: The Master, 1901-1916, London: Rupert Hart-Davis, 1972, p. 362. The Tocqueville quotation is from André Le Vot, "Shakespeare et Melville: Le Thème impérial dans Moby-Dick," Etudes Anglaises, 17 (1964), 552. For more on Shakespeare's reception see Esther Cloudman Dunn, Shakespeare in America, New York: Macmillan, 1939.

The following studies are grouped under the names, listed alphabetically, of major American fiction writers through James who were influenced by Shakespeare or one of his contemporaries.

Cooper

Davie, Donald. The Heyday of Sir Walter Scott. London: Routledge & Kegan Paul, 1961.
See the annotation of this item in Chapter 13, "Sir Walter Scott."

Gates, W. B. "Cooper's Indebtedness to Shakespeare." PMLA, 67 (1952), 716-31.
Gates shows how Cooper drew on his considerable knowledge of Shakespeare in the creation of incident, plot, and character in his novels (which are discussed in chronological order).

Vandiver, Edward P., Jr. "Cooper's The Prairie and Shakespeare." PMLA, 69 (1954), 1302-04.
The most important Shakespearian influence in this novel is to be found in the "pedantic language of Dr. Battius, which is patterned after that of Holofernes in Love's Labour's Lost." However, "although a certain amount of Dr. Battius' pedantry and of the ridicule heaped upon him is fairly entertaining, there is too much of it. If Cooper had devoted less space to Dr. Battius and his speeches, he would have improved the novel."

________. "James Fenimore Cooper and Shakspere [sic]." Shakespeare Association Bulletin, 15 (1940), 110-17.
This is the kind of statistical study that will surely leave readers slack-jawed in amazement and compilers (unless they are helped by their students, as Vandiver was) numb with exhaustion. There is something wonderful in the knowledge that "Cooper probably quotes more widely and more often from Shakspere for chapter mottoes than does any other novelist. Scott, for instance, who was steeped in Shakspere, quotes slightly more than six hundred lines for chapter and book mottoes, whereas Cooper quotes almost eleven hundred lines. Both writers quote from thirty-six different plays; but Cooper, unlike Scott, also quotes from Venus and Adonis and The Rape of Lucrece." Having convinced us that he knows whereof he writes, Vandiver mercifully

concentrates on a single novel to show that it is "indisputable that Cooper's imagination [,] in the process of creating the story and the characters of *The Water-Witch,* turned again and again to Shakspere and particularly to *The Tempest.*"

Crane

Feldman, Abraham. "Crane's Title From Shakespeare?" *American Notes & Queries,* 8 (1950), 185-86.
"It would be interesting to know whether Stephen Crane, in choosing his title *The Red Badge of Courage,* was in any way influenced by the phrase 'murder's crimson badge,' found in Shakespeare's historical tragedy *Henry VI: Part II* (Act III, scene 2, 1. 200)."

Hawthorne

Abel, Darrel. "Immortality vs. Mortality in *Septimius Felton:* Some Possible Sources." *AL,* 27 (1955-56), 566-70.
See the annotation of this item in Chapter 9, "The Eighteenth Century."

Boswell, Jackson Campbell. "Bosom Serpents Before Hawthorne." *ELN,* 12 (1975), 279-87.
See the annotation of this item in Chapter 2, "The Classics."

D'Avanzo, Mario L. "The Literary Sources of 'My Kinsman, Major Molineux': Shakespeare, Coleridge, Milton." *SSF,* 10 (1973), 121-36.
"Seen in relationship to *A Midsummer Night's Dream,* Coleridge's *Biographia Literaria,* and *Paradise Lost,* the story resonates with overtones of meaning that strictly textual criticism or psychological or biographical interpretations cannot fully discern...." Specifically, (1) allusions to Shakespeare's play reinforce the sense of confusion and dreaminess that pervades "My Kinsman, Major Molineux"; (2) the *Biographia* was for Hawthorne "a model commentary on democratic revolution, fanatic excess and cruelty, which he rendered brilliantly into narrative form, expropriating and applying to the American scene the reflections on revolution of the foremost English transcendentalist"; and (3) the echoes of "Milton's hell in *Paradise Lost* ... deepen the meaning of Robin's 'fall' and the sense of cosmic evil of the story that now indelibly tinges his soul."

Davidson, Frank. "Hawthorne's Hive of Honey." *MLN,* 61 (1946), 14-21.
See the annotation of this item in Chapter 8, "Milton and His Age."

Kehler, Dorothea. "Hawthorne and Shakespeare." ATQ, 22 (1974), 104-05.
Hawthorne may have taken the poignant image of a trampled heart from Richard II and used it in "My Kinsman, Major Molineux" and The Scarlet Letter.

Rees, John O., Jr. "Shakespeare in The Blithedale Romance." ESQ, no. 71 (1973), 84-93.
Hawthorne echoes various elements of Antony and Cleopatra, The Tempest, and As You Like It in his novel, which has in common with these "very different Shakespeare plays" a pattern of "double theatricality, when the actors emphatically remind us that we are witnessing performances--that we are being beguiled by the power and flimsiness of stagecraft.... A pattern of stage metaphor and incident pervades The Blithedale Romance."

Reid, Alfred S. The Yellow Ruff and "The Scarlet Letter": A Source of Hawthorne's Novel. Gainesville: University of Florida Press, 1955.
Reid finds counterparts for Hawthorne's characters in the seventeenth-century case of the poisoning of Sir Thomas Overbury. For the actual works on which Hawthorne may have drawn see Reid's companion volume, entitled "Sir Thomas Overbury's Vision" (1616) by Richard Niccols and Other English Sources of Nathaniel Hawthorne's "The Scarlet Letter", Gainesville: Scholars' Facsimiles & Reprints, 1957.

Howells

Hedges, Elaine. "Howells on a Hawthornesque Theme." TSLL, 3 (1961), 129-43.
Howells probably took the title The Shadow of a Dream "from Shakespeare, as was frequently his habit. The phrase, 'the shadow of a dream,' occurs in Hamlet, II, ii, 265. Hawthorne uses the phrase in The Scarlet Letter (Ch. XII), when Dimmesdale is described as walking 'in the shadow of a dream.' The phrase would aptly describe Nevil's condition after Faulkner's death." See Cady and Mathews in chapter 12, "The Romantics."

Hilton, Earl. "Howells's The Shadow of a Dream and Shakespeare." AL, 46 (1974-75), 220-22.
Howells probably took the name of a character and the opening situation of his novel from The Winter's Tale--a play he did not admire, by the way. Hilton speculates that "one could relate all of Shakespeare's late tragi-comedies to the mood and tone of Howells' work in the 1890's."

Irving

Gates, W. B. "Shakespearean Elements in Irving's Sketch Book." AL, 30 (1958-59), 450-58.
Gates finds purely verbal echoes, descriptive material, ideas, and plot elements from Shakespeare in The Sketch Book.

James

Andreach, Robert J. "Literary Allusion as a Clue to Meaning: James's 'The Ghostly Rental' and Pascal's Pensées." CLS, 4 (1967), 299-306.
The two explicit references to and five "echoes" of the Pensées suggest that James may have been making use in his 1876 story of Pascal's distinction between the mathematical and the intuitive ways of thinking. These are not opposed or mutually exclusive entities in Pascal; they are "two poles of knowing" that unite in "one harmonious whole." But James's narrator believes his to be solely a mathematical mind, evidence of its intuitive component notwithstanding. The noodlings of this puzzled fellow, who fails to understand the past (and himself) because he won't allow his intuitive and mathematical modes of perception to cooperate, suggest a mental struggle that is fundamental in later James characters. For example, Isabel Archer in The Portrait of a Lady is betrayed by her tendency toward romantic idealization, whereas Lambert Strether in The Ambassadors saves himself by bringing all of his faculties to bear on his dilemma.

Cargill, Oscar. "The Princess Casamassima: A Critical Reappraisal." PMLA, 71 (1956), 97-117; this essay appears as "The Princess Casamassima" in Cargill's The Novels of Henry James, New York: Macmillan, 1961.
In his preface to the novel James compares Hyacinth Robinson to Hamlet. One may take James to task for what appears to be a self-congratulatory juxtaposition, but only if one overlooks a "European attitude, both critical and creative, extending from Voltaire to Jules Laforgue, which does not correspond with the Anglo-American reverence for the Danish prince. Hamlet, in this European view, is permanently adolescent and too much given to reflection"; Eliot's Prufrock is a perfect example of such a Hamlet. Ivan Turgenev, the Russian realist who influenced James so profoundly, wrote a story entitled "The Hamlet of the Shtchigri District," whose protagonist is a garrulous and self-pitying fellow. Cargill notes that James takes from both Turgenev and Shakespeare in that he makes Hyacinth "pitiable and small" (à la Turgenev) yet endows him with "an acute perceptiveness" (as Shakespeare does Hamlet). See Lerner on James in Chapter 16, "The Realists."

Knoepflmacher, U.C. " 'O rare for Strether!': Antony and Cleopatra and The Ambassadors." NCF, 19 (1965), 333-44.

In Chapter 33 of James's novel Strether mentally transforms Madame de Vionnet's grief for the imminent loss of Chad into "Cleopatra's regal bereavement over the aged Antony's death," a transformation made ironic by his "resulting, unconsciously wishful, self-portrayal as the Antony of his imagined queen." Like Antony, "Strether hovers between two hostile worlds, a world of strict codes and observances and a world of amorality and laxity. Like Antony, he is seduced by the rarefied atmosphere of the older of these two worlds; like Antony, he sees, or professes to see, a 'life' he has ignored in his youth, hoping to 'stretch' its pleasures through his reawakened imagination; like Antony, Strether is ultimately betrayed both by his fancy and by his fancied queen. But Antony acts upon his vision, and his defeat is a triumph which is denied to his American counterpart. For Shakespeare's hero translates imagination into action; he bequeathes his imagination to his queen, stimulates her sacrifice, and, through it, transcends his own ignoble death by becoming a giant 'past the size of dreaming'.... Whereas Antony is thus able to 'stretch,' Strether is not. His imagination, vicarious and powerless, relies solely on the attachments of others and falls outside the realm of will and action." Thus Knoepflmacher shows us the other side of the coin described by Melchiori (below); the disadvantage of keeping the passions in check is that they may stay there.

Lombardo, Agostino. "Henry James, 'The American,' e Il Mito di Otello." In *Friendship's Garland: Essays Presented to Mario Praz on His Seventieth Birthday*, ed. Vittorio Gabrieli, vol. 2. Roma: Edizioni di Storia e Letteratura, 1966.

Lombardo finds evidence of Shakespeare everywhere in James ("in tutta l'opera jamesiana vi sono, così, citazioni ora esplicite ora implicite de drammi shakespeariani, e derivazioni, richiami, allusioni d'ogni sorta"). Though James may have thought *King Lear* the superior work, he seemed most fascinated with *Othello*, and this fascination is evidenced in such novels of his as *The American*. The Othello that interested James was not the jealous man--jealousy is relegated to the subplot of James's novel--but the one who, like Christopher Newman, is cruelly wronged. Othello and Newman reach peaks of success in their lives, astound others with their splendid achievements, and seek wives of comparable magnificence; Mrs. Tristram tells Christopher to "remember what Shakespeare calls Desdemona; 'a supersubtle Venetian.' Madame de Cintré is a supersubtle Parisian." And of course both heroes are done in by intrigue. The Othello figure surfaces again, this time in female form, with Isabel Archer, who (in *The Portrait of a Lady*) is another case of success, marriage, and manipulation; see also Milly Theale in *The Wings of the Dove*. The difference between Othello and Milly is that her story is pervaded by the ultimately victorious power of her innocence ("la vittoriosa forza della sua innocenza"). Christopher Newman, Isabel Archer, and Milly Theale suffer alone and do not cause others to suffer; that is their real success.

Melchiori, Giorgio. "Locksley Hall Revisited: Tennyson and Henry James." Review of English Literature, 6, no. 4 (1965), 9-25.
See the annotation of this item in Chapter 14, "The Victorians."

________. "Shakespeare and Henry James." Shakespeare Newsletter, 17 (1967), 56.
This article is of interest in that it explains (unwittingly) how James could rewrite Othello as he did. Lombardo (above) demonstrates that James's Othello characters achieve an ultimate victory through the force of their innocence. Melchiori notes that the tragic drama represented conflicts openly, whereas the novel was better suited to an age "in which a sense of propriety and personal dignity was the chief of virtues, and social status and economic soundness were of paramount importance"; in the art of such an age, "restraint of feeling took the place of raging passions, and tragedy lay in the repression of passion rather than in its manifestation." And if passions are not manifested, then they need not come into catastrophic conflict, which would destroy all things evil and good. Innocence triumphs in James because it lives to triumph, whereas in Othello innocence is trampled by the brutal passions that are unleashed. (See the comment on Knoepflmacher, above.)

Stafford, William T. "James Examines Shakespeare: Notes on the Nature of Genius." PMLA, 73 (1958), 123-28.
Between April 1873 and September 1896 James reviewed one or more productions of eleven Shakespeare plays. His attitudes toward Shakespeare are most clearly revealed in an introduction that he wrote to The Tempest and in his story "The Birthplace." Characteristically, James says little that is specific about The Tempest in his introduction; instead, he wants to know "why was Shakespeare able to create Lear and Othello," a question that could be answered only if one were to read the works so thoroughly and subtly as to perceive at last "the creative force which lies behind the mask presented to the public by the works." Thus this introduction, even though it appears four years after "The Birthplace" (which was published in 1903), sheds light on that story, in which the custodian of Shakespeare's birthplace refuses to toady to the desire of tourists to have him picture Shakespeare as they would like him to.

Stafford's essay is a source study, then, but one that is quite different from the kind that demonstrates the direct effect of one literary work on another; rather, he points out that James tried to use the plays as a means to an end--the defining of Shakespeare's genius--and reflected that attempt in "The Birthplace."

Tintner, Adeline R. "The Countess and Scholastica: James's 'L'Allegro' and 'Il Penseroso.' " SSF, 11 (1974), 267-76.

See the annotation of this item in Chapter 8, "Milton and His Age."

Warren, Austin. "Henry James: Symbolic Imagery in the Later Novels." In Rage for Order, Chicago: University of Chicago Press, 1948.
See the annotation of this item in Chapter 16, "Scientific Thinkers and Naturalists."

West, Muriel. "Starting Down the Stairs." In A Stormy Night with "The Turn of the Screw." Phoenix: Frye & Smith, 1964.
Is the name Peter Quint suggested by Peter Quince of A Midsummer Night's Dream? To West, at least, "James had turned loose all of Oberon's fairy tribe to romp on the green grass at Bly. Oh, yes--I saw! The Turn of the Screw is indeed a fairy-tale--just as James says it is."

For more on this loony little book see the main annotation in Chapter 11, "The Gothic Novelists."

Melville

Dale, T. R. "Melville and Aristotle: The Conclusion of Moby-Dick as a Classical Tragedy." Boston University Studies in English, 3 (1957), 45-50.
See the annotation of this item in Chapter 2, "The Classics."

Eddy, D. M. "Melville's Response to Beaumont and Fletcher: A New Source for 'The Encantadas.'" AL, 40 (1968-69), 374-80.
In the Barrington Isle sketch in "The Encantadas" the narrator's attitudes toward the buccaneers seem inconsistent: "At one point his comments are sentimental reveries on friendship among the pirates; at another, serious pondering over human frailties." By identifying an epigraph to the sketch whose source was unknown to Jones and Howard (whose studies are discussed in Chapter 5, "Spenser," above) Eddy makes clearer "the ironic and satiric contexts of the Barrington Isle tale." The epigraph is from Beaumont and Fletcher's Wit Without Money (Melville's marked copy is in the Harvard Library), which--like Spenser's Mother Hubberds Tale, which provided three epigraphs for the same sketch--is a satiric look at the various ways of getting money.

Hartman, Jay H. "Volpone as a Possible Source for Melville's The Confidence Man." Susquehanna University Studies, 7 (1965), 247-60.
"Since Jonson and Melville both lived during times when commercialism flourished and threatened traditional values, it is

not surprising that both attacked the insidious attitudes that seemed to be undermining social institutions.... Both the evils Melville attacked and his manner of attack contain striking parallels to Jonson's Volpone. The Confidence Man of the Fidèle could very easily be the Venetian confidence man transplanted to an American setting, so similar is his manner of swindling those about him. It seems quite possible, then, that Melville could have drawn on Ben Jonson's Volpone for ideas as he wrote The Confidence Man."

Head, Brian F. "Camões and Melville." Revista Camoniana, 1 (1964), 36-77.

Melville became familiar with the sixteenth-century Portuguese poet and his epic The Lusiads through Jack Chase, the heroic figure in White-Jacket (1850), of whom Melville wrote: "He talked of Rob Roy, Don Juan, and Pelham; Macbeth and Ulysses; but, above all things, was an ardent admirer of Camoens [the name is spelled this way in the text of the article]. Parts of the Lusiad [sic], he could recite in the original." Melville made reference to the poet and his work throughout his career; for instance, Camoens's description of the stormy Cape of Good Hope is alluded to directly or indirectly in White-Jacket, Moby-Dick, and Billy Budd. In later life Melville addressed two poems to the Portuguese author.

Melville also saw parallels between his situation and that of Camoens: both lived in a declining age (in Camoens's day, the Portuguese empire was disintegrating), and both were insufficiently appreciated by readers. These attitudes, too, are treated in Melville's poetry.

Heflin, Wilson. "A Biblical Source for 'The Whale-Watch' in Moby-Dick." Extracts, 23 (1975), 13.

See the annotation of this item in Chapter 3, "The Bible."

Hughes, Raymond G. "Melville and Shakespeare." Shakespeare Association Bulletin, 7 (1932), 103-12.

A good general introduction to the various Shakespearean echoes in Moby-Dick as well as a chapter-by-chapter listing of some thirty-five allusions to Shakespeare's tragedies.

Jones, Buford. "Spenser and Shakespeare in The Encantadas, Sketch VI." ESQ, no. 35 (1964), 68-73.

See the annotation of this item in Chapter 5, "Spenser."

Kilbourne, W. G., Jr. "Montaigne and Captain Vere." AL, 33 (1961-62), 514-17.

Melville describes Vere as an admirer of Montaigne, described by Kilbourne as "basically a great humanist" yet one who was also "politically pragmatic." Vere's sympathetic qualities notwithstanding, his decision to hang Billy Budd is foreshadowed early in the reference to the French writer.

See Shulman, below.

Le Vot, André. "Shakespeare et Melville: Le Thème Impérial dans Moby-Dick." EA, 17 (1964), 549-63.

Partly out of disdain for those who thought of Shakespeare as a "mere man of Richard-the-Third humps, and Macbeth daggers" Melville downplayed what he saw as staginess in Shakespeare and professed to savor in him only the poet and philosopher who, like Dante or Milton, gave his readers a tragic view of humanity. Yet Melville found it convenient to give some decidedly stagey and Shakespearean qualities to Ahab; he had to make his captain a tragic hero who emphasizes the great problems of his time and all times.

Mansfield, Luther S., and Howard P. Vincent. "Explanatory Notes" to Moby-Dick. New York: Hendricks House, 1952.

The authors note that "of Melville's more general reading [i.e., his noncetological reading], Shakespeare perhaps had the most profound impact" and "the influence of Shakespeare in the book as a whole and particularly in [the character of Ahab] was most apparent in the soliloquies. But it was a pervasive rather than a specific influence." The numerous allusions in Moby-Dick to Shakespeare's plays are discussed in detail in these indispensable notes; so are references to the writings of Sir William Davenant, Donne, Le Sage, Marlowe, Descartes, and Camoens. Montaigne is described as one of several writers who "helped importantly to shape ideas or phrasing" in Moby-Dick.

Matthiessen, F. O. "The Revenger's Tragedy." In American Renaissance: Art and Expression in the Age of Emerson and Whitman. New York: Oxford University Press, 1941.

"Without the precipitant of Shakespeare, Moby-Dick might have been a superior White Jacket. With it, Melville entered into another realm, of different properties and proportions.... His possession by Shakespeare went far beyond all other influences, and, if Melville had been a man of less vigor, would have served to reduce him to the ranks of the dozens of stagey nineteenth-century imitators of the dramatist's stylistic mannerisms. What we actually find is something very different: a man of thirty awakening to his own full strength through the challenge of the most abundant imagination in history." Matthiessen notes various Shakespearean echoes in Moby-Dick's language, scenes, and devices (an example of the latter is "Fedallah's elaboration of the seemingly impossible things that must happen before Ahab can die," which is "reminiscent of Birnam wood [sic] and Dunsinane" in Macbeth). But all of this leaves the reader "on the periphery of Melville's interest" in Shakespeare, which is "the incongruous and often heartrending discrepancies between appearance and truth," as elaborated in such plays as Lear.

Murray, Henry A. "Introduction" to Pierre. New York: Hendricks House, 1949.
This lengthy essay does not examine possible influences very closely, nor does it always distinguish carefully between true influence and mere parallel between some other author's work and Pierre. It makes up for these deficiencies, however, in the sheer number of possible sources mentioned, most of which--given Melville's omnivorous reading habits and his proclivity for using nearly all that he read in one way or another--are undoubtedly to some account. Pierre is a dramatic novel in the tradition of Shakespeare and Seneca, notes Murray, yet "its pervading temper" is that of German romanticism. Disraeli, too, is an important influence--his novels are "the mine from which Melville as novelist extracted more ore (and rubbish) than from any other." Other possible influences include the Bible, Sir Thomas Browne, Byron, Carlyle, Dante, DeQuincey, Godwin, Goethe, Greek mythology, Keats, Mrs. Radcliffe, and the Shelleys, all of which are discussed in impressive detail in the notes that follow the text of the novel.

Olson, Charles. Call Me Ishmael. New York: Reynal & Hitchcock, 1947.
Is it not the poet's job to use figurative language brilliantly and the critic's to use expository language brilliantly, and should not the two jobs be kept separate, by and large? Perhaps the fairest assessment of Call Me Ishmael appears in Robert Berkelman's review of it in The Christian Science Monitor, April 18, 1947, 16: "To those who know Melville and Shakespeare well, there are bits of interest and sudden illumination in the 100 pages that dispose one to feel friendly toward the whole book. But the author's arrangement and style repeatedly turn delight into either irritation or inappropriate amusement. It is not always clear whether he is quoting Melville's notes on Shakespeare or launching into rhapsodic comments on his own. He jumps about. Suddenly, on page 40 he remembers to give thanks to helpful friends. His style ranges from Sears-Roebuck cataloguing to prose as fantastic and willful as e. e. cummings' verse.... He can throw around such fancy words as reify, dromenon, usufruct, sorites. His simpler words often break into CAPITALS. He seems bent upon becoming nominated prose laureate of eccentricity. Old friends of Melville, nevertheless, may run upon fallen fruit in this tangled luxuriant jungle. Others should beware getting lost in the undergrowth."

One of the effects of Olson's study was to stir up Melville scholars with the pronouncement that

> Moby-Dick was two books written between February 1850 and August, 1851.
>
> The first book did not contain Ahab.

It may not, except incidentally, have contained Moby-Dick.

The first book was a simple account of whale fishery, says Olson, whereas the powerful work we have today was precipitated by, among other things, Melville's assimilating Shakespeare's themes and techniques midway in the composition of Moby-Dick. George R. Stewart, in "The Two Moby-Dicks," AL, 25 (1953-54), 417-48, lends credence to Olson when he notes that there are only a few echoes of Shakespeare in the first fifteen chapters and many thereafter, but Edward Stone, in "Moby-Dick and Shakespeare: A Remonstrance," Shakespeare Quarterly, 7 (1956), 445-48, hears clearly the echoes in the early chapters that Stewart does not, thus suggesting that the Shakespeare influence, though important, did not precipitate a "second" Moby-Dick. Olson is defended again in Ann Charter's Olson/Melville: A Study in Affinity, Berkeley: Oyez, 1968. Charter's book is rightly described by Brian Lee in The Year's Work in English Studies, 49 (1968), 396, as something of a "curious work" in itself.

Rice, Julian C. "Moby-Dick and Shakespearian Tragedy." Centennial Review (Michigan State University), 444-68.

If not an ocean, then at least a fair-sized pond of ink has gone into the printing of the various essays on Melville, Shakespeare, and tragedy. All hail, then, to Julian C. Rice, who summarizes concisely the major studies (according to him)--Raymond G. Hughes, "Melville and Shakespeare," Shakespeare Association Bulletin, 7 (1932), 103-13; William Ellery Sedgwick, The Tragedy of Mind, Cambridge: Harvard University Press, 1944; F. O. Matthiessen, American Renaissance, New York: Oxford University Press, 1941; Stanley Geist, Herman Melville: The Tragic Vision and the Heroic Ideal, Cambridge: Harvard University Press, 1939; Charles Olson, Call Me Ishmael, New York: Reynal & Hitchcock, 1947; Kenneth Lash, "Captain Ahab and King Lear," New Mexico Quarterly, 19 (1949), 438-45; Montgomery Belgion, "Heterodoxy on Moby-Dick," Sewanee Review, 55 (1947), 108-25; Julian Markels, "King Lear and Moby-Dick: The Cultural Connection," Massachusetts Review, 9 (1968), 169-76; Edward H. Rosenberry, Melville and the Comic Spirit, Cambridge: Harvard University Press, 1955; and Milton Stern, The Fine Hammered Steel of Herman Melville, Urbana: University of Illinois Press, 1957--and then provides his own correction. All the commentators cited above suggest that Moby-Dick may be approached in the manner of a Shakespearean tragedy, but few explain exactly what Shakespearean tragedy is. Most modern critics--and particularly, as Rice notes with polite but scornful emphasis, "those not directly concerned with drama"--see the tragic hero as "the blind but great hero with the tragic flaw" toward whom we feel pity but also disapproval. But there is another view of the tragic hero that is more applicable to both Lear and Ahab; in this view, as articulated by Isadore Traschen in "The Elements of Tragedy," Centennial Review, 6 (1962), 215-29, the tragic hero is a person "of extreme insight whose vision of reality is supported by the work as a whole." According to Traschen (who applies his theory to Greek and Shakespearean tragedy only), tragedy dramatizes the relations among three attitudes: (1) the profane, which is " 'an attitude shaped by expedience and practicality, by material comforts and social status, or by a violation of orthodox moral standards,' " as embodied (says Rice) in "Stubb most importantly, Flask, the captain of the Bachelor, to a certain extent Ishmael, and various minor figures"; (2) the orthodox, an attitude that " 'unifies life and gives it order' " and is " 'codified through religious and moral doctrine, or codes of honor,' " as seen in the characters of Starbuck and Father Mapple; and (3) the tragic, an attitude that " 'begins with the belief that the orthodox explanation of life is no longer adequate,' " which in Moby-Dick is exclusively the attitude of Ahab. In tragedy the tragic and orthodox views compete directly and openly, while the profane attitude serves as " 'the mocking mirror of tragedy, a parody of it.' "

In Moby-Dick the tragic view prevails because the evil of the world is shown to be cosmic and irrational. Hence the deaths of the profane Stubb, the orthodox Starbuck, and the tragic Ahab; neither the mockery of the first nor the honorable behavior of the second nor the perceptiveness of the third is protection against the blind cruelty of the world. But "if Moby-Dick as tragedy, then, presents a tragic vision of the universe, does Melville supply any alternative to the fate of Ahab? Shakespeare's King Lear, being Lear and a tragic hero, must challenge and be broken by the forces of the universe. Edgar, on the other hand, whose perception of evil is as penetrating as Lear's, can endure. Edgar, like Ishmael in Moby-Dick ... is not crushed when he discovers the lack of absolute justice, divine or human. He is able, in short, to make the best of a bad situation." This is not to say that Ishmael makes it on his own, of course. An important theme of Moby-Dick is one that Ahab calls "mortal interindebtedness," a theme that is treated in many passages throughout the novel and which reaches its culmination in "the epilogue in which Ishmael, enduring because of Queequeg's coffin, is picked up by the ship to which Ahab had refused the mortal debt of charity. Perhaps Melville emphasized this theme of mortal interindebtedness and the need for charity among human beings as the only answer in a world where the orthodox rules can no longer provide a code for action or an easy answer to the unpleasant realities of the universe. As in all tragedy the totality of meaning, though pessimistic, is held short of total bleakness in Moby-Dick by the magnificent dignity of Ahab and the ability of a good character to endure. Ishmael survives with the aid of human beings who in spite of having to contend with evil both in and out of their own natures have a potential for good in an essentially amoral cosmos."

Sedgwick, William Ellery. "Moby Dick." In Herman Melville: The Tragedy of Mind. Cambridge: Harvard University Press, 1945.

See the annotation of this item in Chapter 4, "Dante and the Middle Ages."

Shulman, Robert. "Montaigne and the Techniques and Tragedy of Melville's Billy Budd." CL, 16 (1964), 322-30.
By characterizing Vere as an admirer of Montaigne, Melville cannily invited the sympathy of a wide range of readers, for "there are almost as many Montaignes as there are readers." Ironically, however, Vere responds only to "a limited range of the Essays.... Montaigne's own celebration of the value of compassion, freedom, personal loyalty, private integrity, and individual conscience serves to remind us of what Vere has disregarded."

This essay is intended in part to serve as a corrective to Kilbourne's (above). While their views of Vere are different, Shulman suggests that Kilbourne's main flaw is his drastic oversimplification of Montaigne.

Stevens, Aretta. "The Edition of Montaigne Read by Melville." PBSA, 62 (1968), 130-34.
The edition of the Essays read by Melville was probably the translation by William Hazlitt; both the 1842 and the 1845 impressions are "safely eligible for source study."

Thompson, Lawrance. "God's Stony Heart." In Melville's Quarrel with God. Princeton: Princeton University Press, 1952.
By the time that he was writing Pierre Melville had decided that "Spenser and Dante had become second and third rate poets, now, and only the dark tragedies of Shakespeare or the essays of Montaigne or the words of Solomon fitted his personal category of first rate work, because only such literature reflected for him the ultimate Truth: that 'wisdom which is woe' [Ishmael's words in Moby-Dick]."

Vance, Thomas H. "Prince Hamlet, Melville, and the Ambiguities." In Geschichte und Fiktion: Amerikanische Prosa im 19. Jahrhundert (History and Fiction: American Prose in the 19th Century), eds. Alfred Weber and Hartmut Grandel. Göttingen: Vandenhoeck & Ruprecht, 1972.
Melville took Shakespeare more seriously than Shakespeare did, or perhaps the difference in their viewpoints merely reflects the times they lived in. "Melville's version of Shakespeare's 'Montaigneism' is a good deal heavier on its feet than Shakespeare's own. Pierre has plunged over the brink into nihilism and taken his author with him. But Hamlet's darting paradoxes, whether inspired by Montaigne or by the Renaissance air that the Montaignes had impregnated, are still contained--though it took all Shakespeare's cunning as a dramatic prestidigitator to prevent an overflow--within a firm moral order. There is no danger

that virtue and vice will turn into shadows of nothing: in the great closet scene with the queen Hamlet is in no doubt ... and neither is she when she has felt her heart 'cleft in twain' by his upbraiding words."

Vogelback, Arthur L. "Shakespeare and Melville's Benito Cereno." MLN, 67 (1952), 113-16.

"A study of Babo, the Negro mutineer in Benito Cereno, reveals in a number of ways the striking resemblance which he bears to Shakespeare's notorious villain, Iago." Both are consummate actors; both are intellectually keen; both vow silence when they are apprehended and go silent to their deaths. And thus "Babo takes his place with Jackson in Redburn and Claggart in Billy Budd, those other lineal descendants of Iago by the pen of Melville...."

Watson, Charles N., Jr. "Melville and the Theme of Timonism: From Pierre to The Confidence Man." AL, 44 (1972-73), 398-413.

"Not many Melville readers," says Watson, "would dispute the idea that between 1851 and 1856 Melville's vision of life darkened." Two reasons for Melville's pessimism have already been given by other scholars: (1) "a religious disillusionment, an increasing skepticism about the benevolence and even the existence of God," and (2) growing disbelief in "the ability of literary art to perform the lofty truth-telling function he had conceived for it." In this article Watson explores a third reason for Melville's bleak outlook, namely, "an increasing belief that his career had been betrayed and destroyed by his family, friends, and readers.... More and more, in the works after Moby-Dick, Melville found a metaphor for his disillusionment in the theme of Timonism--a theme which took its name from his reading of Shakespeare's Timon of Athens [one of the plays that Melville read and annotated in the edition of Shakespeare he obtained in 1849] and which implies a betrayal and desertion by one's friends. During these years, with his health and finances precarious and his early literary admirers falling away, he seems to have had an increasing sense of Timon's plight as an analogue to his own. Following such a betrayal, he saw two alternatives: to withdraw, like Timon, into misanthropic solitude; or to engage the public on its own terms, taking on the protective coloring of an artistic confidence-man, playing with a grim humor on the egotism and gullibility of his audience." The withdrawal theme appears in such works as Bartleby the Scrivener, and the confidence theme can be seen in The Confidence-Man, in which "the benignly Satanic survives, plying his artistic trade, leading another unsuspecting reader into the dark." If The Confidence-Man is a grim joke, it is as grim for the writer as it is for the reader, because "as a public author, Melville may well have known that he was taking his last long dive. Though he continued to write poetry until the end of his life and returned to prose fiction in Billy Budd, he never again thought seriously of public success."

Yaggy, Elinor. "Shakespeare and Melville's Pierre." Boston Public Library Quarterly, 6 (1954), 43-51.

Whereas the connection between Hamlet and Pierre; or, the Ambiguities has been discerned by many students of Melville's novel, Yaggy points to the more important influence of Romeo and Juliet. Fate plays a big part in Melville's work as well as Shakespeare's (a point about which critics of both works complain), yet fate shares responsibility for the outcome of each work with the impulsiveness of the main characters; Romeo and Pierre are about equally hotblooded. Then there are other smaller bits of evidence that prove that "Melville's mind was so steeped in the play that it crept in anywhere and everywhere, with or without his volition." To acknowledge the importance of the play's influence is to grasp fully the meaning of Melville's subtitle: "Romeo was a thoughtless youth, unaware yet of the complexity of the world, or to use Melville's word, the ambiguities. He learned that good intentions cannot keep one from being pushed into fatal situations, and that appearance cannot be trusted." After all, does not Romeo think the sleeping Juliet dead?

Poe

Pollin, Burton R. "The Self-Destructive Fall: A Theme from Shakespeare Used in Pym and 'The Imp of the Perverse.' " EA, 29 (1976), 199-202.

Poe's interest in irrationality, stimulated by his consideration of Macbeth and Hamlet, is reflected in the episode of Pym's fall (Chapter 24) and in "The Imp of the Perverse."

Twain

[Author not cited]. "Twain's Version of Hamlet." Twainian, 2, ix (1943), 4-6.

Apparently Twain wrote a new version of Hamlet, which gave prominence to the Dane's younger and more cheerful brother Billy. Nothing is made of it in this article, but one can easily see the connection between this bit of spoofing and the more integral parody of Shakespeare in the King and Duke part of Huckleberry Finn.

Baetzhold, Howard G. Mark Twain and John Bull: The British Connection. Bloomington: Indiana University Press, 1970, passim.

Henry IV and the other historical plays provided archaic language for The Prince and the Pauper. Hamlet is echoed in A Connecticut Yankee, and various Shakespeare plays figured in the composition of Huckleberry Finn.

Schönemann, Friedrich. Mark Twain als Literarische Persönlichkeit. Jena: Verlag der Frommanschen Buchhandlung, 1925.

The author takes it for granted that Twain read and knew Shakespeare, although other critics dispute him. (For a discussion of this disagreement among German scholars see Edgar H. Hemminghaus, Mark Twain in Germany, New York: AMS Press, 1966, p. 102-03.) It could be that, in an attempt to refute the popular image of Twain as unlettered bumpkin, Schönemann assumed too much on too little evidence. Whether or not that is the case, Baetzhold's research (see previous entry) suggests that Twain was indeed familiar with the writings of Shakespeare.

8. MILTON AND HIS AGE

The great works of Milton and Bunyan are remarkable for their intensely felt religiosity; George Herbert's poems often express spiritual struggle as well as sorrow, even anger, at his inability to know God directly; Sir Thomas Browne's Religio Medici is a personal reflection on a potpourri of philosophical and religious themes. Thus it is no wonder that the writers of this age, and particularly its chief author, are cited frequently and often explicitly in the works of our American writers, whose most important single source of literary borrowings, it should be remembered, was the Bible. Of course the writers who most regarded the Bible with skepticism or indifference (even though they had to acknowledge grudgingly its influence on American life and letters) were usually the ones who found it easiest to reject Milton and his contemporaries; conversely, those most receptive to Biblical themes and cadences were by and large equally sensitive to the poetry and prose of the middle and late seventeenth century.

In a country where school children used Paradise Lost as a textbook the reading of Milton by adults may have seemed more dutiful than pleasurable. At least this appears to be the sentiment behind Susan Fenimore Cooper's observation that her father "could seldom be induced to read more than a page or two of Milton at a time." A rebel like Poe had no qualms about pronouncing The Pilgrim's Progress "a ludicrously overrated book," and when Twain wrote to Howells that he "would rather be damned to John Bunyan's heaven" than read James's The Bostonians, he presented his correspondent with a telling example of the lesser of two evils.

So we find that the influence of Milton, Bunyan, and the others is strongest in the works of Hawthorne, Melville, and their contemporaries who swam in the wake of Transcendentalism. These writers were fundamentally religious by nature. Yet theirs is not the faith of adherence, and they interested themselves in conventional religion at least partly because they felt themselves to be in competition with it. As he wrote, Melville thought often of Milton, and his works testify to the Puritan poet's influence. But Melville preferred Milton's merely self-deluded Satan to his cold, vengeful God.

This preface draws on the following sources (see "List of Works Frequently Consulted" for full bibliographic information): Matthiessen, p. 247; Lynn, p. 167; Buell, p. 103; Henry F. Pommer, Milton and Melville, Pittsburgh: University of Pittsburgh Press, 1950, p. 8 (discussed in detail below); Susan Fenimore Cooper,

Pages and Pictures from the Writings of James Fenimore Cooper, New York: W. A. Townsend, 1861, p. 14-15.

The following studies (after the "General" section) are grouped under the names, listed alphabetically, of major American fiction writers through James who were influenced by Milton or one of his contemporaries.

General

Smith, David E. John Bunyan in America. Bloomington: Indiana University Press, 1966.

"American interest in Bunyan," says Smith, "was reflected in rather special and often curious ways. The American wilderness became a symbol for dark Satanic evil. The process of cultivating it into a garden required, from a Puritan standpoint, clearing, weeding, and fencing in." Smith examines five rewrites of Bunyan's classic (a typical one is entitled The Pilgrim's Progress in the Nineteenth Century); they have in common a suspicion of liberalism and reform, and none of them is characterized by what Smith calls "the sustaining force of genius."

For that reason these five works enjoy oblivion today. A work similar in theme yet superior in style to these five is Hawthorne's "The Celestial Railroad"; it and other Hawthorne works are discussed in a chapter that is treated in greater detail below. Concluding chapters deal with Bunyan's impact on Louisa May Alcott and e. e. cummings (The Pilgrim's Progress, says Smith, serves as the organizing pattern for The Enormous Room).

Cooper

Kesterson, David B. "Milton's Satan and Cooper's Demonic Chieftains." South Central Bulletin, 29 (1969), 138-42.

A detailed comparison of Milton's Satan with Magua of The Last of the Mohicans and Mahtoree of The Prairie.

Porte, Joel. "A Paradise for Bachelors." In The Romance in America: Studies in Cooper, Poe, Hawthorne, Melville, and James. Middletown: Wesleyan University Press, 1969.

The author disputes Leslie Fiedler's narrow (to him) reading of The Last of the Mohicans as a miscegenation story. "Despite Cooper's obvious interest in and horror of racial mixing, the not very secret theme of The Last of the Mohicans seems more truly to be the Miltonic one, that sex brought and brings death into the world, with all our woe and loss of Eden. Magua/Satan (the connection is made explicitly by Cooper) brings about the destruction of Uncas/Adam and Cora/Eve, to say nothing of his turning all of Fort William Henry into a fallen world of death and desolation. The only ones really exempt from the effects of sin are Natty and Chingachgook, who have substituted ideal friendship and devotion to manly duty for the baser passions, and seal their compact of purity with almost religious zeal (a firm handshake and scalding tears) over the monitory grave of Uncas, who was noble but tainted by desire."

For Fiedler's version see his _Love and Death in the American Novel_, New York: Stein and Day, 1966.

Hawthorne

Boswell, Jackson Campbell. "Bosom Serpents Before Hawthorne: Origin of a Symbol." _ELN_, 12 (1975), 279-87.

See the annotation of this item in Chapter 2, "The Classics."

Brant, Robert L. "Hawthorne and Marvell." _AL_, 30 (1958-59), 366.

The Scarlet Letter concludes with a description of Hester's grave and its heraldic inscription. Brant cites Marvell's "The Unfortunate Lover" as a source for the latter and suggests that Hawthorne may have wanted to elevate his story to the realm of legend (which is where "The Unfortunate Lover" takes place) rather than merely end on a gloomy note.

Broes, Arthur T. "Journey into Moral Darkness: 'My Kinsman, Major Molineux' as Allegory." _NCF_, 19 (1964), 171-84.

In composing his story Hawthorne borrowed "traditional allegorical episodes and patterns" from the major allegorists. Thus Robin's crossing the river via ferry recalls Dante's descent toward the worst regions of the Inferno, and the townspeople he encounters on the other side recall Spenser's pageant of the Seven Deadly Sins. The city itself is Bunyan's Vanity, and Robin is the pilgrim Christian. Whereas Bunyan's hero attains the Celestial City, however, Hawthorne gives the tale an ironic twist and sends his pilgrim to the city of the damned. "In his later works he was to suggest the possibilities of spiritual regeneration, but in this story there are few flashes of light to illuminate Robin's journey into darkness."

D'Avanzo, Mario L. "The Literary Sources of 'My Kinsman, Major Molineux': Shakespeare, Coleridge, Milton." _SSF_, 10 (1973), 121-36.

See the annotation of this item in Chapter 7, "Shakespeare and the Renaissance."

Davidson, Frank. "Hawthorne's Hive of Honey." _MLN_, 61 (1946), 14-21.

The author suggests the following influences: "Earth's Holocaust" (_Measure for Measure_); "The New Adam and Eve" (_Paradise Lost_, _King Lear_); "Rappaccini's Daughter" (_Paradise Lost_).

Doubleday, Neal Frank. "Hawthorne's Inferno." CE, 1 (1939-40), 658-70.

"Hawthorne's 'The Celestial Railroad' (1843) has been too easily dismissed as a clever parody of Pilgrim's Progress. It is something more than that. Hawthorne makes constant use of his reader's knowledge of Pilgrim's Progress for the ironic contrast that book affords to the religious attitudes of Hawthorne's own generation...." For instance, "the giant Transcendentalist has taken the place of the fearsome Pope and Pagan."

Evans, Oliver. "The Cavern and the Fountain: Paradox and Double Paradox in 'Rappaccini's Daughter.' " CE, 24 (1963), 461-63.

Evans discusses three passages from a single Hawthorne notebook: (1) a quotation from Sir Thomas Browne's Vulgar Errors dealing with an Indian king who sent Alexander a beautiful but fatally intended female who had been fed with poison, (2) Hawthorne's paraphrase of Madame Calderón de la Barca's story (in Life in Mexico) of people who make themselves invulnerable to rattlesnake bite through inoculation with venom, and (3) an original entry in which Hawthorne posited an allegory of the human heart as a cavern--sunny around the entrance, sinister in the interior, Edenic at the center. The first two passages provide the basic situation of the story, the third gives the clue to Beatrice's paradoxical nature. Poor Giovanni--he isn't bright enough to see past Beatrice's poisonous self to her pure center.

Johnson, W. Stacy. "Hawthorne and The Pilgrim's Progress." JEGP, 50 (1951), 156-66.

Bunyan's is the first book Hawthorne read; it is one he reread often; it is the work of fiction that impressed him most profoundly. F. O. Matthiessen (in American Renaissance) noted that Hawthorne tended to refer to Bunyan in describing crises in his fiction. Johnson goes on from there to cite other Bunyan influences on Hawthorne's work--names of characters, allegorical methods, themes--and to conclude that "The Pilgrim's Progress is a major source and inspiration for the art of Hawthorne."

Kloeckner, A. J. "The Flower and the Fountain: Hawthorne's Chief Symbols in 'Rappaccini's Daughter.'" AL, 38 (1966-67), 323-36.

In Book III of Paradise Lost Hawthorne found the flower-fountain symbols that he uses in "Rappaccini's Daughter" and, less centrally, in The Marble Faun and The House of the Seven Gables.

Liebman, Sheldon W. "Hawthorne and Milton: The Second Fall in 'Rappaccini's Daughter.' " NEQ, 41 (1968), 521-35.

In this novel and stimulating study of Hawthorne's tale Liebman notes that the American author borrows the principal Characters from Paradise Lost but gives them new and unexpected roles. Thus Beatrice is the new Adam and Giovanni the Eve who spoils everything, not with an apple but with an antidote given him by Baglioni/Satan. Rappaccini and his garden, thought by most critics to be thoroughly evil, are described as such only by the biased Baglioni and the easily confused Giovanni. Rappaccini is not God, by the way, only a "God-surrogate, defending God's estate, the christian world in which man has fallen only to rise again...." The story illustrates the wrongheadedness of trying to perfect a world that is as perfect as a postlapsarian world can be and that must necessarily contain evil in an amount that is, after all, endurable. The failing of the new Eve and Satan is not their wickedness; paradoxically, it is their inability to tolerate a negligible evil in their world.

________. "Hawthorne's Comus: A Miltonic Source for 'The Maypole of Merrymount.' " NCF, 27 (1972), 345-51.
Milton's work is mentioned several times in Hawthorne's story; it too deals with "the subject of temptation and moral choice." Whereas Milton's Lady is saved by divine intervention, however, Hawthorne's Edgar and Edith are almost entirely responsible for their own salvation. The relation between these two works suggests a larger connection between their authors--both Hawthorne and Milton dwell on the problem of moral choice in their work as a whole.

Matthiessen, F. O. "Hawthorne and Milton." In American Renaissance: Art and Expression in the Age of Emerson and Whitman. New York: Oxford University Press, 1941.
In writing The Marble Faun Hawthorne "unquestionably brooded over the meaning of Paradise Lost." The story of Miriam and Donatello--a remorseful, crime-linked couple, like Adam and Eve--reveals the Puritan viewpoint that Hawthorne shared with Milton. Apropos of the Puritans, Matthiessen echoes Perry Miller in noting that "the impossibility of accepting their explanation of the universe ... should not blind us to the accuracy of their observations of man," whom they saw as "a being radically imperfect, destined to struggle through a long labyrinth of error, and to suffer harsh and cruel shocks." (Matthiessen reminds us that the contrast between this notion and "the one-way optimism of most of Hawthorne's contemporaries could hardly be more striking.")

Mounts, Charles Eugene. "Hawthorne's Echoes of Spenser and Milton." NHJ, 1973, 162-71.
See the annotation of this item in Chapter 5, "Spenser."

Pollin, Burton R. " 'Rappaccini's Daughter'--Sources and Names." Names, 14 (1966), 30-35.
See the annotation of this item in Chapter 12, "The Romantics."

Roulston, C. Robert. "Hawthorne's Use of Bunyan's Symbols in 'The Celestial Railroad.' " Kentucky Philological Association Bulletin, 1975, 17-24.
According to the conventional view, in this story Hawthorne is merely thumbing his nose at Unitarianism and Transcendentalism, and he uses symbols and characters from Bunyan rather mechanically. But Roulston feels that readers who are familiar with The Pilgrim's Progress will recognize the seriousness with which Hawthorne approaches that work; further, they will understand that Hawthorne used Bunyan in order to advance a major theme present in the Puritan's work and his own--the reality of evil.

Smith, David E. "Bunyan and Hawthorne." In John Bunyan in America. Bloomington: Indiana University Press, 1966.
Smith discusses three images from The Pilgrim's Progress that recur in Hawthorne's work: (1) the disingenuous pilgrim; (2) pathways and byways in a labyrinthine wilderness; and (3) the unsuccessful search for the Celestial City. One obvious object of Smith's analysis is "The Celestial Railroad," but he notes that "it would be a mistake to conclude that the influence of Bunyan's work could find reflection only overtly in Hawthorne's art. The Pilgrim's Progress was deeply embedded in his creative consciousness, and we are likely to find unexpected and often luxuriant blossomings from it throughout the range of his imaginative production." Other Hawthorne works discussed in this chapter are Fanshawe, The Scarlet Letter, and The Blithedale Romance.

For an outline of the overall scope of this book see the annotation under the "General" section of this chapter.

Stanton, Robert. "Hawthorne, Bunyan, and the American Romances." PMLA, 71 (1956), 155-65.
Episodes in The Scarlet Letter, The House of the Seven Gables, and The Blithedale Romance are based on Bunyan's notion that there are many seemingly right paths to the Celestial City but only one true road. What Hawthorne depicts in the stories of Dimmesdale and Hester, Hepzibah and Clifford, and Coverdale is the mistaken idea that one can attain the Celestial City easily, a notion shared by several characters in The Pilgrim's Progress, including Hypocrisy, Formalist, Ignorance, and, for a while, Christian himself.

Van Doren, Mark. "Tales and Sketches." In Nathaniel Hawthorne. [No city given]: William Sloane Associates, 1949.
See the annotation of this item in Chapter 5, "Spenser."

James

Tintner, Adeline R. "The Countess and Scholastica: James's 'L'Allegro' and "Il Penseroso.'" SSF, 11 (1974), 267-76.
In this study of James's "Benvolio" Tintner's customarily first-rate scholarship is evidenced once more. Her point is that "in this playful allegory James manages, with the help of Milton's poetry and that classical mythology that Milton himself absorbed, to adjust in his own mind those extremes of human thought and activity that must each play a role in the creative artist's existence." (The title of the James story, as Tintner points out, is an inversion of "Malvolio" from Twelfth Night.)

Veeder, William. Henry James--the Lessons of the Master: Popular Fiction and Personal Style in the Nineteenth Century. Chicago: University of Chicago Press, 1975.
See the annotation of this item in Chapter 14, "The Victorians."

Melville

Mansfield, Luther S., and Howard P. Vincent. "Explanatory Notes" to Moby-Dick. New York: Hendricks House, 1952.
The numerous allusions to Milton and his works as well as those of such contemporaries as Sir Thomas Browne, Bunyan, Dryden, and Hobbes are detailed and explicated in these indispensable notes. (The authors also note that Sir Thomas Browne "helped importantly to shape ideas or phrasing" in Moby-Dick.)

Maxwell, J. C. "Melville and Milton." N&Q, 210 (1965), 60.
Maxwell records a previously unnoticed echo of Paradise Lost in Pierre.

McHaney, Thomas L. "The Confidence-Man and Satan's Disguises in Paradise Lost." NCF, 30 (1975), 200-06.
"It seems clear that Melville drew on Milton's Satan for the introductory chapter of his book and possibly resorted to the same passage again at the ending in order to bring together his images and to underline the identification of the Confidence Man with the devil." As for the disguises, they are the ones traditionally assigned to Satan by the Bible, Milton, and folklore.

Millgate, Michael. "Melville and Marvell: A Note on Billy Budd." ES, 49 (1968), 47-50.
Captain Vere is called "Starry Vere" after a character in Marvell's poem "Upon Appleton House." A portion of the poem that deals with parents and children may have brought out Melville's remorse over the accidental death or suicide of his nineteen-year-old son Malcolm, and in the story "Claggart may represent in part the fault-finding father that Melville knew he had been,

Vere the understanding father he felt he should have been." (Vere shows an unusual form of understanding, since he orders Billy's death. Perhaps it would be more accurate to say that Claggart represents an undue severity, Vere a combination of kindliness and severity found in all fathers.)

Newbery, I. " 'The Encantadas': Melville's Inferno." AL, 38 (1966-67), 49-68.
See the annotation of this item in Chapter 4, "Dante and the Middle Ages."

Perry, Robert L. "Billy Budd: Melville's Paradise Lost." Midwest Quarterly, 10 (1969), 173-85.
In his irrationality, pride, unsuccessful dissembling, and envy Claggart is like Satan. In his personal beauty, innocence, and possession of a tragic flaw Billy is like Adam and Eve. Yet Melville subverts traditional theology when he says that it is wrong to be too good. And when he says that "utter innocence" is but "blank ignorance," he may be echoing Milton's Areopagitica, which speaks of untested virtue as "blank virtue."

Pommer, Henry F. Milton and Melville. Pittsburgh: University of Pittsburgh Press, 1950.
A short, profoundly scholarly work that details the lessons Melville learned from Milton. Of these the two greatest are the Miltonic style, reflected particularly in "Melville's repetitions, cumulations, -ean adjectives, inversions, suspensions, omissions, parentheses, substitutions of parts of speech, words from poetic diction, series of proper nouns, unusual compound words, sonorous passages and passages of dignity, iambic rhythms and epic similes"; and the influence of Satan, particularly on Ahab. "Both Satan and Ahab were hurt in their great pride by powers which they might seem to harm, but could never destroy. Rallying ill-fated followers to their impious revolt, they war against invincibility with which they have no real quarrel." Yet "we are forced to admire their fortitude and sympathy, and to pity them for their inner suffering and their loneliness. Theirs was an inner dynamism compounded not entirely of Hell. Theirs was a consanguinity immeasurable but sure."

Stanton, Robert. "Typee and Milton: Paradise Well Lost." MLN, 74 (May 1959), 407-11.
Stanton expands on the assertion of Pommer (whose book is discussed above) that the valley in Typee resembles specifically Milton's paradise. Melville puts Milton's material to his own use, however, for Typee shows that "modern man and Paradise are mutually destructive," and that "modern man, in spite of his longing for 'a garden of innocence, a paradise of idyllic delights,' would find such a place unbearable."

Vande Kieft, Ruth M. " 'When Big Hearts Strike Together': The Concussion of Melville and Sir Thomas Browne." PLL, 5 (1969), 39-50.

The author begins with F. O. Mattheissen's assertion that "the effect of Browne's works on Melville was an important cause of his shift from the writing of straight adventure to the metaphysical efforts of Mardi, a major influence in the release of Melville's creative energies." But, she says, "Mardi is an oddly mixed book: the allegory is forced, not sufficiently welded to the adventure story; the appeals to legend and authority, the cultivation of tentative states of mind, the wonder-struck attitudes, are somewhat mannered and self-conscious. Browne's influence here seems unassimilated and immature, as though Melville's large quaffing in the cups of the cracked archangel had made him a bit giddy. In Moby Dick, however, the ventriloquism ceases; the assimilation is complete; that specific ingredient in Melville's total vision which may be identified as Browne's influence disappears in the mighty blend of an authentic and original artist."

Poe

Haviland, Thomas. "How Well Did Poe Know Milton?" PMLA, 69 (1951), 841-60.

Pretty well, says Haviland, although the influence is mainly on Poe's poetry and criticism and therefore outside the scope of the present study (though worth a collateral mention).

Twain

Baetzhold, Howard G. Mark Twain and John Bull: The British Connection. Bloomington: Indiana University Press, 1970, passim.

From his study notes for The Prince and the Pauper it is evident that Twain used such works as Pepys's Diary and The English Rogue ("a seventeenth-century compendium of English low-life") as sources for archaic language and other details. The characters of the King and the Duke in Huckleberry Finn take something from portraits in Pepys's Diary of that merry pair Charles II and his brother James, who are often simply referred to by Pepys as "the King and the Duke." And there are elements of Paradise Lost in The Mysterious Stranger. (Baetzhold notes that Twain once planned to write an essay proving that Milton wrote The Pilgrim's Progress and observes sagaciously that "it is probably fortunate that it went no farther than the planning stage.")

Bendixen, Alfred. "Huck Finn and Pilgrim's Progress." MTJ, 18, iii (1976), 21.

Huck's passing mention of Bunyan's narrative (in Chapter 17) may bespeak a greater connection between the works, for "both Huck and Christian are outcasts whose moral superiority is based on a rejection of civilization's values, on a flight from society. Mark Twain's characters are not allegorical representations, but the people fooled by 'The Royal Nonesuch' would have felt comfortable in Vanity Fair.... Bunyan and Mark Twain both knew how hard it was to be a Christian in this world. Like _Pilgrim's Progress_, _Huck Finn_ is fundamentally anti-social. In both works, to affirm virtue is to reject the world."

9. THE EIGHTEENTH CENTURY

The Age of Reason, the Augustan Age, the Enlightenment, the Classical Period (in France), or the Neoclassical (in England): each of these terms suggests without describing adequately the period between Milton and the Romantics, dating roughly from the last quarter of the seventeenth century and continuing for one hundred years. It was an age in which literature, philosophy, political theory, and science put humankind at the center of a universe that had been set in motion long since by a remote God, who had then left this universe--and humankind itself--as fit subject for scrutiny. Such an anthropocentric view led inevitably, in thought and letters, to a certain elegance in expression, a certain bluffness in point of view. It also led to a certain smugness, and when Melville cried, "We want no American Goldsmiths," one wonders if he had in mind that author's best-known character, the Vicar of Wakefield, who looked upon his children as "a very valuable present to my country," yet who was happy when they were humiliated, "as it would give me many opportunities of future triumph, and teach [them] more humility."

Certainly it is both the elegance in style and bluffness in viewpoint of the eighteenth-century authors that resulted in their being relished indiscriminately by writers as different as Hawthorne and Twain. In Twain's case especially one sees how literary style can soften a bluff attitude; one may consider, for example, the last third of Huckleberry Finn, where not only the cruel but also the inevitable maltreatment of slaves is presented in a context of high comedy yet of perceptible bitterness as well. "Strike and conceal your hand," said Voltaire, who, like other French writers of the Ancien Régime, was adept at saying more than he seemed to say. It was a lesson that Twain, among others in America, learned well.

And if Americans sometimes seemed to resemble the sons and daughters of Abysinnia in Johnson's Rasselas, who "rose in the morning, and lay down at night, pleased with each other and with themselves," and who were certain of their superiority to the rest of the world, then a nineteenth-century Johnson, or perhaps several of them, was needed. Johnson thundering against Boswell's foolishness is Johnson exposing the self-deluded "common sense" view of things, the two-and-two-make-four system (as Henry James called it in a scornful letter to his brother William) which, to many, represents all that is worth knowing. The eighteenth-century writers believed in a subtler calculus, one that appealed strongly to the American authors when it came their turn to measure humankind and the universe and humankind.

This preface draws on the following sources (see "List of Works Frequently Consulted" for full bibliographic information): Priestley, p. 54; Matthiessen, p. 187, 206f; Minnie M. Brashear, "Mark Twain and the 'Shadow of Europe,' " in Mark Twain: Son of Missouri, New York: Russell & Russell, 1964; and George R. Havens, The Age of Ideas, New York: Henry Holt, 1955, p. 17-18. For more on the American reception of Johnson and Pope see Agnes Marie Sibley, Alexander Pope's Prestige in America, 1725-1835, New York: King's Crown, 1949; and Robert B. Winans, "Works by and about Samuel Johnson in Eighteenth-Century America," PBSA, 62 (1968), 537-46.

The following studies are grouped under the names, listed alphabetically, of major American fiction writers through James who were influenced by one or more eighteenth-century authors from England or Europe.

Brown

Bernard, Kenneth. "Charles Brockden Brown and the Sublime." The Personalist, 45 (1964), 235-49.

See the annotation of this item in Chapter 11, "The Gothic Novelists."

Brown, Herbert. "Charles Brockden Brown's 'The Story of Julius': Rousseau and Richardson 'Improved.' " In Essays Mostly on Periodical Publishing in America: A Collection in Honor of Clarence Gohdes, ed. James Woodress. Durham: Duke University Press, 1973.

In a letter to his friend Bringhurst (herein reproduced), Brockden Brown sketched a plan for a sentimental romance in epistolary form. The hero and heroine were to be brother and sister, Julius and Julietta. Thus (and I quote from Brown's letter) "the situation was somewhat new, for Rousseau and Richardson had only described that friendship which may subsist between two men or two women, and have given us no striking pictures of sisterly and fraternal love," which, because it exists "in the domestic sphere, must be proportionably [sic] more perfect, as opportunities are here afforded of more frequent converse and entire confidence than in other situations."

Haviland, Thomas P. "Preciositê Crosses the Atlantic." PMLA, 59 (1944), 131-41.

The French heroic romance, or roman de longue haleine, as practiced by Madeleine de Scudêry and others, is a hitherto-overlooked influence on early American letters. Having as their motive force romantic love and characterized chiefly by their lenghthy analytical passages, these romances are consciously or unconsciously imitated in such novels as William Hill Brown's The Power of Sympathy (often called the first American novel) and Charles Brockden Brown's Edgar Huntly and especially his Arthur Mervyn.

Kimball, Arthur G. "Savages and Savagism: Brockden Brown's Dramatic Irony." Studies in Romanticism, 6 (1967), 214-25.
"Brown, like many others at the end of the eighteenth century, was affected by Lockean ideas. But Brown suspected that there were shadowy corners in man's psyche for which Locke's tabula rasa had not provided." More specifically, Brown "sensed a potential source of tyranny in man's nature for which no philosophical system, including Englightenment optimism, could adequately account." In this sense is Brown a transitional figure between the Age of Reason and the Romantic Era.

Levine, Paul. "The American Novel Begins." American Scholar, 35 (1965-66), 134-48.
See the annotation of this item in Chapter 11, "The Gothic Novelists."

Pochmann, Henry A. "Charles Brockden Brown." In German Culture in America. Madison: University of Wisconsin Press, 1957.
Wieland exhibits a characteristic common to the so-called German "rational tale," namely an implicit warning against narrow reliance on only one of the mental faculties. Specifically, Brown's novel may have been directly influenced by Cajetan Tschink's Geisterseher. See Warfel in MLQ, below.

Reid, S. W. "Charles Brockden Brown's Copy of Johnson's Dictionary (1783)." Serif, 11, iv (1975), 12-20.
Reid describes Brown's copy of the abridged dictionary in minute detail; he uses the glyphs and runes that bring joy to the heart of the scientific bibliophile and consternation to everyone else's. However, the close reader of Brown's prose will at least be glad to know which dictionary the novelist probably used and when he acquired it (in 1790, before any of his major works had been published).

Warfel, Harry R. Charles Brockden Brown: American Gothic Novelist. Gainesville: University of Florida Press, 1949.
See the annotation of this item in Chapter 11, "The Gothic Novelists."

_______. "Charles Brockden Brown's German Sources." MLQ, 1 (1940), 357-65.
Brown was influenced by the German Rationalists; in particular,

Wieland may have derived its theme from Cajetan Tschink's Geisterseher, in which various supernatural phenomena are explained away by the use of reason. See Pochmann, above.

Wiley, Lulu Rumsey. Sources and Influences of the Novels of Charles Brockden Brown. New York: Vantage Press, 1950.
Besides having to pay for publishing what others should pay you for, there are two additional reasons for avoiding a vanity press, which is what Vantage is. The first is that you get lousy editing, which explains the curious locutions and factual errors that mar this book. The second is that no one takes you seriously. I have not been able to locate a single review of this book; I can find no reference to it in other Brown scholarship; the interlibrary-loan people had to send all the way to the Bucknell University Library to get a copy (suggesting sales so weak that not a single copy has made it south of the Mason-Dixon line); and that copy gave a strong appearance of having never been checked out before. This is unfortunate; the book isn't that bad. The best part describes five influences on Brown, all forms of fiction that rose out of reaction to the precise and impersonal writing of the Augustans: the sentimental school (Richardson, Fielding, Sterne, Henry Mackenzie), the autobiographical school (Richardson, Defoe, Fielding, Smollett, Sterne), the historical school (Thomas Leland, Maria Edgeworth), the Gothic school (Walpole, Radcliffe, Mrs. Shelley, Maturin), the school of purpose or reform (Mrs. Shelley, Godwin). "From these sources Brown drew inspiration," writes the unlucky author, "and mingled strains from them appear in his novels."

Cooper

Aldridge, A. Owen. "Fenimore Cooper and the Picaresque Tradition." NCF, 27 (1972), 283-92.
Cooper's Autobiography of a Pocket-Handkerchief is in the eighteenth-century English "genre of the peregrinating object" (Aldridge notes that bibliographies of the eighteenth-century English novel include such titles as Adventures of a Black Coat, The Adventures of a Bank Note, and Adventures of a Cork-screw). Thus Cooper's novel is "significant in literary history as a late survival of a minor genre and possibly the only example of the genre in American literature."

Gates, W. B. "A Note on Cooper and Robinson Crusoe." MLN, 67 (1952), 421-22.
In this amusing note Gates points out what can happen when one author allows another to hold sway over him to too great an extent. Under the influence of Robinson Crusoe while writing The Crater, Cooper allowed his character Mark Woolston to mediate Crusoe-like on various aspects of isolation, whereas Woolston is not at all alone, and he has Woolston undergo a religious con-

version à la Crusoe, whereas Woolston had been portrayed as a religious man all along. "Thus, in these incidents, Cooper was following his source so closely that he lost sight of his own previously established situation and character."

Müller, Willi. The Monikins von J. F. Cooper in ihrem Verhältnis zu Gulliver's Travels von J. Swift. Rostock: Carl Hinstorff's Buchbruderet, 1900.
This essay is not only hard to obtain but also printed in the flowery German typeface known as Fraktur. These difficulties notwithstanding, Müller uses the parrallel-passages method to show that Cooper borrowed extensively and sometimes almost verbatim from Swift.

Hawthorne

Abel, Darrel. "Immortality vs. Mortality in Septimius Felton: Some Possible Sources." AL, 27 (1955-56), 566-70.
Abel suggests that Hawthorne's unfinished romance has several sources, notably Swift's Gulliver's Travels (as well as certain of Shakespeare's meditations on death and various accounts of the career of the nineteenth-century visionary Claude-Henri, Comte de Saint-Simon). More significant than Abel's findings, perhaps, is his sensible attitude toward them: recognizing that Septimius Felton has "too little interest and significance to warrant much study," he offers his research as an attempt "to throw light upon the settled preoccupations of Hawthorne and confirm other evidences of what were persistent literary influences upon his work." Like a number of other scholars, Abel notes Hawthorne's tendency to borrow "ideas and effects" but not words and phrases from other authors. Hawthorne relied heavily on his borrowings to create "a rich complication of attitudes" in his work; by disguising his sources so effectively he created another and challenging complication for the source-hunter as well.

Cooke, Alice Lovelace. "Some Evidence of Hawthorne's Indebtedness to Swift." Studies in English (University of Texas), no. 18 (1938), 140-74.
Cooke finds verbal and thematic echoes of Swift in "Dr. Heidegger's Experiment," "The New Adam and Eve," "Earth's Holocaust," "A Select Party," "The Hall of Fantasy," and "The Pygmies." She concludes that Hawthorne and Swift were alike in their analyses of human frailty even though Hawthorne, unlike Swift, thought men and women capable of self-redemption.

Cowley, Malcolm. "Five Acts of The Scarlet Letter." In Twelve Original Essays on Great American Novels, ed. Charles Shapiro. Detroit: Wayne State University Press, 1958.

According to the records of the Salem Athenaeum, Hawthorne read all of Racine as well as other classical French dramatists. Thus The Scarlet Letter may be read as "a Racinian drama of dark necessity." As such, its chapters can be arranged to correspond to standard dramatic form:

Act I, Scene 1: Chapters 1-3
Act I, Scene 2: Chapter 4
Act II, Scene 1: Chapters 7-8
Act II, Scene 2: Chapter 10
Act III: Chapter 12
Act IV, Scene 1: Chapters 14-15
Act IV, Scene 2: Chapters 16-19
Act V: Chapters 21-23

Some chapters (5, 6, 9, 11, 13, 20, and 24, the epilogue) fall outside the dramatic framework; these deal wholly or chiefly with single characters and are narrative or expository in nature. In light of this it seems odd to propose that The Scarlet Letter has "the unity of effect and the strict economy of means of a perfect tale." It would be more accurate to say that the novel represents, as Aristotle wrote, "an action that is serious and also, as having magnitude, complete in itself ... with incidents arousing pity and fear, wherewith to accomplish its catharsis of such emotions." His debt to Racine notwithstanding, Hawthorne, no doubt unwittingly, "recaptured, for his New England, the essence of Greek tragedy."

Davidson, Frank. "Hawthorne's Use of a Pattern from The Rambler." MLN, 63 (1948), 545-48.

"Five sketches in Hawthorne's Mosses [from an Old Manse]--'A Select Party,' 'The Hall of Fantasy,' 'The Christmas Banquet,' 'The Intelligence Office,' and 'A Virtuoso's Collection'--show similarity of design but differ radically in this aspect of their artistry from their companion pieces. Each has a brief introduction and conclusion separated by a somewhat extended section enumerating objects in catalog fashion or presenting a pageant of individual figures who pass in somewhat rapid succession." Hawthorne, who was familiar with most of Dr. Johnson's work, probably took this pattern from Numbers 82 and 105 of The Rambler.

________. "Voltaire and Hawthorne's 'The Christmas Banquet.'" Boston Public Library Quarterly, 3 (1951), 244-46.

Hawthorne had been reading Candide during the months when he composed "The Christmas Banquet," and certainly there are similarities between that story and Chapter 19 of Voltaire's tale: both deal with a dinner to be given for the most miserable, from whom the woefulest man is to be selected and rewarded. However, whereas misery is a condition of life in Voltaire, in Hawthorne it is often subjective and self-induced. Genuine grief, on the other hand, seems necessary to some extent: the most miserable man at Hawthorne's banquet is the one who has been untouched by real grief altogether.

Durham, Frank. "Hawthorne and Goldsmith: A Note." *Journal of American Studies*, 4 (1970), 103-05.
Hawthorne admired, read, and alluded to Goldsmith in his work. For instance, both Governor Bellingham of *The Scarlet Letter* and Mistress Quickly of Goldsmith's "A Reverie at the Boar's Head Tavern in East Cheap" wear ruffs that make the head of each look " 'like that of John the Baptist in a charger' " (the language is the same in both texts).

Fisher, Marvin. "The Pattern of Conservatism in Johnson's *Rasselas* and Hawthorne's *Tales*." *Journal of the History of Ideas*, 19 (1958), 173-96.
Fisher notes Hawthorne's high estimation of Johnson and his familiarity with *Rasselas*; without insisting overmuch on a direct transmission of ideas, he concludes that the conservatism of the later author bears a strong resemblance to that of the earlier: " ... both Johnson and Hawthorne, though they could not condemn every kind of change, urged their fellow human beings to apply checks to all manner of excess, to any radical scheme which promised much at little or no cost. The thought of these two men runs counter to the popular idea of progress, evident in eighteenth-century England and dominant in nineteenth-century America. Like advocates of conservatism today, Johnson and Hawthorne are united not so much by what they advocated as by what they opposed."

Mascheck, J. D. C. "Samuel Johnson's Uttoxeter Penance in the Writings of Hawthorne." *Hermathena: A Dublin University Review*, no. 111 (1971), 51-54.
Johnson's act of penance--his standing bareheaded in the rain on the spot where he had been too proud to help his father sell books fifty years before--is reflected in the public scenes of penance that occur in the marketplace in *The Scarlet Letter*.

Wheeler, Otis B. "Hawthorne and the Fiction of Sensibility." *NCF*, 19 (1964), 159-70.
The eighteenth-century cult of sensibility, which arose as a protest against the low moral tone of Restoration comedy and came to play a significant role in the development of Romanticism, is an acknowledged influence on Hawthorne's early work, yet Wheeler argues with authority that the case is more complex than previously thought. The common view of Hawthorne's work is that *Fanshawe* is an imitative novel lying almost wholly within the tradition of sensibility, but that Hawthorne grows out of his reliance on the tradition as he matures as an artist. This is only partly true. Though some sensibility conventions are obtrusive in

the early work, he rejects some of them from the beginning. Others he comes to reject later. Others he accepts equivocally. Some that he seems to have outgrown appear again in The Marble Faun. Most interesting, as showing the power of a great theme to revitalize hollow or worn-out conventions, is the fact that Hawthorne makes use in his most successful works of certain sensibility conventions that take on a validity in the new context that they never had before.

In The Scarlet Letter, for example, Dimmesdale starts, gasps, clutches at his bosom, and otherwise manifests his emotions as would the hero of an eighteenth-century sentimental novel. He isn't simply upset, however--Dimmesdale is being lashed by the knowledge of a secret sin. Here, then, "we find Hawthorne revitalizing a well-worn convention by connecting it to a theme that takes it far beyond the cult of sensibility."

Irving

Pochmann, Henry A. "Irving's German Sources in The Sketch Book." Studies in Philology, 27 (1930), 477-507.

See the annotation of this item in Chapter 12, "The Romantics."

James

Tintner, Adeline R. " 'High Melancholy and Sweet': James and the Arcadian Tradition." CLQ, 12 (1976), 109-21.
See the annotation of this item in Chapter 2, "The Classics."

________. "Why James Quotes Gibbon in 'Glasses.'" SSF, 14 (1977), 287-88.
By having his narrator refer to a character's "variety of ... inclinations" James alerts the reader to the ironic tone of his story--in The Decline and Fall of the Roman Empire, Gibbon uses this phrase to describe the fleshly appetites of the Roman Emperor Gordianus the Younger, whereas James's narrator applies it to a homely Oxford aesthete.

Warren, Austin. "Henry James: Symbolic Imagery in the Later Novels." In Rage for Order. Chicago: University of Chicago: University of Chicago Press, 1948.
See the annotation of this item in Chapter 16, "Scientific Thinkers and Naturalists."

Melville

Bell, Millicent. "Pierre Bayle and Moby Dick." PMLA, 66 (1951) 626-48.

In his distaste for the Transcendental denial of evil Melville may have found a soulmate in Pierre Bayle; certainly the dialectic of good and evil in Moby-Dick recalls the viewpoint set forth by Bayle in many of the articles in his Dictionnaire Historique et Critique, an English translation of which Melville bought in 1849. In this article Bell points out philosophic and even stylistic similarities between Melville and Bayle, of whom one might say, as Hawthorne said of Melville, "he can neither believe nor be comfortable in his disbelief." See Frederick, below.

Dillingham, William B. "Melville's Long Ghost and Smollett's Count Fathom." AL, 42 (1970-71), 232-35.
Dr. Long Ghost, the "congenial rogue" of Melville's Omoo, is based on both a real person named John Troy and the hero of Tobias Smollett's The Adventures of Ferdinand Count Fathom. Melville's novel refers to Smollett's explicitly, and there are a number of subtler parallels.

Frederick, John T. "Melville's Early Acquaintance with Bayle." AL, 39 (1967-68), 545-47.
Nearly twenty years before his purchase of Bayle's Dictionnaire (see Bell, above) Melville may have made the acquaintance of the French skeptic in a fictitious dialogue between "Locke and Bayle" that can be found in Lindley Murray's English Reader, a text used at the Albany Academy when Melville studied there.

Isani, Mukhtar Ali. "The Naming of Fedallah in Moby-Dick." AL, 40 (1968-69), 380-85.
See the annotation of this item in Chapter 12, "The Romantics."

Mansfield, Luther S., and Howard P. Vincent. "Explanatory Notes" to Moby-Dick. New York: Hendricks House, 1952.
Among the eighteenth-century figures alluded to in Moby-Dick and discussed in these indispensable notes are Addison, Boswell, Dr. Johnson, Goldsmith, Pope, Sterne, Locke, Kant, Pierre Bayle, Voltaire, Le Sage, and Schiller.

Moore, Richard S. "Burke, Melville, and the Power of Blackness." ATQ, 29 (1976), 30-33.
Melville owned a copy of Edmund Burke's Enquiry into the Origins of Our Ideas of the Sublime and Beautiful, which may have influenced the aesthetics of Moby-Dick. For one thing, Burke assumed that "terror is a far more intense emotional state than that pleasure which is evoked by beauty"; thus "Burke's analytic of the sublime defined the vast, the powerful, and the obscure of nature as legitimate artistic resources."

Pochmann, Henry A. "Herman Melville (1819-1891)." In German

Culture in America. Madison: University of Wisconsin Press, 1957.

The author notes interesting parallels between Melville's work and Kant's. In Moby-Dick the thesis of Kant's Critique of Pure Reason is borne out, for the universe is inscrutable, and one cannot even validate the usefulness of reason as a tool to penetrate it. Of course Kant said in his Critique of Practical Reason that one must preserve moral order and believe in God and immortality even though their existence can't be proved, but when Melville tested this idea in Pierre he came up, as the novel's subtitle suggests, with ambiguities. Melville agreed with Kant's metaphysic but seemed dubious of his ideas on morals. "Rightly or wrongly interpreted," says Pochmann, "Kant furnished Melville with the backbone upon which to build his anatomy of despair."

Thomas, Russell. "Melville's Use of Some Sources in The Encantadas." AL, 3 (1931-32), 432-56.

See the reference to this item in the annotation of Leon Howard, "Melville and Spenser--A Note on Criticism," MLN, 46 (1931), 291-92, in Chapter 5, "Spenser."

Welsh, Alexander. "A Melville Debt to Carlyle." MLN, 73 (1958), 489-91.

See the annotation of this item in Chapter 14, "The Victorians."

Poe

Allen, Mrs. Mozelle Scaff. "Poe's Debt to Voltaire." Studies in English (University of Texas), no. 15 (1935), 63-75.

The author lists quotations and paraphrases of Voltaire by Poe, possible borrowings (such as the miraculous return to life by Dr. Pangloss in Candide, which appears to be paralleled in "Loss of Breath" and "Some Words with a Mummy"), and similarities in critical and other attitudes.

Hirsch, David H. "The Pit and the Apocalypse." Sewanee Review, 76 (1968), 632-52.

See the annotation of this item in Chapter 3, "The Bible."

Jeffrey, David K. "The Johnsonian Influence: Rasselas and Poe's 'The Domain of Arnheim.' " Poe N, 3 (1970), 26-29.

The garden of Arnheim recalls the pastoral paradise of Amhara in Rasselas. Importantly, Arnheim is constructed rather than discovered--while the landscape is the same, then, the difference to which the two artists put it suggests "differences between the ages of sensibility and romanticism, the mirror and the lamp."

Pollin, Burton R. "Dean Swift in the Works of Poe." N&Q, 20 (1973), 244-46.

A brief survey of Poe's several references, in both fiction and criticism, to Swift's works.

________. "Poe and Daniel Defoe: A Significant Relationship." Topic, 16, xxx (1976), 3-22.

Early on Poe reviewed Robinson Crusoe at length and thereafter cited Defoe or his writings twelve times in letters and in print. What he admired most in Defoe was his verisimilitude, which Poe thought was achieved more through a controlling viewpoint than an amassing of detail. He must have learned Defoe's lesson well; when The Narrative of Arthur Gordon Pym appeared, numerous reviewers praised it for resembling Robinson Crusoe.

Twain

Baetzhold, Howard G. "Postscript I." In Mark Twain and John Bull: The British Connection. Bloomington: Indiana University Press, 1970.

"In Chapter Eight of Huckleberry Finn Huck's stumbling across the ashes of Jim's campfire on Jackson's Island parallels Crusoe's discovery of Friday's footprint." More importantly, Defoe's masterpiece provided a model for A Connecticut Yankee: Hank Morgan sees himself as Crusoe, and he sets out with Clarence as his man Friday to civilize the island on which he is stranded.

Beau Tibbs in Goldsmith's The Citizen of the World may have provided Twain with the basis for Colonel Sellers of The Gilded Age and The American Claimant.

Brashear, Minnie M. "Mark Twain and the 'Shadow of Europe.' " In Mark Twain: Son of Missouri. New York: Russell & Russell, 1964.

"To say that Mark Twain's treatment of his materials may have been influenced by suggestions that filtered through to him out of the preceding century appears at first thought absurd. Such seeming lawlessness of manner, the casual reader feels, can have no spring in the Augustan Age. But certain of Mark Twain's characteristic types, the character, the informal essay, the apologue, the maxim, and the picaresque-like narrative as adapted by Defoe and Smollett--models which had already established themselves in American humorous writing--appear to be more akin to eighteenth-century forms than to those of the nineteenth century." What follows is a general discussion of the influence on Twain of specific eighteenth-century English authors (Defoe, Fielding, Goldsmith, Pope, Smollett, Sterne, Swift) as well as that of certain earlier writers (Cervantes, Le Sage).

Briden, Earl F. "Huck's Island Adventure and the Selkirk Legend." *MTJ*, 18, iii (1976), 12-14.
"William Cowper's 'Verses Supposed to be Written by Alexander Selkirk, During His Solitary Abode in the Island of Juan Fernandez' (first published in 1782) condense in two opening stanzas ideas not expressly treated in Crusoe's tale yet strikingly echoed in Huck's: first, the ironic relationship between the islander's pathetic isolation and his autonomous authority; secondly, his equally ironic experience of strangely tame creatures of the wilderness."

Cowper, Frederick Augustus Grant. "The Hermit Story as Used by Voltaire and Mark Twain." In *In Honor of the Ninetieth Birthday of Charles Frederick Johnson*, ed. Odell Shepard and Arthur Adams. Hartford: Trinity College, 1928.
"Voltaire's *L'Hermite* [Chapter 20 of *Zadig*] is probably the chief source of Mark Twain's *The Mysterious Stranger*."

Krause, Sydney J. "Boys, Girls, and Goldsmith." In *Mark Twain As Critic*. Baltimore: Johns Hopkins Press, 1967.
In writing "Goldsmith's Friend Abroad Again," a series of seven "letters" dealing with the mistreatment of the Chinese, Twain aped *The Citizen of the World*. In borrowing Goldsmith's form, speculates Krause, Twain probably learned to detest his mannered style.

Laverty, Carroll D. "The Genesis of *The Mysterious Stranger*." *MTQ*, 8, iii and iv (1947), 15-19.
Possibly still useful, though largely superseded by subsequent scholarship, this article suggests that Twain's assertions in *The Mysterious Stranger* that animals are often superior to humans came from Swift. Other possible sources of the story include Wilbrandt's *The Master of Palmyra* and Greek myth.

Parsons, Coleman O. "The Background of *The Mysterious Stranger*." *AL*, 32 (1960-61), 55-74.
"Twain's sources were formative, corroborative, and illustrative. They shaped his outlook, supported and clarified attitudes already formed, and afforded graphic instances of life as he understood it. The shaping influences on *The Mysterious Stranger* were probably (1) from life: Twain's Presbyterian upbringing, boyhood friendships and experience, horror of fire, remorse, conversations with Macfarlane, suffering and loss in maturity; and (2) from literature: Voltaire's *Zadig*, the *Apocryphal New Testament*, *Paradise Lost*, *Gulliver's Travels*, Prospero's speech, and possibly Jane Taylor's 'The Mysterious Stranger,' as well as *Micromegas* and other works by Voltaire. Corroborative influences were Carlyle, Ingersoll, *Faust*, Wilbrandt's *Der Meister von Palmyra*, Lecky's *History of European Morals*, and possibly

Michelet's La Sorcière and the Clairville-Selby play. Illustrative matter came from sources already mentioned, as well as from Emperor Norton's happy insanity, the life of Luther, Macdonald's At the Back of the North Wind, Scott's Letters on Demonology and Witchcraft, and possibly from Verne's Cinq Semaines en Ballon and Alcott's Little Men. The greatest influence was the heredity or experience which gave Samuel Clemens a sense of guilt and a desire to escape from it, and the next in potency was Voltaire."

Salomon, Roger. "Twain and the Whig Hypothesis." In Twain and the Image of History. New Haven: Yale University Press, 1961.

See the annotation of this item in Chapter 14, "The Victorians."

Schönemann, Friedrich. Mark Twain als Literarische Persönlichkeit. Jena: Verlag der Frommannschen Buchhandlung, 1925.

In dealing with Goldsmith's influence on Twain, Schönemann may have assumed too much again (see the annotation of the Schönemann entry in Chapter 7, "Shakespeare and the Renaissance"). But at least Goldsmith may have affected Twain's style and his adoption of certain of the more casual literary forms--the sketch, the anecdote, the travel letter, and so on.

For a commentary on Schönemann's treatment of the Twain-Goldsmith connection see Edgar H. Hemminghaus, Mark Twain in Germany, New York: AMS Press, 1966.

Taylor, Coley Banks. Mark Twain's Margins on Thackeray's "Swift." New York: Gotham House, 1935.

No particular influence is discussed here, though some might be imputed in light of Twain's thorough and spirited scribblings in the margins of Thackeray's essay. His final remark is, "Void of every tender grace, every kindly, humanizing element, what a bare, glittering iceberg is mere intellectual greatness--& such was Swift's." Did not Twain perceive the kinship between himself and Swift that modern scholars do, or is he simply not saying?

10. JANE AUSTEN

Austen's most notable single contribution to American literature is that her work served as a model for Cooper's *Precaution* (see the articles by Hastings and Scudder, below); she thus helped to start one of the most prolific careers in American letters. Her greatest appeal, however, was to a later generation of authors. Howells called her "the dear, the divine, the only Jane Austen herself," and when he plumped for realism and modernism in fiction and turned his back on many of the great English novelists that he had admired once, Austen was the only one who retained his loyalty. He described her as a great artist because a truthful one; in effect, he thought of her as a realist, a writer who was neither sentimental nor melodramatic--though the epithet belongs to the academicians of this century, to Howells Austen was surely the last great novelist of the Enlightenment.

In the sense that William Gilmore Simms used the phrase in his preface to *The Yemassee* (1835), Howells admired an Austen novel because it was "a felicitous narrative of common and daily occurring events" rather than a poeticized or epical work like the romances of Scott. If such a mild formula for fiction seems calculated to arouse only the indifference of such handlers of great themes as Hawthorne and Melville, it must have been little more than anathema to Twain, who wondered why Howell's divine Jane was allowed to die a natural death and said, "When I take up one of Jane Austen's books, I feel like a barkeeper entering the kingdom of Heaven."

But the same prescription for writing became something quite different in the mind of Henry James, who, like Austen, was a faithful reporter of the mores of a specific social class, yet was interested in more than the merely "felicitous narrative." His *The Europeans*, for instance, suggests Austen rather vividly, yet the added satire is pure James. Which is to say that Austen provided James with at least some of the tools that he used, in his own highly idiosyncratic way, to expose the foibles of society as he saw it.

This preface draws on the following sources (see "List of Works Frequently Consulted" for full bibliographic information): Wagenknecht, *Howells*, p. 17, 87, 94-95; Wagenknecht, *Twain*, p. 38-39; Oscar Cargill, *The Novels of Henry James*, New York: Hafner, 1971, p. 67.

The following studies are grouped under the names, listed alphabetically, of major American fiction writers through James who were influenced by Jane Austen.

Cooper

Hastings, George E. "How Cooper Became a Novelist." AL, 12 (1940-41), 20-51.

The story of Cooper's decision to become a novelist is well known, but the facts are hazy. His daughter reported that one day the author-to-be threw down an English novel that he found unsatisfactory and proclaimed that he could write a better book himself. Challenged by his wife, Cooper persisted in his resolve, and a long and productive career was the result.

Various attempts, mostly half-hearted, have been made to identify the English novel that Cooper rejected; Hastings reviews the work to date and then presents in minute detail his own findings. His conclusion: "I think it highly probable that Cooper when he wrote Precaution had read some of Mrs. Opie's tales, that he was familiar with more than one of Jane Austen's novels, and that he may have known Mrs. Brunton's Discipline; but I am fairly convinced that in Precaution he attempted 'an elaborate imitation in plot and character' of a definite English novel, and that that novel is Jane Austen's Persuasion."

Scudder, Harold H. "What Mr. Cooper Read to His Wife." Sewanee Review, 26 (1928), 177-94.

See previous item. Scudder believes that Pride and Prejudice served as the model for Precaution. (Of course one may allow that Pride and Prejudice influenced Cooper and still agree with Hastings's conclusion.)

James

Simon, Irène. "Jane Austen and The Art of the Novel." ES, 43 (1962), 225-39.

If we think of the prefaces collected in The Art of the Novel as James's justification for his own kind of fiction, and if we note how often that these prefaces describe the kind of novel that Jane Austen wrote, then perhaps we may assert the existence of an influence not heretofore noted: "... she uses the indirect approach no less than he does, and ... her purpose like his is to make us see." (Yet "the main difference is surely that James insists on the single point of view, whereas Jane Austen continually shifts hers.")

West, Muriel. A Stormy Night with "The Turn of the Screw." Phoenix: Frye & Smith, 1964.

See the annotation of this item in Chapter 11, "The Gothic Novelists."

11. THE GOTHIC NOVELISTS

Typically the Gothic novel sets forth the most unimaginable horrors--the dead returning to life, skeletons in monks' garb, statues dripping blood--in the polished periods of the eighteenth century; it suggests that the clear-eyed Man of Reason has discovered new and discomforting truths with the same old tools of inquiry. And it would appear to have been about time for a change of subject matter. A study of the tastes of contemporary readers indicates a growing desire to step out of the drawing room in search of subterranean passages, trapdoors, and dungeons--the catalog of a late-eighteenth-century circulating library in America, for example, shows an increased interest in Gothic novels of the kind written by "Monk" Lewis and Mrs. Radcliffe.

For a time, however, the restraints of reason held strong against the flood of Romanticism that was to come and of which the Gothic tendency was an obvious and often heavy-handed precursor. In 1798 Charles Brockden Brown sent a copy of his _Wieland_, with its emphasis on madness, mesmerism, and autocombustion, to Thomas Jefferson. It is not known whether Jefferson ever read Brown's novel, yet one cannot but speculate on the book's reception by one who thought that the purpose of imaginative literature was, in his own words, to present "virtue in the best and vice in the worst forms possible." It is inconceivable that Brown had such a chillingly rational goal in mind. Evidently the Republic was not ready for, say, a Poe--not yet, at least. That Brown, Poe, and others were ready for the Gothics, however, is incontestable.

This preface draws on the following sources (see "List of Works Frequently Consulted" for full bibliographic information): Fiedler, p. 140; Marvin Mudrick, "Introduction" to Horace Walpole's _The Castle of Otranto_, New York: Collier, 1963, p. 9-10; Herbert Ross Brown, _The Sentimental Novel in America, 1789-1860_, Durham: Duke University Press, 1940, p. 22.

The following studies (after the "General" section) are grouped under the names, listed alphabetically, of major American fiction writers through James who were influenced by the Gothic novelists.

General

Coad, Oral Sumner. "The Gothic Element in American Literature Before 1835." _Journal of English and Germanic Philology_, 24 (1925), 72-93.

"The aim of this paper is to follow the Gothic convention during one of its most prolific periods as it manifested itself in America before reaching its apogee at the hands of Poe and Hawthorne." Coad's view is the traditional one, namely, that Charles Brockden Brown and others mishandled the Gothic mode, which never came into its own in America until after 1835, when "to Gothic literature was added the grave moral beauty and the exotic art of Poe." Interestingly, she points out that there are Gothic elements in the first American novel, The Power of Sympathy (1789), which Coad attributes to Sarah Wentworth Morton but which is now known to have been written by William Hill Brown.

Coad mentions such specific influences as Goethe and Byron but notes that "the dominant influence on the whole body of American Gothic literature was Mrs. Radcliffe."

Malin, Irving. "American Gothic Images." Mosaic, 6, iii (1973), 145-71.
Malin discusses three images: the voyage, the masquerade, and the castle; the latter, he notes, is "adopted from the novels of Walpole, Mrs. Radcliffe, and Monk Lewis."

Redden, Sister Mary Maurita. The Gothic Function in the American Magazines (1765-1800). Washington, D.C.: Catholic University of America Press, 1939.
Redden notes the earmarks of English Gothic fiction--castles, animated portraits, swoons, prophetic dreams, tyrants, criminal priests, and so on. (In the copy I examined some helpful person had added "the manuscript," "the crime (mysterious)," and "Italians.") She then makes a similar list for American Gothic fiction, which retains most of the English characteristics and adds a few native ones. As might be expected, Indians supply at least some of the Gothic terror in the American tales. Significantly, while English Gothic fiction refers occasionally to harems, seraglios, and eunuchs, American Gothic fiction does not; one sees the hand of John Calvin in this. About half of this book is given over to plot summaries of some seventy-five stories that appeared in American magazines between 1765 and 1800.

Brown

Bernard, Kenneth. "Charles Brockden Brown and the Sublime." The Personalist, 45 (1964), 235-49.
Often praised for his description of the American landscape in his novels, Brown actually uses all the pictorial commonplaces of eighteenth-century English writing ("fantastic cliffs, gloomy hollows, rushing streams, dangerous chasms, mists, dead trees, moss, storms, mazes, and so on"). However, in his functional use of scenery Brown differs from a writer like Mrs. Radcliffe, who uses it purely as backdrop: in Edgar Huntly, for example,

the rise and fall of the physical terrain suggests the mental landscape of the novel's tortured protagonist.

Hume, Robert D. "Charles Brockden Brown and the Uses of Gothicism: A Reassessment." ESQ, no. 66 (1972), 10-18.
In the manner of those excellent studies that show how an author appropriated an influence and put it to his or her own use, this essay points out that "Brown's Gothicism is not mere window-dressing. Unlike such popular writers as Clara Reeve and Sophia Lee, Brown does not produce sentimental romances in which scary episodes and mock-supernaturalism add a *frisson* for the customer's greater entertainment. When he employs such devices, his object is to produce a reaction on the *character*, not the reader. Considered as suspense stories, or proto-Poe, Brown's novels seem pretty poor stuff. But to view them this way is unjust, for what Brown really seems to be after in each of his six major novels is close attention to the psychology of his characters--and it is this concentration which makes any reader but the most captious critic relatively unworried by Brown's botched structures and loose ends. Brown's perpetual emphasis on the reactions of his characters to events rather than on the events themselves accounts for the curious role of the Gothic in his novels. For though the Gothic does not serve a merely decorative function, it is employed not for the affective purposes we expect, but to provide situations, problems, and trials for the characters to respond to."

Levine, Paul. "The American Novel Begins." American Scholar, 35 (1965-66), 134-48.
In his early novels Charles Brockden Brown evidences certain influences: from William Godwin he borrowed "Utopian notions about the power of human reason"; from Samuel Richardson an interest in psychological motivation; from Mrs. Radcliffe a concern with abnormal psychology. Ultimately, however, he separates himself from these influences by emphasizing the internal rather than the external nature of terror. Significantly, his "last and best gothic tale," *Edgar Huntly*, is also "the first American novel in which the theme of pursuit and flight is absolutely central." And this theme, says Levine, is the distinguishing feature of the American novel from Brown and Cooper through Ralph Ellison and Jack Kerouac.

Warfel, Harry. *Charles Brockden Brown: American Gothic Novelist*. Gainesville: University of Florida Press, 1949.
Although a biography, this work refers in passing to Brown's sources. Of particular interest to Warfel are the ways in which Brown adapted his sources to his own ends: "Contemporary story patterns, especially the seduction motif essential to every eighteenth-century novel and play, were molded into new shapes and then subtly universalized by subordinating melodramatic action

to psychological probing into the springs of abnormal conduct.... Instead of ghosts and other supernatural or pseudo-supernatural manifestations, he used the wonders of nature and of human power which seem supernatural to the inexpert observer. Some of these, which were described in medical treatises, were ventriloquism, spontaneous combustion of the human body, identity of fate in twins, religious mania, homosexuality, and sleepwalking. Each incident had its counterpart in reported experience, so that while adhering to the principle of basing stories on fact, he could fulfill an ambition to 'excite and baffle curiosity without shocking belief.' "

Wiley, Lulu Rumsey. Sources and Influences of the Novels of Charles Brockden Brown. New York: Vantage Press, 1950.
See the annotation of this item in Chapter 9, "The Eighteenth Century."

Hawthorne

Allen, M. L. "The Black Veil: Three Versions of a Symbol." ES, 47 (1966), 286-89.
Both Hawthorne and Dickens read The Mysteries of Udolpho and both used in their own stories the symbol of the black veil. Thus "in both countries, novelists were finding in the Gothic mode the cónstituents of a symbolic convention, but the difference in symbolic direction shown by these two stories suggests one difference between the two traditions. The Minister's Black Veil, like The Scarlet Letter and Moby Dick, uses symbol and mystery to explore the ambiguous relationship of the abstract (is evil metaphysical and universal?) and the psychological (or is it a manifestation of limitations and compulsions of the individual psyche?). The Black Veil, like Wuthering Heights and Bleak House, is less profoundly obsessed with these aspects of experience, but brings its symbolism directly to bear on a social situation."

Autrey, Max L. "A Source for Roger Chillingworth." ATQ, 26 (1975, supplement), 24-26.
See the annotation of this item in Chapter 14, "The Victorians."

Doubleday, Neal Frank. "Hawthorne's Use of Three Gothic Patterns." CE, 7 (1946), 250-62.
The patterns are "(1) mysterious portraits, (2) witchcraft, and (3) the esoteric arts or researches which would break through the limitations of mortality." In particular, Doubleday discusses the possible influence of Melmoth the Wanderer on "Ethan Brand."

Fiedler, Leslie A. "The Power of Blackness: Faustian Man and the Cult of Violence." In Love and Death in the American Novel. New York: Stein and Day, 1966.

"The Faustianism of Hawthorne is the melodramatic Faustianism of the gothic romances: of Lewis, whom he read avidly, and of Maturin, from whose _Melmoth the Wanderer_ he borrowed the name of a minor character in _Fanshawe_. Not only Lewis and Maturin, but Mrs. Radcliffe and Brockden Brown were favorite authors of the young Hawthorne; and from them he learned how to cast on events the lurid lights, the air of equivocal terror which gives _The Scarlet Letter_ its 'hell-fired' atmosphere. The very color scheme of the book, the black-and-whiteness of its world illuminated only by the baleful glow of the scarlet letter, come from the traditional gothic palette; but in Hawthorne's imagination, those colors are endowed with a moral significance. Black and white are not only the natural colors of the wintry forest settlement in which the events unfold, but stand, too, for that settlement's rigidly distinguished versions of virtue and vice; while red is the color of sexuality itself, the fear of which haunts the Puritan world like a bloody specter."

Goldstein, J. S. "The Literary Source of Hawthorne's _Fanshawe_." _MLN_, 60 (1945), 1-8.

"Investigation reveals that Maturin's novel [_Melmoth the Wanderer_] contains almost all the major plot elements and character portraits that went into Hawthorne's first important work."

Lundblad, Jane. "Hawthorne and the Tradition of Gothic Romance." In _Nathaniel Hawthorne and European Literary Tradition_. New York: Russell & Russell, 1965.

"Gothic Romance formed an important substratum of Hawthorne's productions--perhaps not always consciously used, but ever present and often employed for definite purposes.... the properties that are usually comprised under the term Puritan formed a strange and strong counterweight to his bent for the fantastical, and it is in the mingling and interaction of such influences from many quarters, but chiefly of these two currents, that Hawthorne's genius is to be sought and found. The amalgamation was made with great conscious artistry and followed carefully prepared lines.... Hawthorne's use of the Gothic elements was comparatively profuse in his first short stories; it waned during the middle period of his productions, to be revived in his latest works."

Turner, Arlin. "Hawthorne's Literary Borrowings." _PMLA_, 51 (1926), 543-62.

Turner identifies a variety of both native and foreign elements in Hawthorne's fiction, including "virtually all the methods and devices peculiar to the Gothic romancers." For example:

1. "The studious and solitary youth bothered about questions of fame" (Fanshawe, Oberon in "The Devil in Manuscript" and "Fragments from the Journal of a Solitary Man").

2. "The colorless heroine" (Ellen in Fanshawe).
3. "The fate-driven villain who is thwarted on the verge of success--usually he attempts the seduction of a child-like woman" (Butler in Fanshawe, Westervelt in The Blithedale Romance).
4. "The old woman reveling in sorrow" (the old women at the death of Widow Butler in Fanshawe and the old maid in "The White Old Maid").
5. The alchemists who use the occult sciences as a means to knowledge (Dr. Dolliver, various characters in "Rappaccini's Daughter," "The Prophetic Pictures," "The Birthmark," and "The Artist of the Beautiful"); those who use the devil (in "Young Goodman Brown") or his agent (the wizard in "Alice Doane's Appeal").
6. "An old man as guardian of innocent children" (Melmoth in Fanshawe, Dr. Grimshawe).
7. "Analysis of sensation" (the analysis of Redclyffe's sensation while he is intoxicated and again after he has been shot in Doctor Grimshawe's Secret).
8. "Use of dramatic foreshadowing and premonition" (the entrance of the proud lady in "Lady Eleanore's Mantle," the forewarning of the mother in "The Ambitious Guest," the omen in "The Lily's Quest").
9. "Second sight" (in "Howe's Masquerade" and in the rumor regarding Priscilla in The Blithedale Romance).
10. "Supernatural demonstrations" (the vision in the sky that Dimmesdale sees, the ghost of Alice and Maule's Well in The House of the Seven Gables, the legend of the Bloody Footstep in The Ancestral Footstep and elsewhere, supernatural pictures in "The Prophetic Pictures" and "Edward Randolph's Portrait").
11. "Mesmerism" (in the stories of the Veiled Lady in The Blithedale Romance and Alice in The House of the Seven Gables).
12. "The shroud" (in "The Wedding Knell" and "The Shaker Bridal").
13. Other "funeral situations" (the death of Widow Butler in Fanshawe, of Judge Pyncheon in The House of the Seven Gables, of the young lover in "The White Old Maid," of the bride in "The Shaker Bridal"; see also the flowers growing from a grave in Septimius Felton and the vegetation that supposedly grew from the heart of the buried Zenobia in The Blithedale Romance).
14. "Mysterious manuscripts" (the lost deed and the manuscript containing the story of Alice in The House of the Seven Gables, the manuscript taken from the body of the dead British soldier in Septimius Felton).
15. "Gloomy houses" (the House of the Seven Gables, the old house beside the graveyard in Doctor Grimshawe's Secret, the ancestral mansions in England with their hidden doors, concealed rooms, and long dark passages in Doctor Grimshawe's Secret and The Ancestral Footstep).
16. "Graveyards" (the one in Doctor Grimshawe's Secret, the

catacombs and the Capuchin burial ground in The Marble Faun).
17. "Musty libraries" (in Doctor Grimshawe's Secret).

Irving

Clendenning, John. "Irving and the Gothic Tradition." Bucknell Review, 12, ii (1964), 90-98.
By consciously parodying the Gothic mode yet retaining in his stories the terror that is essential to it, Irving serves as a link between the original Gothic novelists and writers like James and Faulkner, whose often-frightful worlds are the result of genuine terror rather than the cause of it.

Pochmann, Henry A. "Irving's German Sources in The Sketch Book." Studies in Philology, 27 (1930), 477-507.
See the annotation of this item in Chapter 12, "The Romantics."

Ringe, Donald A. "Irving's Use of the Gothic Mode." Studies in the Literary Imagination, 7, i (1974), 51-65.
Irving adhered to the Scottish "common sense" philosophy that stressed the objective reality of the physical world and denied the existence of such nonmaterial creatures as those who populate the Gothic tales of The Sketch Book and Bracebridge Hall. The ostensible author of these books, Geoffrey Crayon, half regrets the passing of belief in such phantasms, but as a common-sense sort he must attribute them to ignorance or faulty perception. By consciously working within the Gothic mode while gently ridiculing it, Crayon/Irving is having his ghostly cake and eating it too.

James

Nettels, Elsa. "Romance: I." In James & Conrad. Athens: University of Georgia Press, 1977.
"We can readily appreciate James's accomplishment if we briefly compare The Portrait of a Lady with the romances it most closely resembles. The novels of Ann Radcliffe, especially The Mysteries of Udolpho, which Madame Merle undoubtedly has in mind when she humorously questions Isabel about an ideal lover and his 'castle in the Apennines' ..., at once suggest themselves. Another well-known Gothic work, J. S. Le Fanu's novel Uncle Silas (1864), bears even more marked resemblances in plot and relationship of characters to James's novel."

West, Muriel. A Stormy Night with "The Turn of the Screw." Phoenix: Frye & Smith, 1964.
As humor, this is the kind of writing at which only English professors laugh, but as criticism, A Stormy Night is funnier than

and no doubt as informative as much of that produced by the Dryasdust school. Purportedly a manuscript by "H. K. Y." (a hokey author, it would seem) that was found and edited by West, A Stormy Night is one writer's on-the-spot account of his reading of The Turn of the Screw and recalling, as he goes along, various writings that James might have parodied in his thriller. The sources include the plethora of studies of unexplained phenomena that appeared toward the end of the nineteenth century as well as James's own story "Gabrielle de Bergerac," but more important than these is the Gothic school of fiction. Turn contains "the most characteristic, the most typical, of the stock situations and devices of Gothic: the ancient manuscript so useful in turning back time and giving a shot in the arm to latent credulity, the old house at Bly with its two towers, the remarkable synchronization between horrifying events and natural phenomena--the candles blown out at critical moments, the blasts of icy wind announcing or attending the apparitions, and the inevitable fixed stare of these creatures, to say nothing of the nervous tremors of the governess and her remarkable aspects as a heroine."

To my mind, H. K. Y./West isn't emphatic enough about James's skill in making these creaky devices come alive, but his/her general idea is sound. Specific novels mentioned include those by Radcliffe, Le Fanu, and Austen.

Melville

Arvin, Newton. "Melville and the Gothic Novel." NEQ, 22 (1949), 33-48.

The explicit reference in Billy Budd to Mrs. Radcliffe and The Mysteries of Udolpho starts Arvin on a consideration of just how much of Melville is Gothic in nature, and while he does not overestimate this particular influence, he does find that Melville's fiction is pervaded by Gothic characters, symbols, themes, and moods--all transformed into Melville's terms, of course (dungeons become vermin-infested forecastles, for instance).

Mansfield, Luther S., and Howard P. Vincent. "Explanatory Notes" to Moby-Dick. New York: Hendricks House, 1952.

The authors note "many superficial resemblances" between Ahab and the cruel caliph who is the subject of William Beckford's Vathek.

Rose, Edward J. " 'The Queenly Personality': Walpole, Melville, and Mother." Literature and Psychology, 15 (1965), 216-29.

In White-Jacket, writing of shipboard sexual high jinks, Melville notes: "There are evils in men-of-war, which, like the suppressed domestic drama of Horace Walpole, will neither bear representing, nor reading, and will hardly bear thinking of. The landsman who has neither read Walpole's Mysterious Mother, nor Sophocles's Oedipus Tyrannus, nor the Roman story of Count

Cenci [sic], dramatised by Shelley, let that landsman guardedly remain in his ignorance of even worse horrors than these, and forever abstain from seeking to draw aside this veil." The reader of this article will no doubt acknowledge the relationship between The Mysterious Mother and Melville's novel of incest, Pierre, whether or not he agrees that "in Walpole, Sophocles, and Shelley, Melville saw confirmed his own deepest psychic experiences."

Shetty, Nalini V. "Melville's Use of the Gothic Tradition." In Studies in Honour of William Mulder, eds. Jagdish Chander and Narindar S. Pradhan. Delhi: Oxford University Press, 1976.

Melville used "the best elements of the Gothic genre without the medieval trappings and hackneyed forms. His own personal experience led him to feel the powerful enmity and evil present in the world and the elusive nature of reality. Part of the novelist's attempt to present this terror-ridden and baffling universe is done by the frequent use of Gothic techniques and themes--the persecution of the innocent, the use of desolated ships, etc." Ships are Melville's Gothic castle, says Shetty; the San Dominick of Benito Cereno (which is the story discussed in greatest detail here) is described as "battered and mouldy, the castellated forecastle seemed some ancient turret, long ago taken by assault and then left to decay."

Poe

King, Lucille. "Notes on Poe's Sources." Studies in English (University of Texas), no. 10 (1930), 128-34.

"Students of Poe have doubtless observed resemblances between 'Metzengerstein' and Walpole's The Castle of Otranto. There are four principal points of similarity which indicate an indebtedness to Walpole's novel: the Gothic castle of romance, the prophecy, the animated picture, and the fall of the castle along with the extinction of the family."

Whitt, Celia. "Poe and The Mysteries of Udolpho." Studies in English (University of Texas), no. 17 (1937), 124-31.

Poe borrowed a number of details from Mrs. Radcliffe's novel while composing his story "The Assignation." Poe's Mentoni resembles her Montoni, for instance, and both works feature a peculiar sort of glass that bubbles and reacts violently when poison is poured into it.

12. THE ROMANTICS

When someone asked the eighteenth-century French author Fontenelle if he never laughed, Fontenelle replied, "Non, je ne fais jamais Ah-ah-ah." To go Ah-ah-ah was a private function, in effect: if it had to be done at all, it was done secretly and the fact was not mentioned to others. The essential difference between the Classical or eighteenth-century viewpoint and the Romantic one is the difference between a worldly and commonsensical and a dreamy, often drunken use of the conscious mind to perceive reality; it is perhaps best characterized by Shelley's self-conscious decision to invoke "light and fire from those eternal regions where the owl-winged faculty of calculation dare not ever soar." This change from repression to release, like the abandonment of the Ptolemaic system in favor of the Copernican, marks one of the seams of history.

For the present purpose, the rise of Romanticism is accompanied by the first instances of substantial cross-pollination between the English and Continental writers and their American counterparts. In 1820 the likable but by then rather anachronistic Sydney Smith was asking, "In the four quarters of the globe, who reads an American book?" For Wordsworth and Coleridge in England and Chateaubriand in France had already read and made use of William Bartram's Travels (1791), the botanist's account of his journey through the southern United States. Keats pronounced Charles Brockden Brown's Wieland a work of "powerful genius"; Thomas Love Peacock believed that Goethe, Schiller, and Brown were the authors who influenced Shelley most profoundly; Byron thought of Irving's "The Broken Heart" as "one of the finest things ever written on earth" and said that he could not hear it without weeping.

Of course Romanticism takes many forms. It is possible, and from time to time it is fashionable, to discriminate among "romanticisms" as if no one of Romanticism's avatars had characteristics in common with any of the others. But if it is true that both John and Jane are "human," that statement does not become less true just because one is shown to be "male" and the other "female." The rise of Romanticism was neither an isolated nor a strictly aesthetic phenomenon. It was one aspect of a worldwide revolution in politics, religion, economics, manners, and morals (and, to be sure, aesthetics). Thus it matters less that, for example, the German Romantic writers and philosophers, who provided the impetus for European and American Romanticism, represented an urban and cosmopolitan viewpoint that sought the refinement of preexisting culture, whereas the American Romantics espoused a largely Rousseauistic attitude intended to serve as the basis for the establishment of a culture. What matters more is that both groups of writers and thinkers had the same goal in mind, namely, an end to, or at least an amelioration of, what they saw as the hypocrisy, conformity, and philistinism of the "decadent" cultures in which they lived.

In Cervantes's day the Romantic hero had to struggle with his mythic counterpart for the public's attention (see the preface to Chapter 6, "Cervantes"). Actually, the clear-sighted Rationalists of the eighteenth century helped the Romantics by scoffing at or ignoring the overblown mythic hero; thus they cleared the stage for the battle with the real foe, the smug bourgeois with their narrow ideas and abiding contempt for the ideas of others.

With the Romantics, that battle began in earnest.

This preface draws on the following sources (see "List of Works Frequently Consulted" for full bibliographic information): Cunliffe, p. 41-43; Wager, p. 54, 61; Zipes, p. 144-48; F. L. Lucas, The Decline and Fall of the Romantic Ideal, Cambridge: Cambridge University Press, 1963, p. 55, 96. Various studies deal generally with the American reputations of specific Romantic figures and their influence on thought and culture in this country. Among these are Julia Power, Shelley in America in the Nineteenth Century: His Relation to American Critical Thought and His Influence, New York: Haskell House, 1964; Hyder E. Rollins, Keats' Reputation in America to 1848, Cambridge: Harvard University Press, 1946; and Paul M. Spurlin, Rousseau in America, 1760-1809, University: University of Alabama Press, 1969.

The following studies (after the "General" section) are grouped under the names, listed alphabetically, of major American fiction writers through James who were influenced by the English and Continental Romantics.

General

Clements, Robert J. "Il Romanticismo Italiano e l'America." In Il Romanticismo: Atti del Sesto Congresso dell'Associazione Internazionale per gli Studi di Lingua e Letteratura Italiana (Budapest e Venezia, 10-17 ottobre 1967). Budapest: Akad. K., 1968.

This succinct article may be helpful to some scholars, but it is so general that one oughtn't to learn Italian solely to read it. The author mentions mainly the Americans who traveled in Italy; after touching briefly on the careers of Cooper, Hawthorne, Irving, Harriet Beecher Stowe, and others, he concludes that "the major exponents of American Romanticism found the means to put themselves in direct contact with Italian Romantic thought and incorporate it into their masterpieces."

Lombard, C. M. "The American Attitude Towards the French Romantics." RLC, 39 (1965), 358-71.

"Several factors would explain the enthusiasm with which the French Romantics were often received. Much in their writing was marvelously suited to the literary and social outlook in America. Their revolt against classicism was appreciated in a country with fresh memories of a successful revolution. In the wilderness of the New World the praises of nature sung by Rousseau, Chateaubriand, Hugo, and Lamartine acquired new meaning. Adventurous spirits clamoring for social justice welcomed the liberal views of Mme de Staël and George Sand. Devout Americans distrustful of the Enlightenment and Jacobinism were once more favorably disposed towards French culture by the religious themes in Chateaubriand and Lamartine."

________. "The Image of the French Romantics in America (1800-1870)." Bulletin of Bibliography, 25 (1967), 25-29.
An indispensable checklist of books and articles about early American attitudes toward French literature and culture. There are eight subdivisions: "General Background," "General Views on French Romantics," "Precursors of French Romanticism," "Cousin," "Hugo," "Lamartine," "George Sand," and "Miscellaneous."

________. "Mme de Staël's Image in American Romanticism." College Language Association Journal, 19 (1975), 57-64.
Madame de Staël was received favorably by a Protestant society often hostile to foreign writers. One reason for this was that she was seen as a defender of religious values; another is that, unlike other European intellectuals, she encouraged Americans to develop their own national literature.

Brown

Berthoff, Warner. "Brockden Brown: The Politics of the Man of Letters." The Serif, 3 (1966), 3-11.
Brown embraced the liberalism of Godwin (whose Enquiry Concerning Political Justice advocated not violent revolution, as in France, but moral and psychological revolution through education and other means), yet "a characteristic American practicality and ideological reserve" kept him from turning doctrinaire. Besides, such novels as Wieland evince Brown's belief that "there was always some self-generating demonism in the man of energy, some fatality at the root of his experience, which would resist public disciplining and subvert any compromise or armistice imposed by social decorum."

Brown, Herbert. "Charles Brockden Brown's 'The Story of Julius': Rousseau and Richardson 'Improved.' " In Essays Mostly on Periodical Publishing in America: A Collection in Honor of Clarence Gohdes, ed. James Woodress. Durham: Duke University Press, 1973.

See the annotation of this item in Chapter 9, "The Eighteenth Century."

Kimball, Arthur G. "Savages and Savagism: Brockden Brown's Dramatic Irony." Studies in Romanticism, 6 (1967), 214-25.
See the annotation of this item in Chapter 9, "The Eighteenth Century."

Levine, Paul. "The American Novel Begins." American Scholar, 35 (1965-66), 134-48.
See the annotation of this item in Chapter 11, "The Gothic Novelists."

Cooper

Fridén, Georg. James Fenimore Cooper and Ossian. Upsala: Lundequistska Bokhandeln; Cambridge: Harvard University Press, 1949.
The speech of Cooper's Indians shows the influence of Ossian as well as the Ossian imitations of Byron and the Ossian-influenced works of Scott. Other aspects of Cooper's Leatherstocking tales suggest the same influence: nature metaphors, the evocation of a dying race, an active spirit-world. "Taken together, these similarities seem to constitute another instance of the influence of European Romanticism on American literature."

Hayne, Barrie. "Ossian, Scott and Cooper's Indians." Journal of American Studies, 3 (1969), 73-87.
In the Leatherstocking series Cooper was trying to write his country's epic. As models he had Macpherson's Ossian and Scott's novels. The works of all three authors are concerned with past glory, a dying race, and the sublimity of nature. Interestingly, Ossian may have been influenced by magazine accounts of Indian life and speech; thus its impact on Cooper is possible evidence of a curious round-trip effect in literary influence.

Crane

Stone, Edward. "Crane and Zola." ELN, 1 (1963), 46-67.
See the annotation of this item in Chapter 16, "Scientific Thinkers and Naturalists."

Hawthorne

Anderson, Norman A. " 'Rappaccini's Daughter': A Keatsian Analogue?" PMLA, 83 (1968), 271-83.

Conceptual, textual, and character parallels enable the reader to add Keats's "Lamia" to the by-no-means-inconsiderable list (which Anderson reviews here) of sources already suggested for Hawthorne's story.

Bowen, James K. "More on Hawthorne and Keats." ATQ, 2 (1969), 12.
Bowen mentions the Smith and Anderson articles (see entries) and then cites parallel passages from Hawthorne's American notebooks and Keats's "Isabella; or The Pot of Basil" to show that Hawthorne considered writing a story on the dead-lover-as-fertilizer theme.

Cohen, Hubert I. "Hoffmann's 'The Sandman': A Possible Source for 'Rappaccini's Daughter.' " ESQ, no. 68 (1972), 148-53.
Hawthorne may have read E. T. A. Hoffmann's tale of a student (named Nathaniel, interestingly enough) who fell in love with an automaton that had been constructed by an evil scientist. Or he may have seen Sir Walter Scott's summary of "The Sandman" in his essay "Novels of Ernest Theodore Hoffmann." Either way, there are too many similarities between Hoffmann's story and Hawthorne's for anyone to deny that the former is a likely source of the latter.

D'Avanzo, Mario L. "The Literary Sources of 'My Kinsman, Major Molineux': Shakespeare, Coleridge, Milton." SSF, 10 (1973), 121-36.
See the annotation of this item in Chapter 7, "Shakespeare and the Renaissance."

Fogle, Richard Harter. "Coleridge, Hilda, and The Marble Faun." ESQ, no. 71 (1973), 105-11.
There are several affinities between The Marble Faun and the life and work of Coleridge, but the most important are the Coleridgean ideas behind Hilda's work as a copyist. "Her pictures are pure Romantic symbols, purged of all accidentality or imperfection," and "Hilda in her painting goes back through the surfaces of the aesthetic object to the vital germ of the original inspiration."

Kern, Alexander. "The Sources of Hawthorne's 'Feathertop.' " PMLA, 46 (1931), 1253-59.
Kern proceeds as carefully as Hawthorne himself might have in order to show how both the conception and the ultimate composition of a literary work is often "a process of slow evolution" rather than one of "sudden inspiration." Briefly, he points to three sources for "Feathertop": an 1840 notebook entry, Hawthorne's reading of "a tale of [Ludwig] Tieck" (probably Die

Vogelscheuche) in 1843, and another notebook entry made in 1849. "Feathertop" itself appeared in 1852.

Krumpelmann, J. T. "Hawthorne's 'Young Goodman Brown' and Goethe's 'Faust.' " Die Neueren Sprachen, 5 (1956), 516-21.
Hawthorne may have drawn details from the Walpurgisnacht scene in Faust for use in his story.

Lombard, C. M. "Hawthorne and French Romanticism." Rivista di Letterature Moderne e Comparate, 24 (1971), 311-16.
Hawthorne borrowed fragmentarily from Chateaubriand and Hugo but owed much to Madame de Staël and George Sand, both of whom depict contrasting female types (e.g., Zenobia and Priscilla in Hawthorne) as well as the emotionally and intellectually superior woman (e.g., Hester Prynne).

Lundblad, Jane. "Hawthorne and Mme de Staël." In Nathaniel Hawthorne and European Literary Tradition. New York: Russell & Russell, 1965.
The prototype for the "dark, glamorous, intellectual, and free" woman in Hawthorne (e.g., Zenobia in The Blithedale Romance and Miriam in The Marble Faun) is Corinne, Madame de Staël's idealized self-portrait in the novel of the same name. In contrast with what Lombard says (above), Hester Prynne is not affected by de Staël--she, of Hawthorne's heroines, is "the one most free from discernible literary or factual influences."

Matenko, Percy. Ludwig Tieck and America. Chapel Hill: University of North Carolina Press, 1954.
Matenko discusses a number of general and possible influences; he notes, for instance, that "The House of the Seven Gables shows the combination of the realistic and the imaginary so characteristic of Tieck's best novellistic [sic] style." The one definite source he discusses is Tieck's Die Vogelscheuche, which inspired Hawthorne's "Feathertop," though here it is a matter not of stylistic influence but of similarity in content (both works treat the idea of a scarecrow transformed into a human being).

Noyes, Russell. "Hawthorne's Debt to Charles Lamb." Charles Lamb Bulletin, 4 (1973), 69-77.
"Of Lamb's essays, 'Dream Children' and 'The South Sea House' appear to have been the most richly suggestive to Hawthorne for his own sketches. Hawthorne found especially attractive Lamb's delight in reverie, his nostalgic love of the past, and his sympathetic insight into human character. Technically, Lamb offered Hawthorne certain rhetorical figures, an enrichment of vocabulary, and a mellow informality of style. Direct observation was, without a doubt, the foundation of Hawthorne's art, but

books in abundance and the play of a vigorous imagination were required in the construction of a finished house of art."

Pfeiffer, Karl G. "The Prototype of the Poet in 'The Great Stone Face.' " *Research Studies of the State College of Washington*, 9 (1941), 100-08.
Hawthorne's description of the poet and his poetry in "The Great Stone Face" indicates a thorough familiarity with Wordsworth's writings and suggests "that Wordsworth may have exercised a greater influence on Hawthorne than has so far been recognized."

Pochmann, Henry A. "Nathaniel Hawthorne (1804-1864)." In *German Culture in America*. Madison: University of Wisconsin Press, 1957.
Pochmann acknowledges the possible (and widely discussed) influence of Hoffmann and Tieck on Hawthorne. Concerning Goethe, he notes that Hawthorne's late handling of the Faust theme is closer to Goethe's than to that of earlier writers such as Marlowe. In *The Scarlet Letter* the wages of sin is death, but in *The Marble Faun* the characters triumph over sin only by recognizing it through experience. Thus it is in Goethe's *Faust*, whose hero errs but is saved.

Pollin, Burton R. " 'Rappaccini's Daughter'--Sources and Names." *Names*, 14 (1966), 30-35.
Here Pollin considers "a few of the possible sources [of Hawthorne's story] which serve chiefly to underscore the theme of the transformation or re-creation of human life, these being Mary Shelley's *Frankenstein*, Godwin's *St. Leon*, and Milton's *Paradise Lost*."

Scheuermann, Mona. "Outside the Human Circle: Views from Hawthorne and Godwin." *NHJ*, 1975, 182-91.
The author examines the influence of Godwin's *Caleb Williams* on *The Scarlet Letter*. Both novels stress the need for individuals to have some sort of productive intercourse with their community and both dramatize a collapse of that intercourse, which forces the individuals out of the community and places them in a state that is never truly remediable. This, writes Scheuermann, is the result of "a rather pessimistic outlook that Hawthorne, conditioned by his Puritan heritage, finds so compatible in Godwin."

Schwarz, Peter. "Zwei Mögliche 'Faust'-Quellen für Hawthornes Roman The Scarlet Letter." *Jahrbuch für Amerikastudien*, 10 (1965), 198-205.
There are a variety of possible sources for the Faust plot--original German accounts, Marlowe's play, Goethe's--and this

essay differentiates among them. First (and unnecessarily) it is established that Dimmesdale is no Faust; he is tempted by mere sexual passion and a "dream of happiness" with Hester rather than the desire for spiritual emancipation and revolt. But Dimmesdale has in him much of the Faust of the folk story, as seen particularly in the motif of the sorrowful voice (das Motiv der Klagenden Stimme), the voice which has an underlying pathos and plaintiveness in it at all times.

It is from Goethe that Hawthorne takes his ending, in which it is made clear that salvation is possible because God's grace is greater than the sins of the individual (this ending contrasts with that of Marlowe's play, in which Faust is taken to hell). Hawthorne's outlook is not as bright as Goethe's, however: whereas Faust can restore himself to God's grace in life, the damage done to a soul like Dimmesdale's " 'is never, in this mortal state, repaired.' "

Smith, Julian. "Keats and Hawthorne: A Romantic Bloom in Rappaccini's Garden." ESQ, no. 42 (1966), 8-11.

Keats's "Lamia" provides "not mere details but helps form the basic structure, characterization, and theme of Hawthorne's story." Take the endings as one example: "Lamia disappears, Lycius dies, the guests stand agast [sic], Apollonius is triumphant; Beatrice dies, Rappaccini and Giovanni stand by helplessly, Baglioni looks on triumphantly."

Stein, William Bysshe. Hawthorne's Faust: A Study of the Devil Archetype. Gainesville: University of Florida Press, 1953.

Hawthorne gave the Puritan preoccupation with good and evil a new form as a result of his contact with both the New England Goethe cult and the various European Faust-motivated novels of the late eighteenth and early nineteenth centuries (both influences are discussed succinctly yet convincingly by Stein in Chapters III and IV of the book). In a word, "a fluid conception of the Faust myth is the dynamic principle of composition ruling Hawthorne's creative imagination."

Stein emphasizes the fluidity of Hawthorne's notion of the Faust story. For instance, there are no one-to-one equivalences between the characters in the Faust story and those of The Scarlet Letter; on the other hand, each of the main characters in the latter has distinct Faustian attributes.

Stewart, Randall. "Recurrent Themes in Hawthorne's Fiction," in his Introduction to The American Notebooks by Nathaniel Hawthorne. New Haven: Yale University Press, 1932.

One of Hawthorne's recurrent themes is that of the elixir of life. His treatment of that theme in the unfinished Dolliver Romance, whose hero was to become a child again in order to apprehend some secret known only to children, may have been prompted by Wordsworth's "Ode: Intimations of Immortality."

See the index of the Notebooks for other, less significant references to Wordsworth.

Stock, Ely. "The Biblical Context of 'Ethan Brand.' " AL, 37 (1965-66), 115-34.
See the annotation of this item in Chapter 3, "The Bible."

Wheeler, Otis B. "Hawthorne and the Fiction of Sensibility." NCF, 19 (1964), 159-70.
See the annotation of this item in Chapter 9, "The Eighteenth Century."

White, Robert L. " 'Rappaccini's Daughter,' The Cenci, and the Cenci Legend." SA, 14 (1968), 63-86.
A "major determinant" of Hawthorne's story is the nineteenth-century romantic legend of Beatrice Cenci and particularly Shelley's verse drama The Cenci, here considered (in great detail) as a possible source of characters, plot, setting, and so on.

Howells

Cady, Edwin H. "Howells and Tragedy." In The Realist at War: The Mature Years--1885-1920--of William Dean Howells. Syracuse: Syracuse University Press, 1958.
Howells took the title The Shadow of a Dream from Endymion, Keats's meditation on spiritual love. In the novel Faulkner dreams that his wife Hermia and friend Nevil are in love and that their marriage and his funeral take place simultaneously; after Faulkner's actual death, his dream casts such a shadow over the love of Hermia and Nevil (which doesn't develop until after Faulkner is dead) that they can only grasp at but not seize what is, in Keats's phrase, "a hope beyond the shadow of a dream." See Mathews, below.

Mathews, James W. "Another Possible Origin of Howells' The Shadow of a Dream." AL, 42 (1970-71), 558-62.
Correcting Hedges (see Chapter 7, "Shakespeare and the Renaissance") and Cady (above), Mathews thinks that Howells took his title from Shelley's "The Sensitive Plant" because this poem (which contains the lines, referring to life, "Where nothing is but all things seem, / And we the shadows of the dream") features elements--a devoted woman, plants that decay when love dies--that are also important to the novel. Too, Shelley's poem is pessimistic, like the novel, as opposed to Keats's Endymion, an optimistic poem and the one that Cady favors as the novel's source. As for Hedges, Mathews notes that she "offers lines from Hamlet and The Scarlet Letter as possible origins of the title, though the narrative and theme of neither are similar to those of The Shadow of a Dream."

Irving

Matenko, Percy. "Tieck and American Authors." In Ludwig Tieck and America. Chapel Hill: University of North Carolina Press, 1954.

"Tieck possibly had a secondary influence upon [Irving]" in that he may have "helped to confirm and fortify the tendencies which Irving already possessed and had developed independently prior to his acquaintance with the German author."

Pochmann, Henry A. "Irving's German Sources in The Sketch Book." Studies in Philology, 27 (1930), 477-507.

From the beginning the American short story was linked with the German tale, because Irving, Poe, and Hawthorne had to deal with charges of plagiarism from German sources. In this article Pochmann begins by describing the genesis of Irving's serious interest in matters German; almost certainly it stems from his meeting Sir Walter Scott, himself a sort of lay Germanist by dint of his frequent choice of fey subjects as well as his outright scholarly interest in contemporary German literature. "Whatever the reason," notes Pochmann, "Irving's visit to Scott was followed by a wild effort to take German [sic] by storm."

Evidently Irving's study paid off; Pochmann locates the following German sources for specific tales: (1) "Peter Klaus," from Otmar's Volks-Sagen ("Rip Van Winkle"); (2) "The Wild Hunter of Hacklenburg," also from Otmar ("The Legend of Sleepy Hollow"); (3) Bürger's Lenore ("The Spectre Bridegroom").

By way of conclusion Pochmann advises wisely that "the three stories discussed, while they are all inspired by the romantic literature of Germany, are by no means out-and-out romantic stories. Irving never quite got away from the influence of the literary tradition under which he began writing; and the stories of The Sketch Book, while they are primarily romantic, have still much of what is common to the English classical period. Irving never allows his romantic heart to run away with his classical good-sense; he does not lose himself in his subject. Over all, there plays the quiet, genial humor of Washington Irving, laughing at his characters, at his situations, at himself, and at his reader. 'Rip Van Winkle,' 'The Legend of Sleepy Hollow,' and 'The Spectre Bridegroom' are contributions to the Gothic, not however, of the type of Walpole's Gothic, or Lewis's, or Mrs. Radcliffe's. They may be classed as belonging to the sportive Gothic, a genre in which Irving has scarcely been surpassed. The three stories remain classic examples of this type."

This discussion appears, with some changes, in Pochmann's German Culture in America, Madison: University of Wisconsin Press, 1957, which the reader may also want to consult.

________. "Irving's German Tour and Its Influence on His Tales." PMLA, 45 (1930), 1150-87.

"In passing from the period of The Sketch Book and Bracebridge Hall to that of the Tales of a Traveller, we proceed from the first stage of Irving's development as a romanticist to the second. Of the intervening period the greater part of the years 1822 and 1823 was spent in Germany. Irving went to Germany a lukewarm romanticist, more interested in the grotesquely sportive and burlesque romantic than in the truly romantic, but he returned from Dresden two years later an out-and-out romanticist." Among other influences Pochmann finds in Goethe's Wilhelm Meister, Tieck's Phantasus, and Schiller's Die Räuber sources for Tales of a Traveller--a work that he, positing a judgment with which Reichart (below) would doubtless agree, finds "a book of pieces, ill-arranged, badly classified, and, all in all, a patch-work quilt."

As noted in regard to the previous item, this essay appears (with some alteration) in Pochmann's authoritative German Culture in America, Madison: University of Wisconsin Press, 1957.

Reichart, Walter A. Washington Irving in Germany. Ann Arbor: University of Michigan Press, 1957.

Irving made good use of German legends, fairy tales, and ballads in his writing of The Sketch Book, which includes his masterpieces, "Rip Van Winkle" and "The Legend of Sleepy Hollow." (Reichart observes in his introduction that no doubt for many readers it will be "surprising and disappointing to know that these narratives with their Catskill and Hudson Valley scenes, considered so genuinely American, were in part suggested to Irving by his German reading.") Emboldened by the success of The Sketch Book, Irving set out for Germany--which he had not visited before--to gather material for a sequel. But Tales of a Traveller, which both Irving and his readers hoped would be a " 'German Sketch Book,' " turned out to be a failure marked by "a lack of originality and spontaneity," a "heterogeneous group of flimsy stories that lack interest or literary distinction." This study is more biographical than critical, though it takes into account and responds to points raised by the two Pochmann articles (above).

James

Briggs, Anthony D. "Alexander Pushkin: A Possible Influence on Henry James." Forum for Modern Language Studies (University of St. Andrews, Scotland), 8 (1972), 52-60.

None-too-careful critics have garbled the origins of James's The Aspern Papers, but over the years research has established at least three geneses: an incident involving the burning of a Byron letter, an anecdote about a Shelley enthusiast's attempts to lay his hands on some of the poet's letters, and James's own concern over the existence of possibly indiscreet letters from him to Constance Fenimore Woolson. Brigg suggests a fourth source (which doesn't necessarily exclude any of the others): Pushkin's

The Queen of Spades, which is also the story of a young man laying siege to an older woman's home and trifling with the affections of the woman's companion.

D'Avanzo, Mario L. "James's 'Maud-Evelyn': Source, Allusion, and Meaning." Iowa English Yearbook, 13 (1968), 24-33.
See the annotation of this item in Chapter 14, "The Victorians."

Deakin, Motley F. "Daisy Miller, Tradition, and the European Heroine." CLS, 6 (1969), 45-59.
See the annotation of this item in Chapter 15, "The Realists."

Feuerlicht, Ignace. " 'Erlkönig' and The Turn of the Screw." Journal of English and Germanic Philology, 58 (1959), 68-74.
Feuerlicht doesn't argue direct influence, but he does point out that Goethe's ballad and James's story are similar "in the mood of 'old sacred terror,' in the basic themes, in the reality of the 'apparitions,' in the motives [sic] of supernatural evil, of extraordinary beauty of children, of sexual perversion, and of sudden and mysterious death, and in the abrupt ending."

Leeming, David Adams. "Henry James and George Sand." RLC, 43 (1969), 47-55.
The younger and more romantic James based much of his early writing on the model of Sand. In midcareer he seemed affronted by her frankness, but it is evident from his late fiction that he was fascinated by heroines who, like Sand, strove to make an art of life.

Mooney, Stephen L. "James, Keats, and the Religion of Consciousness." MLQ, 22 (1961), 399-401.
In The Golden Bowl James refers to Adam Verver's "peak in Darien" which refers to the moment when Adam became an aesthetic being as well as a purely mercantile one. James's allusion to "On First Looking into Chapman's Homer" is "central not only to Adam's consciousness but to the meaning of the entire novel," for "although on the surface quiet, mild, and almost neutrally serene, [Adam] possesses an inner vision that transcends the spectacular power of his position as one of the richest men in the world and endows him with secret faculties for perceiving moral and aesthetic quality," and "throughout The Golden Bowl it is Adam's consciousness that creates the possibilities of life for Maggie, the Prince, and Charlotte."

Tintner, Adeline R. "Keats and James and The Princess Casamassima." NCF, 28 (1973), 179-93.
"James was immensely moved by Keats's poetry, his life, and

his death," notes Tintner in this richly documented essay, and his interest accounts for a definitely "Keatsian strain" in The Princess Casamassima. Once one is aware of the "recognizable allusions to Keats's poetry and to the legend of Keats's life," one understands what James intended with his hero, Hyacinth Robinson, who, like Keats, died at twenty-five with his conflicts unresolved.

Veeder, William. Henry James--the Lessons of the Master: Popular Fiction and Personal Style in the Nineteenth Century. Chicago: University of Chicago Press, 1975.
See the annotation of this item in Chapter 14, "The Victorians."

Melville

Betts, William W., Jr. "Moby Dick: Melville's Faust." Lock Haven Bulletin, no. 1 (1959), 31-44.
The author begins with a useful survey of Melville's knowledge of German authors and goes on to demonstrate convincingly that "Melville's conception of Ahab (as one whose soul was fired by an insatiable desire for truth) has been affected by the saga of Faust, and the whole design of the novel by Goethe's Faust especially," even down to such details as Fedallah being the devil with his tail tucked away to escape detection.

Conarroe, Joel O. "Melville's 'Bartleby' and Charles Lamb." SSF, 5 (1968), 113-18.
"Both in tone and in structure Bartleby is patterned on the familiar story as written by Lamb."

D'Avanzo, Mario L. "Ahab, the Grecian Pantheon and Shelley's Prometheus Unbound: The Dynamics of Myth in Moby-Dick." Books at Brown, 24 (1971), 19-44.
See the annotation of this item in Chapter 2, "The Classics."

________. "Pierre and the Wisdom of Keats's Melancholy." Extracts, 16 (1973), 6-9.
At the point in Pierre (Book IV, "Retrospective," I and II) where Pierre is "on the threshold of dark knowledge after 19 years of pastoral innocence," there are a number of allusions to Keats's "Ode on Melancholy," notably to the image of Joy's grape bursting on one's palate fine, which in both works is used in such a way as to suggest that "intensity of melancholy is directly related to one's potential to feel joy and sense delight deeply."

Duerksen, Roland A. "Caleb Williams, Political Justice, and Billy Budd." AL, 38 (1966-67), 372-76.

Duerksen does not insist on a "direct line of influence," but he notes similarities between Melville's novel and William Godwin's Caleb Williams (a copy of which Melville had obtained in London in 1849). Both novels relate the tale of a likable young man who impulsively slays an antagonist whose long-standing animosity toward his killer seems to be without basis. Too, both books deal with the dilemma of trying a formally guilty but essentially innocent party--a dilemma treated in more general terms in Godwin's Political Justice.

Fiess, Edward. "Byron's Dark Blue Ocean and Melville's Rolling Sea." ELN, 3 (1966), 274-78.
Byron's "Address to the Ocean," a set piece often declaimed by schoolchildren in Melville's day, is referred to overtly several times in Melville's writings; in addition, its language and imagery recur frequently in the American author's prose. "In a writer whose prose often achieves its ends by the means of poetry, it is not odd to find that the remembered language of poetry, in this case Byron's language, once played a subtly influential role."

________. "Melville as a Reader and Student of Byron." AL, 24 (1952-53), 186-94.
A discussion of Melville's annotations in his sixteen-volume set of Byron's Life and Works.

Finkelstein, Dorothee. Melville's Orienda. New Haven and London: Yale University Press, 1961.
See the annotation of this item in Chapter 1, "The Oriental Heritage."

Isani, Mukhtar Ali. "The Naming of Fedallah in Moby-Dick." AL, 40 (1968-69), 380-85.
The author examines possibilities for the source of the Parsee harpooner's name and points out that the most likely are a tale in The Spectator and, more importantly, Thomas Moore's Lalla Rookh, which deals with Zoroastrianism and features characters named Fadladeen and Abdalla, whose names Melville may have combined.

Mansfield, Luther S., and Howard P. Vincent. "Explanatory Notes" to Moby-Dick. New York: Hendricks House, 1952.
Thomas DeQuincey and Goethe are cited as two writers who "helped importantly to shape ideas or phrasing" in Moby-Dick; the authors also note that Melville "could get from books of such slight literary merit as Robert Southey's The Doctor ... abundant stimuli that set his mind to work." Other Romantic figures alluded to in these indispensable notes are Byron, Coleridge,

Hazlitt, Keats, Lamb, Rousseau, the Shelleys, and Madame de Staël.

Mogan, Joseph, J., Jr. "Pierre and Manfred: Melville's Study of the Byronic Hero." PLL, 1 (1965), 230-40.
"Not only do Manfred and Pierre have the same blood in their veins; Manfred is clearly Pierre's progenitor." There are a number of ways in which the two works are similar, and though both protagonists "are prey to essentially the same conflict" (i.e., the conflict between their ideals and reality), in fact "Melville's use of symbolism and ambiguity has complicated and universalized Pierre to much broader dimensions than Manfred."

Monteiro, George. "Melville and Keats." ESQ, no. 31 (1963), 55.
The Old Dansker in Billy Budd calls Claggart "Jemmy Legs." In naval slang a "jimmy-legs" is a master-at-arms. Melville may have got his slightly altered version from a Keats letter (to Benjamin Bailey, January 23, 1818).

Moore, Maxine. "Melville's Pierre and Wordsworth: Intimations of Immortality." New Letters, 39 (1973), 89-107.
Moore speculates that "Melville wrote Pierre, or, The Ambiguities as a parody on the life and work of Wordsworth," though she is careful to term Wordsworth the "hidden metaphor" in Pierre.

Murray, Henry A. "Introduction" to Pierre. New York: Hendricks House, 1949.
See the annotation of this item in Chapter 7, "Shakespeare and the Renaissance."

Noone, John B., Jr. "Billy Budd: Two Concepts of Nature." AL, 29 (1957-58), 249-62.
Billy Budd represents the clash between two eighteenth-century concepts of humanity: that of Rousseau, whose noble savage is apotheosized in Melville's hero, and that of Hobbes, who sees evil as an omnipresent element (witness Claggart's motiveless and persistent hatred of Billy) that must be checked by rationalism, represented in the novel by Captain Vere. The fate of Billy is Melville's acknowledgment that Western culture is "a one-way historical path away from the primitive." Thus "Billy is an anachronism. His death is not a redemptive act but the symbolic certification of a historical fact"; it is easy to point up the symbolic significance of Billy's transfer from Rights of Man of the Indomitable, but one should bear in mind that "with the French army everywhere triumphant on the Continent, only the British Navy stood between England and national oblivion" and that "the Rights as a merchant ship is free to sail the seas

only on condition that the sealanes are kept open by such a vessel as the Indomitable."

But if Billy's death meant the simple end of an anachronism, then surely Vere's decision would be less problematic. Clearly Billy and Vere represent two extremes, Rousseauvian instinctualism and Hobbesian rationalism, that cry out for synthesis. This synthesis is found in the person and career of Lord Nelson, which explains a lengthy digression in Billy Budd that has puzzled and irritated generations of readers, says Noone.

Incidentally, Noone posits no direct connection between the works of the two eighteenth-century thinkers and that of Melville, but he argues persuasively that Melville juxtaposes in Billy Budd the ideas of Rousseau and Hobbes as they exist in "some vague 'climate' or 'stream' of intellectual history."

Pochmann, Henry A. "Herman Melville (1819-1891)." In German Culture in America. Madison: University of Wisconsin Press, 1957.

Without being very specific Pochmann notes that Melville "paid a good deal of attention to Goethe and was alternately attracted and repulsed by him" and quotes Melville as saying, in a letter to Hawthorne, "as with all great genius, there is an immense deal of flummery in Goethe, and in proportion to my own contrast with him, a monstrous deal of it in me."

Ridge, George Ross and Davy S. "A Bird and a Motto: Source for 'Benito Cereno.' " Mississippi Quarterly, 13 (1960), 22-29.

One cannot do otherwise than agree with the Ridges, who lay down their argument like workers laying stones for a path. In fact, they lay it down twice. The first paragraph notes that "the case for proposing The Rime of the Ancient Mariner as a source for Benito Cereno is of course circumstantial.... But the circumstantial evidence is so extensive that it perhaps requires a greater act of faith to reject than to accept this thesis." And the last paragraph reminds us that "it ultimately requires a greater act of faith, we believe, to reject than to accept the notion that the Ancient Mariner is a source for Benito Cereno." In between, these points are made: that the Mariner and Cereno look and act alike, that the themes are similar and similarly developed, that descriptions are parallel.

Rockwell, Frederick S. "DeQuincey and the Ending of 'Moby-Dick.' " NCF, 9 (1954), 161-68.

DeQuincey's "The English Mail-Coach," which Melville read in December 1849 or January 1850, describes a situation that may have been used in the last pages of Moby-Dick. "In this situation we have a man of superhuman power, maimed as if by supernatural powers in retaliation for his human presumption, sleepless for three days, driving his coachful of helpless humanity to swift catastrophe. Let us put the situation in terms of the sea, as Melville would intuitively have done, with the suggestion provided by DeQuincey's passing description of it. Do we not have something strikingly suggestive of maimed Ahab driving his crew through the three days' Chase to final disaster?"

Rose, Edward J. " 'The Queenly Personality': Walpole, Melville, and Mother." Literature and Psychology, 15 (1965), 216-29.
See the annotation of this item in Chapter 11, "The Gothic Novelists."

Sealts, Merton M., Jr. "Melville's Neoplatonic Originals." MLN, 67 (1952), 86-92.
Melville took some technical terms from Thomas Taylor the Platonist's introduction to and glossary of The Six Books of Proclus on the Theology of Plato (as well as from the opening pages of the text itself) and used them in his own writings to satirize unintelligible philosophizing; see the annotation of this item in Chapter 2, "The Classics."

Thomas, Russell. "Melville's Use of Some Sources in The Encantadas." AL, 3 (1931-32), 432-56.
See the reference to this article in the annotation of Leon Howard's "Melville and Spenser--A Note on Criticism," MLN, 46 (1931), 291-92, in Chapter 5, "Spenser."

Welsh, Alexander. "A Melville Debt to Carlyle." MLN, 73 (1958), 489-91.
See the annotation of this item in Chapter 14, "The Victorians."

Poe

Cobb, Palmer. The Influence of E. T. A. Hoffmann on the Tales of Edgar Allan Poe. Chapel Hill: University of North Carolina Press, 1908. Also published as an issue of Studies in Philology, 3 (1908).
Cobb discusses the previous work done on the Hoffmann-Poe connection, the increasing interest in German literature in England and America from about 1825 on, and Poe's knowledge of German, following which he devotes separate chapters to the relationships between specific works: "Elixiere des Teufels" and "William Wilson," "Magnetiseur" and "Tale of the Ragged Mountains," "Die Jesuiterkirche in G_____" and "The Oval Portrait," and "Doge und Dogaressa" and "The Assignation." He rejects the notion that Hoffmann influenced Poe's style (see Gruener, below).

Gerber, Gerald E. "The Coleridgean Context of Poe's Blackwood Satires." ESQ, no. 60 (1970, supplement), 87-91.

The satires in question are "The Psyche Zenobia" and "The Scythe of Time," which sometimes echo "arguments presented and in a few instances language used in the Biographia."

Gruener, Gustav. "Notes on the Influence of E. T. A. Hoffmann upon Edgar Allan Poe." PMLA, 19 (1904), 1-25.

"If the sequence of reasoning in this paper has been logical, it has proved, and it is hoped by tangible evidence, that Poe acknowledges the kinship of his tales to those of Hoffmann, when he calls them 'fantasy pieces;' that he took from Hoffmann the idea of the Tales of the Folio Club; that through Hoffmann he seems to have hit upon the name Tales of the Grotesque and Arabesque, and from him to have received many a suggestion and inspiration for his own 'weird tales;' finally, that his very style seems to have been affected and molded in a very marked manner by that of the German author; in short, that Hoffmann exerted a deep-reaching influence upon the young Poe, an influence which he grew away from, but never entirely outgrew."

Cobb (above) agrees largely with Gruener's points although he refutes the idea of stylistic influence by showing that the key device of repetition (" 'Hear me, Emily, hear me!' ") is too common in fiction to be a distinguishing feature of either Hoffmann's prose or Poe's.

Lombard, Charles. "Poe and French Romanticism." Poe N, 3 (1970), 30-35.

After a succinct and informative discussion of the popularity of French Romantic authors in America Lombard discusses Poe's distaste for much of the sentimentalism of French Romanticism as well as his borrowings, notably from the works of Victor Hugo. Lombard guesses that Baudelaire and Mallarmé were drawn to Poe "partly by a perceptible Gallic cast in his works."

Matenko, Percy. "Tieck, Poe and Hawthorne." In Ludwig Tieck and America. Chapel Hill: University of North Carolina Press, 1954.

"Direct evidence of influence is contained in the reference in The Fall of the House of Usher to Tieck's The Journey into the Blue Distance and two references to Tieck in Poe's criticism of Hawthorne."

Newlin, Paul A. "Scott's Influence on Poe's Grotesque and Arabesque Tales." ATQ, 2 (1969), 9-12.

See the annotation of this item in Chapter 13, "Sir Walter Scott."

Pochmann, Henry A. "Edgar Allan Poe (1809-1849)." In German Culture in America. Madison: University of Wisconsin Press, 1957.

Surveying the various authorities, Pochmann ends by siding with one who concludes that Poe knew enough German to read easy prose at sight and to translate more difficult passages. There is no discernible German influence in Poe's extravagant and satirical tales nor in the stories of ratiocination, but there is palpable "Germanism" in his tales of disease, madness, and occult occurrences. Hoffmann and Tieck are obvious influences here.

Pochmann also notes the influence of the ideas of August Wilhelm von Schlegel, who said that unity of action and totality of effect come not from a cause-and-effect relation of events but from a great number of impressions that have a cumulative effect on the reader.

Pollin, Burton R. Discoveries in Poe. Notre Dame and London: University of Notre Dame Press, 1970.

As the title suggests, there is no coherent theme to this collection of essays, though most of the individual studies try to locate sources, mainly Romantic, for Poe's fiction, poetry, and criticism.

The germane discoveries include the following: (1) Poe borrowed from Victor Hugo (Notre-Dame de Paris, Hernani) in composing "The Masque of the Red Death," "The Pit and the Pendulum," and "The Cask of Amontillado"; (2) "The Masque of the Red Death" was also shaped by Byron's poem "Darkness" and Mary Shelley's novel about the death by plague of all humankind save the narrator, The Last Man; and (3) "the themes and atmospheres of Poe's tales [derive in part from] William Godwin's 'nightmare' novels."

Stovall, Floyd. "Poe's Debt to Coleridge." Studies in English (University of Texas), no. 10 (1930), 70-127.

This long article is devoted largely to Poe's criticism, though it deals with his poetry and fiction as well. Here are three Poe stories that Stovall discusses and the sources for them that he locates in Coleridge's writings: "MS. Found in a Bottle" ("The Rime of the Ancient Mariner"); "Silence--A Fable" ("The Wanderings of Cain"); and "The Masque of the Red Death" ("Allegoric Vision").

Suther, Judith D. "Rousseau, Poe, and the Idea of Progress." PLL, 12 (1976), 467-75.

"In a Platonic dialogue called 'The Colloquy of Monos and Una,' Poe echoes the arguments against progress found in Rousseau's Discours sur les sciences et les arts."

Thompson, G. R. Poe's Fiction: Romantic Irony in the Gothic Tales. Madison: University of Wisconsin Press, 1973.

Thompson is, to use a word that Poe would have loved, a resurrectionist. Critics have often dismissed Poe as being "merely" gothic, that is to say, less interested in substance than in cheap thrills. What these critics have missed, says Thompson, is the influence of German Romanticism and particularly its development of a comic perspective based on an "apprehension of the comic, the ironic, and the absurd in an otherwise melancholy and even sinister world." This perspective is called Romantic Irony and it is best expressed in the writings of two of Poe's favorite authors, the dramatist and novelist Ludwig Tieck and the critic August Wilhelm von Schlegel. In brief, Romantic Irony consists in an author's positing both an orthodoxy and its opposite and subscribing equally to the validity of each; thus Tieck's play The World Turned Topsy-Turvy, which features such "form-breaking ironies" as actors who are simultaneously spectators, etc. This sportiveness is actually the culmination of eighteenth-century German admiration for Cervantes, Swift, Fielding, and Sterne--and, in turn, it is reflected in the works of Coleridge, Carlyle, and Hazlitt, whom Poe also read. The intent of such sportiveness is anything but frivolous, for "the thrust of the philosophy, the criticism, and the literature of German Romanticism was, for a while, toward an ultimate harmony involving a unification of opposites, an annihilation of apparent contradictions and earthly limitations, and a merging of the subjective human personality and objective rational understanding into a penetrating view of existence from the height of the ideal--but always with an eye to the terrors of an ultimately incomprehensible, disconnected, absurd, probably decaying, and possibly malevolent universe. The only attainable harmony out of all this deceptiveness and chaos was a double vision, a double awareness, a double emotion, culminating in an ambivalent joy of stoical self-possession--in irony." Thus the Romantic ironists were much more than simple mockers, for they aimed at "transcendental mastery of the world and oneself through simultaneous detachment and involvement.... Through simultaneous ironic detachment and involvement, the German ironists thought, the Romantic artist achieves a liberating transcendental perception of the dark paradox of human existence."

Hence the suggestion in Poe's works that "the deceptive perversity of the universe and of the mind can only be transcended by the godlike imagination of the ironic artist, who yokes together contrarieties and sees beyond hope and despair, beyond good and evil, by deceptively intruding the comic into the tragic, the satiric into the demonic," for only in terms of interpenetrating opposites can the truth about humanity's place in the world be told.

Vitt-Maucher, Gisela. "E. T. A. Hoffmanns 'Ritter Gluck' und E. A. Poes 'The Man of the Crowd': Eine Gegenüberstellung." German Quarterly, 43 (1970), 35-46.

A year after Poe alluded in print to the works of Hoffmann (in an 1839 review of Longfellow's Hyperion) he published "The Man of the Crowd," a story so unmistakably similar in basic idea and structure to Hoffman's "Ritter Gluck" that a direct influence must be assumed.

Zeydel, Edwin H. "Edgar Allan Poe's Contacts with German as Seen in His Relations with Ludwig Tieck." In Studies in German Literature of the Nineteenth and Twentieth Centuries: Festschrift for Frederic E. Coenen, ed. Siegfried Mews. Chapel Hill: University of North Carolina Press, 1970.

In the back-and-forth battle over whether or not Poe knew German, Zeydel comes down on the negative side. (Of far greater importance, it seems to me, is whether Poe read any German authors at all, regardless of the language in which their works appeared.) It is Zeydel's conclusion that Poe "may have read some of Hoffmann's tales in English translation, and two of Tieck's but most of what he knew, or thought he knew [!], about these authors was derived at second or third hand."

Twain

Baetzhold, Howard G. "Postscript II." In Mark Twain and John Bull: The British Connection. Bloomington: Indiana University Press, 1970.

Among the Romantic poems that Twain admired and made use of (though mainly in his travel books and his minor and unpublished writings) are many of Burns's, Coleridge's The Ancient Mariner, Wordsworth's The Excursion, several poems each by Byron and Thomas Moore, and Leigh Hunt's "Abou Ben Adhem."

Liljegren, S. B. "The Revolt Against Romanticism in American Literature as Evidenced in the Work of S. L. Clemens." Studia Neophilologica, 17 (1944-45), 207-58.

A too-long article chiefly useful for its reprinting of Twain's little-known parodies of poems by Thomas Moore and Coleridge.

13. SIR WALTER SCOTT

At the beginning of the history of our imaginative literature an American author had two principal English models to imitate, Austen and Scott. It is significant that Cooper began by imitating the first, failed, and then turned to the second. It is fair to say, then, that the American novel is founded, if somewhat anomalously, on the example of Sir Walter Scott, and, indeed, his influence is pervasive. Hawthorne, for example, adopted from Scott's works numerous devices (many of which are, in turn, echoes of Shakespeare's plays): the tendency to group characters and develop the story of each group separately; the method of plot development via dramatic, emotion-charged scenes; the occasional introduction of low-comic characters into otherwise serious stories. From time to time American acclamation of Scott bordered on the hyperbolic: both Poe and Emerson, for instance, compared _The Bride of Lammermoor_ with Aeschylus.

Yet in a letter to Brander Matthews, Twain said this about Scott's work: "Lord, it's all so juvenile! so artificial, so shoddy; and such wax figures and skeletons and spectres." And Howells found Scott not only melodramatic but politically reactionary. Why this strong division of opinion? Perhaps the answer is suggested by Irving's attitude toward Scott, whom he admired but whose manner he wanted to avoid. If Scott's influence was great, perhaps it was too great. Despite his admiration for _The Bride_, Poe rejoiced in the depletion of Scott's stock, noting in an essay that there have been "the Ratcliffe [sic] dynasty, the Edgeworth dynasty, and the Scott dynasty; each, like the family of the Caesars, passing from good to bad, and from bad to worse, until each has run out." This is perhaps wishful thinking on Poe's part, but at least it is evidence of the desire to throw off what he regarded as a baleful influence. To a number of our authors Scott was a childhood author who had to be outgrown; his very harmlessness is suggested by the fact that Harriet Beecher Stowe's clergyman-father forbade her all novels save those of Scott. As adults the majority of our writers found Scott insufficiently penetrating. No doubt many would have concurred with Thomas Carlyle's words: "One knows not what idea worthy of the name of great, what purpose, instinct, or tendency, that could be called great, Scott was ever inspired with. His life was worldly; his ambitions were worldly. There is nothing spiritual in him; all is economical, material, of the earth earthy." For an increasingly skeptical group of authors, the all-too-comfortable example of Scott was to be derided, especially since it could not be forgotten.

This preface draws on the following sources (see "List of Works Frequently Consulted" for full bibliographic information): Matthiessen, p. 203; Wagenknecht, Poe, p. 127, 128; Wagenknecht, Twain, p. 38; Wagenknecht, Howells, p. 17, 85; Wagenknecht, Irving, p. 70; Cunliffe, p. 186; James Grossman, James Fenimore Cooper, Stanford: Stanford University Press, 1949, p. 21; Emery Neff, Carlyle, New York: Russell & Russell, 1968, p. 182.

The following studies (after the "General" section) are grouped under the names, listed alphabetically, of major American fiction writers through James who were influenced by Sir Walter Scott.

General

Orians, G. Harrison. "Walter Scott, Mark Twain, and the Civil War." South Atlantic Quarterly, 40 (1941), 342-59.

Though Twain is mentioned in the title of this article, it is actually a general study of Scott's impact on the Southern way of life. The article has three literary ancestors: (1) Twain's complaint in Life on the Mississippi about Scott's reactionary influence on Southern culture and politics; (2) Hamilton James Eckenrode's "Sir Walter Scott and the South," North American Review, 206 (1917), 595-603, an angry expansion of Twain's original charge; and (3) Grace Warren Landrum's "Sir Walter Scott and His Literary Rivals in the Old South," AL, 2 (1930-31), 256-76, a refutation of the two previous items based on a careful survey of contemporary periodicals, newspapers, and archive materials.

In this article Orians agrees with Landrum's assertions that (1) Scott was popular in the South but that he was also popular everywhere else, and (2) he shared the stage with such rivals as Byron, Bulwer, and Carlyle, all exponents of Romanticism and Medievalism as much as Scott was. Then Orians discusses the cotton culture, an institution far more influential on the South's anti-industrial stance than the novels of Scott.

Cooper

Davie, Donald. The Heyday of Sir Walter Scott. London: Routledge & Kegan Paul, 1961.

Davie devotes to Cooper the last three chapters of this study of Scott's influence on other authors. The intent of these three chapters is to argue affinities between Scott and Cooper even when direct influence is not observable. Briefly, Davie points out that The Pioneers, of all the Leatherstocking books, is structurally closest to a Scott novel; that The Deerslayer is the book whereby Cooper "worked his way ... out of the world of Scott"; but that even The Water-Witch, a novel governed more by the conventions of comic opera and Shakespearean comedy than by those of any other tradition, has a certain rapport with Scott's St. Ronan's Well.

Dekker, George. James Fenimore Cooper: The Novelist. London: Routledge & Kegan Paul, 1967.

Scott comes and goes in this book as his influence on Cooper waxes and wanes. Scott's best works, writes Dekker, were the Waverley novels, such as Old Mortality and Waverley, which register "complex historical change by focusing on a brief but crucial period of transition." The Pioneers (1823) is Cooper's "most impressive imitation of the Waverley-type novel"; like Guy Mannering, for instance, it is rich "in well-remembered scenes of a vanished way of life--primitive, prodigal, egalitarian" and is "centrally concerned with that period of the recent past when the present order achieved a manifest supremacy." (Almost parenthetically, Dekker notes that "if Cooper inherited these fictional preoccupations from Scott, Scott inherited them from Maria Edgeworth, whose Castle Rackrent and The Absentee furnished the direct models for Guy Mannering and The Bride of Lammermoor.")

In The Last of the Mohicans (1826) and The Prairie (1827) Cooper abandons the " 'wavering hero' " of the Waverley novels and The Pioneers, thereby losing a strong organizing center but gaining both a more-fully-developed main character and "a more sympathetic and inward-seeming portrait of the American Indians than would otherwise have been possible." The "wavering hero" makes a comeback in The Pathfinder (1840), which, however, with its "less ambitious scope and its focus on personal rather than communal or even national problems," is not at all like a Waverley novel or even the earlier Leatherstocking tales.

Fridén, Georg. James Fenimore Cooper and Ossian. Upsala: Lundequistska Bokhandeln; Cambridge: Harvard University Press, 1949.

See the annotation of this item in Chapter 12, "The Romantics."

Hayne, Barrie. "Ossian, Scott and Cooper's Indians." Journal of American Studies, 3 (1969), 73-87.

See the annotation of this item in Chapter 12, "The Romantics."

Orians, G. Harrison. "The Angel of Hadley in Fiction: A Study of the Source of Hawthorne's 'The Grey Champion.' " AL, 4 (1932-33), 257-69.

See the annotation of this item in the Hawthorne section of this chapter (below).

Hawthorne

Cohen, Hubert I. "Hoffmann's 'The Sandman': A Possible Source for 'Rappaccini's Daughter.' " ESQ, no. 68 (1972), 148-53.

See the annotation of this item in Chapter 12, "The Romantics."

Grant, Douglas. "Sir Walter Scott and Nathaniel Hawthorne." *University of Leeds Review*, 8 (1963), 35-41.
Grant points to specific debts: the best parts of *Fanshawe* owe much to Scott, and there are numerous similarities between *The Heart of Midlothian* and *The Scarlet Letter*. More importantly, he notes that Scott set an example by doing for Scotland what Hawthorne was to do for New England. Prior to that example Scots had appeared largely as provincials in English literature. "But Scott, in *Waverley*, had at a blow vindicated the history, types, manners, customs, speech, and scenery of his own country as eminently suitable for romance, with such effect that the literary world--of Europe, let alone England--was soon wearing the tartan." Hawthorne must have pondered his own chances of playing such a role in America, which explains both his care in studying Scott's works as well as his lifelong admiration of them.

Jones, Buford. "The *Faery Land* of Hawthorne's Romances." *ESQ*, no. 48 (1967), 106-24.
See the annotation of this item in Chapter 5, "Spenser."

________. " 'The Man of Adamant' and the Moral Picturesque." *ATQ*, 14 (1972), 33-41.
See the annotation of this item in Chapter 5, "Spenser."

Koskenlinna, Hazel M. "Setting, Image, and Symbol in Scott and Hawthorne." *ESQ*, no. 70 (1973), 50-59.
The author shows how the two novelists make similar use of rocks, cliffs, forests, gardens, water, and snakes in their works.

Orians, G. Harrison. "The Angel of Hadley in Fiction: A Study of the Source of Hawthorne's 'The Grey Champion.' " *AL*, 4 (1932-33), 257-69.
An actual historical event--the appearance of a mysterious stranger who rallies a New England congregation against Indian attack--was used by Scott in *Peveril of the Peak*, which work subsequently influenced Cooper's *The Wept of Wish-ton-Wish* and Hawthorne's "The Grey Champion."

________. "Scott and Hawthorne's *Fanshawe*." *NEQ*, 11 (1938), 388-94.
Fanshawe is more interesting as evidence of Scott's impact on the readers and writers of the 1820s than it is as part of the Hawthorne canon. Orians notes that there is "almost a consanguinity" between Fanshawe and Scott's Waverley.

Turner, H. Arlin. "Hawthorne's Literary Borrowings." *PMLA*, 51 (1936), 543-62.

"Hawthorne's chief debt to Sir Walter Scott [who is only one of numerous sources treated in this article] lies in his interest in the history of his native locality and in his effort to preserve in his works the romantic features of that history; but, whereas Scott placed greatest emphasis on the historical and romantic significance, Hawthorne laid most stress on the moral possibilities of the history. Each had an unbounded interest in local traditions and legends, and each made considerable use of the supernatural.

"Hawthorne very probably profited by the example of the Scottish romancer in the matter of technique. Throughout Fanshawe and in the Market Place scenes of The Scarlet Letter he divides his characters into groups and carries the actions of the several groups along separately; and he takes from Scott the method, illustrated well in The Scarlet Letter, of unraveling a plot by a series of well-defined dramatic scenes. The long and frequently elaborate speeches in Hawthorne's works--speeches which contain much of the subjective element--are also suggestive of Scott. Both stop not infrequently for personal comments, telling the reader in what light to consider the characters and the actions; and both reflect again and again their personal hobbies."

Irving

Pochmann, Henry A. "Irving's German Sources in The Sketch Book." Studies in Philology, 27 (1930), 477-507.

See the annotation of this item in Chapter 12, "The Romantics."

James

Veeder, William. Henry James--the Lessons of the Master: Popular Fiction and Personal Style in the Nineteenth Century. Chicago: University of Chicago Press, 1975.

See the annotation of this item in Chapter 14, "The Victorians."

Melville

Mansfield, Luther S., and Howard P. Vincent. "Explanatory Notes" to Moby-Dick. New York: Hendricks House, 1952.

Melville's passing references to Scott's works are identified and discussed in these indispensable notes.

Poe

Newlin, Paul A. "Scott's Influence on Poe's Grotesque and Arabesque Tales." ATQ, no. 2 (1969), 9-12.

In a letter to T. W. White, Poe argues that commercially successful fiction deals with "the ludicrous heightened into the grotesque; the fearful colored into the horrible; the witty exaggerated into the burlesque; and the singular heightened into the strange and mystical." Newlin suggests that Poe derived these ideas from Scott's article "On the Supernatural in Fictitious Composition; and particularly on the Works of Ernest Theodore William [sic] Hoffmann."

Twain

Baetzhold, Howard G. Mark Twain and John Bull: The British Connection. Bloomington: Indiana University Press, 1970, passim.

His avowed distaste for Scott notwithstanding, Twain saw ways in which his writings might be useful. For instance, "in study notes for The Prince and the Pauper, he twice considered the possibility of incorporating examples of chivalric combat from Ivanhoe, and also jotted down page numbers from Kenilworth, Quentin Durward, and The Fortunes of Nigel where he might find descriptions of dress and armor, the wording of 'a stately proclamation,' and an account of Alsatia (Whitefriars) as a place of refuge for criminals." Twain also borrowed from Scott when he wrote A Connecticut Yankee and Huckleberry Finn (the silent, gliding undertaker in Chapter 27 of Huckleberry Finn is clearly modeled on Oliver Le Dain, the councilor of Louis XI in Quentin Durward).

14. THE VICTORIANS

The mutual admiration between American and English writers that began in the Romantic era continued to intensify. In 1841 Dickens wrote Irving: "There is no living writer, and there are few among the dead, whose approbation I should feel so proud to earn. And with everything you have written upon my shelves, and in my thoughts, and in my heart of hearts, I may honestly and truly say so." Carlyle, when he learned of Irving's death, wrote: "It was a dream of mine that we two should be friends." Thackeray thought Leatherstocking "better than anyone in 'Scott's lot.' " The sober Macaulay was but one of a number of notable Englishmen who took Uncle Tom's Cabin as gospel. Edward Bellamy's Looking Backward is known for having inspired William Morris's News from Nowhere. Kipling could recall phrases and sentences from Howells's Venetian Life decades after he read it. The same author, having read Sarah Orne Jewett's The Country of the Pointed Firs, wrote her that "it's immense--it is the very life.... I don't believe even you know how good that work is!" When Oscar Wilde declared publicly that no living English novelist could be mentioned with James and Howells he was guilty of a typically Wildean overstatement. Yet it was the kind of hyperbole that countered, because it gave the lie to, Sydney Smith's earlier assertion that no one ever read an American book.

What else, besides mutual understanding and admiration, did these two groups of mid- and late-century writers inherit from the Romantics? For one thing, an intensified moral concern, whether it be the antimaterialist thunderings of Carlyle (influenced, as he was, by the German Idealists), or, more directly to the point, the societal critiques of Morris and Ruskin and the sympathetic portrayals of the lower classes by Dickens, both of which have at their roots a disgust for the evils of the Industrial Revolution. The Americans followed suit: certainly James was as eloquent in denouncing American vulgarity as Arnold was in attacking English philistinism. And in the early romances of Howells as well as in the novels of George Eliot the reader notes a fond lingering over the Indian and the peasant that has its roots in, yet is something more than, the merely Wordsworthian picturesque. In writings like these the growth of Realism (discussed in the next chapter) is evident, and Realism is of necessity a morally concerned mode of thinking and writing if one understands it as James did when he said, in discussing Flaubert, that "every out-and-out realist who provokes serious meditation may claim he is a moralist."

Another Romantic legacy that the later writers shared was the belief in the autonomy of art and the artist that was to become the art-for-art's-sake idea, just as an interest in the picturesque and déclassé became the Realistic movement in literature. At first glance the two tendencies may seem unrelated or even opposed, but in fact they are inextricably linked, not only because they are found simultaneously in so many writers on both sides of the Atlantic--consider Howells and William Morris, for example--but also because a claim for the autonomy of art is very likely to be the social critic's first line of defense. Moreover, each of these ostensibly unrelated beliefs (artists are answerable only to themselves, the masses must be hearkened to) bespeaks the desire, ever present in the serious artist yet particularly intense at this time, to pique the complacent bourgeois, to see him squirm.

This preface draws on the following sources (see "List of Works Frequently Consulted" for full bibliographic information): Wager, p. 61-61, 64, 107, 165, 140, 160, 141, 129; Leon Edel, Henry James: The Conquest of London, 1870-1881, Philadelphia: Lippincott, 1962, p. 126, 129; Robert Falk, The Victorian Mode in American Fiction 1865-1885, East Lansing: Michigan State University Press, 1965, p. 45, 61. Students of Browning's work may be interested in Louise Greer, Browning and America, Chapel Hill: University of North Carolina Press, 1952.

The following studies are grouped under the names, listed alphabetically, of major American fiction writers through James who were influenced by the Victorians.

Crane

Colvert, James B. "The Origins of Stephen Crane's Literary Creed." Studies in English (University of Texas), no. 34 (1955), 177-88.

Colvert begins by disputing Ahnebrink's claim that Crane was highly influenced by Zola (see the entry on Ahnebrink's book in Chapter 16, "Scientific Thinkers and Naturalists"). Rather, this "unusually ill-read" author modeled himself after Dick Heldar of Kipling's The Light That Failed. "Dick is an Impressionist painter in revolt against the canons of nineteenth-century respectability. He chooses Bohemian life for the freedom it gives him in his enthusiastic pursuit of fame, and with great determination he seeks the truth about life in the slums of London and on the battlegrounds of remote deserts. He is proud, independent, and free in the expression of inconoclastic opinions." Thus "Kipling is Crane's chief literary ancestor."

Osborn, Scott C. "Stephen Crane's Imagery: 'Pasted Like a Wafer.' " AL, 23 (1951-52), 362.

Crane concludes Chapter 9 of The Red Badge of Courage with this sentence: "The red sun was pasted in the sky like a wafer." A striking image in itself, the sun as wafer has been accepted by critics as a literary watershed that divides the older mode of realism from the newer one of impressionism. Yet Kipling, not Crane, should be credited with the first use of this image; a sentence in The Light That Failed reads: "The fog was driven apart for a moment, and the sun shone, a blood-red wafer, on the water." Crane was enthusiastic about Kipling's writings and probably borrowed the image unconsciously.

Interestingly, this temperately written article managed to provoke two rather hysterical ones that say little about either Crane or Kipling although they do argue (fiercely) the merits and follies of source hunting. The reader may wish to see R. W. Stallman, "The Scholar's Net: Literary Sources," CE, 17 (1955), 20-27, and F. W. Bateson, "The Discrimination of Literary Sources: Mr. Stallman's Muddles," CE, 17 (1955), 131-35.

Stone, Edward. "Crane and Zola." ELN, 1 (1963), 46-47.
See the annotation of this item in Chapter 16, "Scientific Thinkers and Naturalists."

Hawthorne

Autrey, Max L. "A Source for Roger Chillingworth." ATQ, 26 (1975, supplement), 24-26.
Hawthorne's source is James Malcolm Rymer's Varney the Vampire: Or, The Feast of Blood (1847). That novel also has a Dr. Chillingworth who has dabbled in the black arts.

Berthold, Dennis. "Hawthorne, Ruskin, and the Gothic Revival: Transcendent Gothic in The Marble Faun." ESQ, no. 74 (1974), 15-32.
"One of Hawthorne's most treasured discoveries in Europe was Gothic architecture.... The Gothic material reveals more than this, however. When studied in the context of Hawthorne's whole career, it is evident that his appreciation for the Gothic mode grew and developed in the broad cultural ferment of the Gothic Revival, particularly as led by John Ruskin. In his early fiction, Hawthorne exhibited the commonplace American suspicion of Gothic forms; but during the 1850's, when Ruskin's influence was at its peak in both England and America, Hawthorne began to see the vital spiritual and aesthetic truths expressed in the Gothic and to understand their relevance to his own symbolic vision. The development of this 'Gothic feeling,' through Hawthorne's American fiction and European notebooks to its culmination in The Marble Faun, thus demonstrates his awareness of and sensitivity to the shifting cultural tastes of his time and reveals the process by which he transmuted the raw material of life into the powerful symbols of art." For both Hawthorne and Ruskin "the Gothic was true because it denied nothing, however grotesque."

Howells

Gardner, Joseph H. "Howells: The 'Realist' as Dickensian." MFS, 16 (1970), 323-43.
In his fiction Howells bodies forth his theory of complicity, which holds that the discrete entities of the universe are intimately connected; corollary to this theory is the belief that providence controls all. This is "the most explicitly Dickensian motif" in Howells's novels and it is synonymous with what another commentator calls Dickens's philosophie de noël. Dickens himself abandoned this "teleological optimism" for "the tragic vision typified by Little Dorrit." But Howells, while criticizing Dickens's overreliance on the workings of a benevolent providence in his early works, exploited the same device in his own writings.

James

Allott, Miriam. " 'The Lord of Burleigh' and Henry James's 'A Landscape Painter.' " N&Q, 200 (1955), 220-21.
Tennyson's poem about a rich man in disguise who falls in love with a simple maid served as the basis of James's tale, although the American reconstructed Tennyson's naive fable "with a youthfully dry sophistication."

________. "Mrs. Gaskell's 'The Old Nurse's Story': A Link Between 'Wuthering Heights' and 'The Turn of the Screw.' " N&Q, 206 (1961), 101-02.
A fascinating study of a story by Mrs. Gaskell that appeared in Dickens's periodical Household Words in 1852, two years after she had received a copy of Wuthering Heights from Charlotte Brontë and several decades before the publication of The Turn of the Screw. The Gaskell story has numerous elements in common with both Brontë's novel (most notably a phantom child tapping at a window and crying to be let in) and James's (which is also about a young woman trying to save children from malevolent spirits). The Gaskell story, incidentally, like The Turn of the Screw, was supposed to be "a Christmas entertainment."

________. " 'Romola' and 'The Golden Bowl.' " N&Q, 198 (1953), 124-25.
James borrowed and put to his own use two elements of Eliot's novel: the idea of "something precious," which becomes the golden bowl, and the character of Tito Melema, who resembles Prince Amerigo.

________. "A Ruskin Echo in 'The Wings of the Dove.' " N&Q, 201 (1956), 87.
James's description of Maud Lowder is based on Ruskin's " 'God-

dess of Getting-on' or 'Britannia of the Market' " (in The Crown of Wild Olive).

Auchincloss, Louis. "Washington Square and 'The Aspern Papers.'" In Reading Henry James. Minneapolis: University of Minnesota Press, 1975.

See the annotation of this item in Chapter 15, "The Realists."

Berland, Alwyn. "Henry James and the Aesthetic Tradition." Journal of the History of Ideas, 23 (1962), 407-19.

James was familiar with the classical tradition of stoicism, but his variety was not the stringent stoicism of Seneca. It was instead an aspect of the aestheticism of Ruskin and Pater and Arnold, who saw culture as the new religion and stoic renunciation of the vulgar and merely material as part of that religion. See also the annotation of the Cox article on James's stoicism in Chapter 2, "The Classics."

Cargill, Oscar. "The Portrait of a Lady: A Critical Reappraisal." MFS, 3 (1957), 11-32.

Cargill takes issue with those who would have Isabel Archer based solely on either James's dead cousin Minnie Temple or George Eliot's heroine, Gwendolyn Harleth of Daniel Deronda. In actuality she is based on both of these as well as on Bathsheba Everdene of Hardy's Far from the Madding Crowd. And no wonder, says Cargill: all the characters of The Portrait are composites, "as one would expect them to be in a novel which is in a way a summary of all the novelist had learned in his apprenticeship."

D'Avanzo, Mario. "James's 'Maud-Evelyn': Source, Allusion, and Meaning." Iowa English Yearbook, 13 (1968), 24-33.

James's bizarre story of a man who meets the parents of a dead girl whose suitor, husband, and widower he becomes has as its source Browning's poem "Evelyn Hope." The story takes to task the Romantic idealism of Wordsworth and Browning and Shelley while acknowledging the power of that idealism to comfort the aggrieved.

Engleberg, Edward. "James and Arnold: Conscience and Consciousness in a Victorian 'Künstlerroman.'" Criticism, 10 (1968), 93-114.

In Chapter 6 of Roderick Hudson, the hero announces: "I'm a Hellenist; I'm not a Hebraist." With this reference to the terms that Matthew Arnold discussed in Culture and Anarchy (1869) James announces explicitly the poles of the dialectic that serves as the book's organizing principle: Hellenism, or consciousness, represented in the novel by Roderick; and Hebraism, or conscience, represented by Rowland Mallet, Roderick's patron. This "very un-Hegelian" dialectic results in no synthesis, however, only annihilation. Consciousness and conscience must go together in the individual; "when the patron becomes the conscience of his protégé's consciousness, neither can prevail." Roderick Hudson is "the first serious Künstlerroman in English" (though each dealt with the problem in his own way, neither Poe nor Hawthorne wrote a full-scale novel with the artist as hero) and thus "prepared the way for a significant progeny."

Kenney, Blair Gates. "The Two Isabels: A Study in Distortion." Victorian Newsletter, no. 25 (1964), 15-17.
Kenney notes many correspondences between Trollope's The Duke's Children and The Portrait of a Lady. The "distortion" involves James reversing Trollope's theme of age deferring to youth by sacrificing the young people in his novel to the desires of the old.

Kirby, David K. "A Possible Source for James's 'The Death of the Lion.' " CLQ, series 10 (1973), 39-40.
The germ of this story may be an anecdote recounted by the Victorian narrative painter William Powell Frith in his autobiographical volume A Victorian Canvas. There Frith describes the poet Thomas Moore as "a lion thoroughly lionised" and "a fish out of water." James untangles the metaphors: he retains the lion image to describe specifically an artist mobbed by his admirers and uses the fish-in-distress idea to suggest the helplessness of other characters.

Lainoff, Seymour. "James and Eliot: The Two Gwendolens." Victorian Newsletter, no. 21 (1962), 23.
Gwendolen Erme of James's story "The Figure in the Carpet" owes part of her characterization to Gwendolyn Harleth in Daniel Deronda.

Leavis, F. R. "Daniel Deronda and The Portrait of a Lady." In The Great Tradition. London: Chatto & Windus, 1955.
In discussing "the great tradition" of the English novel, which is to say the novel as written by Jane Austen and in which formal and moral preoccupations are precisely matched, Leavis makes "an assertion of fact and a critical comparison: Henry James wouldn't have written The Portrait of a Lady if he hadn't read Gwendolyn Harleth (as I shall call the good part of Daniel Deronda), and of the pair of closely comparable works, George Eliot's has not only the distinction of having come first; it is decidedly the greater." This fact, notes Leavis with the modesty of a man who changes the titles of novels at liberty, "can hardly be questioned." See Levine (below).

Leavis, Q. D. "A Note on Literary Indebtedness: Dickens, George Eliot, Henry James." Hudson Review, 8 (1955), 423-29.

In this impressionistic but nonetheless challenging essay Leavis juxtaposes and meditates on three similar scenes--ones in which a heroine broods over the ruins of Rome--from Little Dorrit (1857), Middlemarch (1872), and The Portrait of a Lady (1881). She concludes that while Eliot, in borrowing from Dickens, improved upon his trick of using scenery to precipitate an emotional experience for his heroine, James, in borrowing from Eliot, wrote a passage that is merely picturesque rather than poetic and is, at base, "parasitic."

Levine, George. "Isabel, Gwendolyn, and Dorothea." ELH, 30 (1963), 244-57.

This essay complements F. R. Leavis's study (above) of the relation between Daniel Deronda and The Portrait of a Lady. Levine finds so many correspondences between The Portrait and Eliot's Middlemarch that the reader must acknowledge the influence of the last-named novel as well. Wisely, Levine lends credibility to his argument by discussing differences as well as similarities; for instance, whereas both of Eliot's are novels of "social analysis" that depend upon the existence of strong ties between individual minds and the world at large, James's novel depicts a "private moral struggle" that is "peculiarly divorced from a solidly realized historical time and place." Too, whereas the "bad" husbands conveniently die in Middlemarch and Daniel Deronda, the "bad" husband of The Portrait does not, forcing Isabel to face her fate and the reader to contemplate it. So James took characters and a basic fictional situation from two classically Victorian novels by George Eliot, but he put these elements to use in a strikingly modern way.

Melchiori, Giorgio. "Browning e Henry James." In Friendship's Garland: Essays Presented to Mario Praz on His Seventieth Birthday, vol. 2. Rome: Edizioni di Storia e Letteratura, 1966.

Melchiori emphasizes the influence of certain Browning works ("My Last Duchess," "Andrea del Sarto," "A Light Woman," "Pictor Ignotus," Men and Women, The Ring and the Book) on the writings of the younger James ("The Story of a Masterpiece," "Osborne's Revenge," A Landscape Painter," "The Madonna of the Future," Roderick Hudson). In addition to referring outright to Browning in a number of his fictions, James also adopted several of Browning's situations and even his methods. The dramatic monologue, for instance, becomes the diary entry; both devices result in involuntary disclosures by the one who speaks or writes.

________. "Locksley Hall Revisited: Tennyson and Henry James." Review of English Literature, 6, 4 (1965), 9-25.

A sensitive discussion of James's borrowing from Shakespeare but especially from Tennyson in "A Passionate Pilgrim," a story that reverses the Laureate's paean to Victorian progress and optimism. Melchiori shows how James operates in the tradition of "transferring a line or passage already charged with its own meaning into a new context, thereby adding to its suggestiveness."

Pisapia, Biancamaria. "George Eliot e Henry James." *SA*, 13 (1967), 235-80.

Pisapia notes a tendency on the part of critics (such as F. W. Dupee) to underplay the impact of Eliot's writings on James in favor of the influence of such authors as Hawthorne and Balzac. She counters this with a thorough consideration of James's fascination with Eliot based largely on his reviews of her work. In discussing specific influences she observes that the heroine of "Madame de Mauves" resembles Dorothea Brooke in *Middlemarch* (both are deluded in marriage) and that James's story is a step in the path leading from Eliot's novel to *The Portrait of a Lady*, where the English author's influence is of even greater account. The debt continues in the maturer novels, in which numerous male characters (Hyacinth Robinson, Nick Dormer, Merton Densher, Prince Amerigo) recall Tito Melema of *Romola* while certain female ones (Fleda Vetch, Milly Theale, Rosanna of *The Ivory Tower*) owe something to Dorothea Brooke. A bigger influence than any of these, however, is that of Gwendolyn Harleth (of *Daniel Deronda*) on the character of Kate Croy.

Thematically, James owes to Eliot the opposition of "sympathy" (associated with Rowland Mallet, Lambert Strether, Milly Theale) to "narrowness" (associated with Osmond, Madame Merle, Roderick Hudson, Kate Croy, Prince Amerigo, and Charlotte Stant). In both authors sympathy is not an innate capacity but one that is developed through training and practice.

Ross, Michael L. "Henry James's 'Half-Man': The Legacy of Browning in 'The Madonna of the Future.' " *Browning Institute Studies*, 2 (1974), 25-42.

More than anyone else Browning "provided James with ... the most brilliant and fully-realized evocation of the fictional opportunities latent in an Italian locale." Ross sees James's tale as a reversal of "Andrea del Sarto"--Browning's protagonist has skills that surpass his ability to conceive artistically, whereas James's hero is capable of plans that are out of proportion to his limited technical resources.

Selig, Robert L. "The Red Haired Lady Orator: Parallel Passages in *The Bostonians* and *Adam Bede*." *NCF*, 16 (1961), 164-69.

In an 1866 essay James comments on the lack of "dramatic progression" in the character of Dinah Morris. Obviously Verena Tarrant is based on Dinah, but in developing her character James avoided the static quality that he considered a flaw in Eliot's portrait of her heroine.

Thorberg, Raymond. "Germaine, James's Notebooks, and The Wings of the Dove." CL, 22 (1970), 254-64.
Thorberg is able to trace the evolution of James's novel from its genesis in Edmond About's Germaine (both the novel and the dramatized versions) to its final form via the "bridge" of James's notebook entries and his story "Georgina's Reasons."

Tintner, Adeline R. "Arsène Houssaye's 'Capricieuse' and James's 'Capricciosa.' " RLC, 50 (1976), 478-81.
In an article in PQ, 38 (1959), 488-96, Bebe Spano points out a probable connection between the real-life Princess Belgiojoso and The Princess Casamassima. Here Tintner guesses that James's description of his character as a "capricciosa" is based on Arsène Houssaye's designation (in Les Confessions) of the real-life princess as a "capricieuse." So this is "another instance of how the sources for James's characters or plots, even when drawn from life, are supported by literary correlates."

________. "Henry James's Use of 'Jane Eyre' in 'The Turn of the Screw.' " Brontë Society Transactions, 17, i (1976), 42-45.
Just before he wrote or while he was writing his celebrated ghost story James reviewed Clement Shorter's book on Charlotte Brontë. From it, from Mrs. Gaskell's Life of Charlotte Brontë, and from Jane Eyre, James took a number of details and perhaps even his story's central idea--in Chapter 17 of Jane Eyre there is a spirited discussion of the danger of liaisons between governesses and tutors and their corrupting effect on young children.

________. "Octave Feuillet, La Petite Comtesse, and Henry James." RLC, 48 (1974), 218-32.
When James was fifteen he read Feuillet's novel (which he mentions, some years later, in The Princess Casamassima). From it he took two character types--the capriciossa or flirtatious female and the man who resists love until it is too late, an example of this latter type being John Marcher in The Beast in the Jungle.

Veeder, William. Henry James--the Lessons of the Master: Popular Fiction and Personal Style in the Nineteenth Century. Chicago: University of Chicago Press, 1975.
This excellent book begins by identifying two literary styles that were characteristic of Victorian fiction and that James adopted for his own use. The first is a "reassuringly precise" style that Veeder calls "equipoise"; derived from neoclassical literature, it is the style that provides the average Victorian reader with the feeling of security, that "God is in His heaven or at least that order remains on earth." The second is a "breathtakingly gaudy" style that Veeder calls "extravagance"; it is the style that encourages readers, once they are assured of their

security, to indulge their emotions. In establishing the rapport between James and other Victorian practitioners of these two styles Veeder refers "primarily to three novels which James definitely read by 1871--those favorites The Heir of Redclyffe by Charlotte Yonge, The Initials by Baroness von Tautphoeus, and The Wide, Wide World by Susan Warner. Then, to establish how representative of the popular tradition these works are, I draw often upon two best-sellers which James apparently had not read--St. Elmo by Augusta Jane Evans and Ishmael by E. D. E. N. Southworth. Occasional examples also come from other popular novels which James knew, particularly Holmes' Elsie Venner, Cherbuliez' Le Roman d'une honnête femme, Charlotte Brontë's Villette, and Mrs. Gaskell's Ruth."

Veeder also discusses character in the writings of James and his peers. He is especially good on The Portrait of a Lady, showing how Isabel Archer and Gilbert Osmond both combine and transcend popular stereotypes, thus making The Portrait "the last great Victorian novel," which nonetheless "announces the advent of modern fiction." Veeder's remarks on the complicated genealogies of the names in The Portrait are fascinating; one can only stand in awe of the astounding number of trashy novels Veeder must have read. His handling of details is no less than phenomenal. In discussing Madame Merle, for instance, he notes that the names of villainous characters often begin with "M" and then gives thirty-eight examples. He cites five places in the text where Madame Merle's smile is described as curving to the left and then notes that "the crooked curl of the villain's sardonic smile derives ... from Milton's Satan and reappears in Byron, Scott, and in virtually every popular novel that I know, including The Heir, The Initials, St. Elmo, and The Wide, Wide World."

Melville

Barbour, James, and Leon Howard. "Carlyle and the Conclusion of Moby-Dick." NEQ, 49 (1976), 214-24.

Carlyle's influence on Melville in Moby-Dick extends beyond mere similarities of rhetoric and humor. There are parallel incidents in Sartor Resartus and Melville's novel; too, "the philosophical conclusion of Moby-Dick is filled with ambiguities" provoked at least in part by Melville's reading of Carlyle, which he undertook in 1850 during a break in the composition of his whale story.

The authors discuss at length two borrowings: Carlyle's idea of an emblematic universe, which became Ahab's insistence that all visible things are but as pasteboard masks; and the weaver god in Sartor Resartus (in Chapter 93, "The Castaway," Pip sees " 'God's foot upon the treadle of the loom' ").

D'Avanzo, Mario L. " 'The Cassock' and Carlyle's 'Church-Clothes.' " ESQ, no. 50 (1968, supplement), 74-76.

Melville attacks Carlyle's superficial insistence on the importance of outward forms by having a sailor in Moby-Dick dress himself in the penis skin of a whale before slicing up its blubber, thus "suggesting that society is based on sexual and economic concerns. It is not the church and church clothes, but the vestiture of the phallus and the labors of the working man in his phallic coat that causes or allows society to exist. Procreation and work, to Melville, are the real basis and origin of society."

________. "Melville's 'Bartleby' and Carlyle." In Melville Annual 1965 / A Symposium: Bartleby the Scrivener, ed. Howard P. Vincent. Kent: Kent State University Press, 1966.
The sources of Melville's story are Carlyle's Sartor Resartus and Heroes and Hero Worship, and "Bartleby's malaise is an ironic inversion of the spiritual development of Professor Diogenes Teufelsdröкh [sic] and the Carlylean hero as a man of letters."

Doubleday, Neal F. "Jack Easy and Billy Budd." ELN, 2 (1964), 39-42.
The relationship between Billy Budd, Claggart, and Captain Vere in Melville's Billy Budd is like that between Jack Easy, Mr. Smallsoul, and Captain Wilson in Marryat's Mr. Midshipman Easy (1836), which Melville would have read "a little before or about the time of his first voyage." Whereas Jack Easy's loss of innocence is treated comically, however, Billy Budd's is handled with characteristically Melvillean sobriety and fatalism.

Fite, Olive L. "Billy Budd, Claggart, and Schopenhauer." NCF, 23 (1968), 336-43.
Billy Budd is Schopenhauer's "beautiful soul," the good man who lives in "a world of friendly individuals, whose well-being he regards as his own"; Claggart is the evil man who "feels himself surrounded by strange and hostile individuals and his only hope is centered in his own good." To read Billy Budd in Schopenhauerian terms is to understand the development of Claggart's envy of Billy (Melville marked a passage on envy in his copy of Schopenhauer) as well as Billy's altruistic decision to die for the well-being of others.

Lane, Lauriat, Jr. "Melville and Dickens' American Notes." Extracts, 12 (1972), 3-4.
"There is a real chance that Dickens may have influenced Melville's writings.... In fact, almost every criticism of America in American Notes has at least a rough parallel somewhere in Melville's writings: in Redburn, the situation of emigrants and other ship passengers; in Mardi, the government in Washington and the issue of slavery; in "Bartleby," the prisons of New York; in Pierre, the prisons, underworld, and newspapers of New York and the general self-assertiveness; and in The Confidence-Man, almost all of these along with literary transcendentalism, com-

mercial trickery and general distrust. Dickens and Melville were, after all, writing about the same reality, but these parallels deserve a closer look for the kinship they display between Dickens' and Melville's views of mid-19th-century America."

Ledbetter, Kenneth. "The Ambiguity of Billy Budd." TSLL, 4 (1962-63), 130-34.

A salutary attempt to refute overly neat interpretations of Melville's last work, this essay argues that Billy Budd is shot through with ambiguity because "Melville was strongly influenced during these last years by his reading of Schopenhauer and tried in his final work [but failed] to accept and define the dark necessity he found there." Evidently Billy's dual need to die and to live neutralized each other.

Mansfield, Luther S., and Howard P. Vincent. "Explanatory Notes" to Moby-Dick. New York: Hendricks House, 1952.

There are passing references to Dickens in Moby-Dick; Carlyle, however, is alluded to so frequently that the authors of these indispensable notes consider his impact on the novel almost as great as Shakespeare's.

Murray, Henry A. "Introduction" to Pierre. New York: Hendricks House, 1949.

See the annotation of this item in Chapter 7, "Shakespeare and the Renaissance."

Rosenthal, Bernard. "Melville, Marryat, and the Evil-Eyed Villain." NCF, 25 (1970), 221-24.

By means of the parallel-texts method Rosenthal establishes that Frederick Marryat's The Phantom Ship provided Melville with "the prototype for his mysteriously demonic man threatening an innocent youth" in Redburn.

Sutton, Walter. "Melville and the Great God Billy Budd." Prairie Schooner, 34 (1960), 128-33.

See the annotation of this item in Chapter 1, "The Oriental Heritage."

Thompson, Lawrance. Melville's Quarrel with God. Princeton: Princeton University Press, 1952, passim.

"Melville's violent [and sustained] reaction against the essentially orthodox Christian viewpoint underlying Carlyle's Sartor Resartus is reflected throughout Moby-Dick and Pierre."

Welsh, Alexander. "A Melville Debt to Carlyle." MLN, 73 (1958), 489-91.

In writing Chapter 69 of Moby-Dick ("The Funeral") Melville borrowed from Carlyle's essay on "Boswell's Life of Johnson" the image of the sheep who illustrate the stubborn survival of meaningless traditions because they "leap over a vacuum, because their leader originally leaped there when a stick was held" (the quote is from "The Funeral").

Welsh notes that we can add Carlyle's Critical and Miscellaneous Essays to the list of books Melville is known to have read; further, we should examine those essays "as a source for [Melville's] notions of continental philosophy, Goethe and Voltaire, and all the lesser personalities whom Carlyle introduced in extravagant terms to the writers of England and America."

Norris

Graham, D. B. "Frank Norris's Afternoon of a Faun." PLL, 10 (1974), 307-12.

In one scene from the first chapter of The Octopus Norris appears to be reworking Mallarmé's best-known poem, "L'Après-midi d'un Faune: Eglogue" (1876).

Poe

Grubb, Gerald D. "The Personal and Literary Relationship of Dickens to Poe (Part Three: Poe's Literary Debt to Dickens)." NCF, 5 (1950), 209-21.

This is the last of a three-part article; its main purpose is to deal with Poe's reviews of Dickens's work (which were generally favorable) as well as their correspondence and their friendship, which, though never "deep and abiding," seemed genuine. Poe's debt to Dickens is not large, although there are certain traceable connections, e.g., between the raven in Barnaby Rudge who croaks "Nobody" and Poe's celebrated bird.

Ada B. Nisbet's "New Light on the Dickens-Poe Relationship," which is on pages 295-302 of this same volume, deals with the disputed authorship of some notices of Dickens's work that Poe may or may not have written but adds nothing specific about the American's debt to his English contemporary.

Krappe, Edith Smith. "A Possible Source for Poe's 'The Tell-Tale Heart' and 'The Black Cat.' " AL, 12 (1940-41), 84-88.

It's Dickens's "A Confession Found in a Prison." See Senelick (below).

Senelick, Laurence. "Charles Dickens and 'The Tell-Tale Heart.' " Poe S, 6 (1973), 12-14.

In his review of Dickens's Master Humphrey's Clock, Poe singled out for praise a slight tale entitled "A Confession Found in a Prison," which bears a resemblance to his own (and superior) story, which appeared a couple of years later. See Krappe (above).

Soule, George H., Jr. "Another Source for Poe: Trelawney's The Adventures of a Younger Son." Poe S, 8 (1975), 35-37.
Using the parallel-passages method, Soule offers convincing evidence that Trelawney's "popular tale of life as a corsair in Malaysian waters" may have provided details for "MS. Found in a Bottle," The Narrative of Arthur Gordon Pym, "Metzengerstein," "William Wilson," and other works by Poe.

Strickland, Edward. "Dickens' 'A Madman's Manuscript' and 'The Tell-Tale Heart.' " Poe S, 9 (1976), 22-23.
In his review of The Pickwick Papers Poe quoted almost three quarters of "A Madman's Manuscript." His own story resembles Dickens's in detail and narrative strategy--each is "a first-person narration by a madman of a murderous assault" as well as "a deranged parody of methodical self-analysis."

Twain

Aspiz, Harold. "Lecky's Influence on Mark Twain." Science and Society, 26 (1962), 15-25.
A lucid explanation of the relation between Twain's Connecticut Yankee and Lecky's History of European Morals from Augustus to Charlemagne, from which Twain borrowed not only characters, incidents, and details but also a theme--that theoretically humanity *can* be perfected through democratic social organization and scientific progress, even though human nature is stubborn and intractable and will always revert at the last moment to outworn and discredited thought patterns that cannot be shaken off.

Baetzhold, Howard G. Mark Twain and John Bull: The British Connection. Bloomington: Indiana University Press, 1970, passim.
It would be difficult to overpraise this fine source study. It is an exemplary book, both for its original insights and its careful inclusion of the work of such earlier source hunters as Walter Blair and Sydney J. Krause (discussed below). Baetzhold treats virtually all of Twain's literary sources (see the specific references in other chapters), but of course the emphasis is on Twain's involvement with his contemporaries. In discussing Twain's travels, reading, correspondence, and friendships Baetzhold portrays convincingly a writer's mind; he shows how an author discovered, discarded, and incorporated into his own work the things he saw and read and heard about. Readers come away with a sense of the fallible but fruitful process that yields art. This book supports and extends Minnie Brashear's pioneering effort (discussed

above in Chapter 9, "The Eighteenth Century") to prove that Twain was not, as even he pictured himself, an unlettered funny man.

Concerning the Victorians in particular, Baetzhold deals with the major influences--Carlyle, Dickens, and Lecky--as well as others, such as Charlotte M. Yonge, whose *The Little Duke* inspired *The Prince and the Pauper*. Baetzhold considers such troublesome phenomena as Twain's career-long "discussion with Lecky," during which the novelist vacillated between Lecky's "intuitive" view of morality, which says that moral choices are governed by an inner sense of right and wrong, and the "utilitarian" view that the disillusioned Twain leaned toward in his later years, according to which men and women possess no innate sense of virtue and instead base their morality on the increase of their own happiness and the lessening of their pain. Baetzhold focuses on concrete influences as well: for instance, he recalls and elaborates on Walter Blair's discovery that the incident in Chapter 10 of *Huckleberry Finn*, in which the disguised Huck is shown to be a male when Mrs. Loftus throws a lump of lead into his lap and he joins his knees instead of spreading them as a girl might, is based on an identical one in Chapter 63 of Charles Reade's *The Cloister and the Hearth*.

Other Victorian authors who affected Twain's writing include Macaulay, Kipling, Trollope, Tennyson, Mrs. Humphrey Ward, Browning, FitzGerald, Arthur Conan Doyle, Gilbert and Sullivan, and George Standring, whose *The People's History of the English Aristocracy* crystalized the anti-English sentiments that appear in *A Connecticut Yankee*.

Blair, Walter. "The French Revolution and *Huckleberry Finn*." *MP*, 55 (1957), 21-35.

Twain's reading of Carlyle's *The French Revolution*, Dickens's *A Tale of Two Cities*, and other works is reflected throughout *Huckleberry Finn*, and not solely in the "inferior burlesque chapters."

________. "So Noble ... and So Beautiful a Book." In *Mark Twain and Huckleberry Finn*. Berkeley and Los Angeles: University of California Press, 1960.

In Chapters 1-3 of *Huckleberry Finn* Huck is already debating whether he will follow a more intuitive line in matters of morality, as the Widow Douglas suggests, or adhere to Miss Watson's Calvinist notions. The terms of this dilemma, which becomes more important as the book progresses, were borrowed by Twain from Lecky's *History of European Morals*. In Chapter 16, when Huck rejects the promptings of his conscience--which, according to Lecky, is formed by the community one lives in--and follows his natural urge to save Jim from recapture, it is a triumph of what Lecky described as the "*natural* power of perceiving that some qualities such as benevolence, chastity, or veracity, are better than others" (emphasis added).

Cooper, Lane. "Mark Twain's Lilacs and Laburnums." MLN, 47 (1932), 85-87.

Twain's A Double-Barreled Detective Story parodies The Seamy Side, by Walter Besant and James Rice. Twain's tale begins: "It was a crisp and spicy morning in early October. The lilacs and laburnums," etc. The English novel begins: "It was a quiet morning in very early June. The lilacs and laburnums...." See Kraus (below).

Davis, Chester. "Mark Twain's Religious Beliefs as Indicated by the Notations in His Books." Twainian, 14 (1955), 1-4 (May-June issue), 1-4 (July-August issue), 1-4 (September-October issue).

It is regrettable that the author of this detailed three-part article felt obliged to pepper it with his own horrified reactions to Twain's mildly skeptical marginalia in Lecky's History of European Morals. For instance, Davis quotes Lecky as writing "But whatever may be thought of the justice of the Catholic conception of death or of its influence upon human happiness, it is plain that it is radically different from that of the pagan philosophers. That man is not only an imperfect but a fallen being, and that death is the penal consequence of his sins, were doctrines profoundly new to mankind, and they have exercised an influence of the most serious character upon the moral history of the world." Davis writes, "The sensational revelation is that Mark has crossed out the word 'serious' and has substituted the word 'rotten.' Certainly no person would do what Mark has done to his own personal book from his own library, with the feeling no one in the world would know, unless he was expressing his innermost feelings and convictions. Members are also cautioned not to jump to any conclusions as to the feelings of your Secretary [Davis, evidently], he is doing his duty of reporting in what he believes to be the true purpose of the 'Research' included as a part of the name of our organization."

All this editorial unctuousness notwithstanding, one does come away with a sense of how close a reader the supposedly unlettered Twain was.

Hill, Hamlin, and Walter Blair. "Literary Sources." In The Art of Huckleberry Finn. 2d ed. San Francisco: Chandler, 1969.

The authors enumerate several literary sources for Twain's novel, including three from the Victorian period, and quote actual passages that may have influenced the composition of Huckleberry Finn. The Victorian authors, the works excerpted, and the chapters of Huckleberry Finn that may have been affected are as follows:

(1) Dickens, A Tale of Two Cities; HF, Chapters 2, 3, 35, and 40 (but why not 5 and 6, in which Pap Finn comports himself much like Dickens's Jerry Cruncher?)

(2) Carlyle, The French Revolution: A History; HF, Chapters 6, 14, and 21 (but why not 22, where Colonel Sherburn gives a very Carlylean speech on the nature of mobs?)

(3) Lecky, History of European Morals; HF, Chapters 2, 8, 12, 15, 16, 22, 23, and 31.

Kraus, W. Keith. "Mark Twain's 'A Double Barreled Detective Story': A Source for the Solitary Oesophagus." MTJ, 16, ii (1972), 10-12.

Twain may have borrowed a phrase or two from Besant and Rice's The Seamy Side (see the article by Cooper, above), but his two-part story shows a greater overall resemblance to Arthur Conan Doyle's two-part "A Study in Scarlet."

Krause, Sydney J. "Macaulay: Living History by Antitheses." In Mark Twain as Critic. Baltimore: Johns Hopkins Press, 1967.

"If there was one writer Twain would rather have been other than himself, I believe it would have been Macaulay. He read and reread him early and late, in season and out, and never tired of what he called the 'glittering pageantry' of his prose.... Perhaps the best demonstration of the kind of appeal Macaulay had for Twain is to be inferred from his having come under Macaulay's influence, both aesthetically and philosophically. A reading of the essays on Hastings and Clive inspired him to write a lyric and symbolic poem (no small feat for Twain). In addition, all three of Twain's historical novels, The Prince and the Pauper, A Connecticut Yankee, and Joan of Arc, were composed on the Macaulayan theory that history should provide an imaginative vivification of the past.... In A Connecticut Yankee, he specifically relied on the Whiggish concept of progress, which Macaulay had done so much to popularize, and on a moral interpretation of history which William Hartpole Lecky had directly inherited from Macaulay. There was a like equivalence in method, for in noting how he wanted to deal with history in the Yankee, Twain asserted that his main object (like Macaulay's) had been to present a 'contrast'; modern times being a commentary on ancient times, with the 'juxtaposition emphasiz[ing] the salients of both.'"

Laverty, Carroll D. "The Genesis of The Mysterious Stranger." MTQ, 8, iii and iv (1947, combined issue), 15-19.

See the annotation of this item in Chapter 9, "The Eighteenth Century."

McKeithan, D. M. "Mark Twain's Tom Sawyer Abroad and Jules Verne's Five Weeks in a Balloon." Studies in English (University of Texas), no. 28 (1949), 257-70.

In 1868 Twain began a "balloon story" (a popular genre at the time) but was discouraged enough to abandon it when Verne's novel appeared. Yet his Tom Sawyer Abroad, written in 1892, seems to incorporate a number of details from Five Weeks in a Balloon.

Rogers, Rodney O. "Twain, Taine, and Lecky: The Genesis of a Passage in *A Connecticut Yankee*." *MLQ*, 34 (1973), 436-47.

While writing *A Tramp Abroad* Twain included a passage on the abuse of serfs by feudal nobles, the information for which he took from Hippolyte Taine's *L'Ancien Règime*. The passage was cut, but Twain revised and used it in *A Connecticut Yankee*. The changes that Twain made, such as the introduction into the revised version of the Catholic Church as a force of feudal oppression, are largely attributable to his reading of Lecky's *History of European Morals*. Lecky's outlook is the Whig one, whereby history is "the natural evolution of liberty. democracy, and Protestant individualism." Yet this evolutionary process comes to smash in *A Connecticut Yankee*, in which Twain's optimism first peaks and then plummets ("as a consequence the novel is frequently spoken of as a watershed between the humor of the earlier writings and the rage and despair of Twain's later works"). Interestingly, a reading of both the excised *Tramp* chapter and the whole of the *Yankee* (as well as other passages in Twain, such as the "Lynching Bee" episode in *Huckleberry Finn*) indicates a common theme that is "the strongest current in Twain's social thought," namely, the average person's meekness and capacity for self-enslavement, and thus the doubtfulness of any social system that "would make common men the engineers of progress."

Salomon, Roger. "Twain and the Whig Hypothesis." In *Twain and the Image of History*. New Haven: Yale University Press, 1961.

"Between Twain and the Enlightenment stood the Whig historians, for whom history recorded the development of knowledge and political liberty." Twain embodies this idea (articulated by Macaulay and others) in *A Connecticut Yankee*: "In the figure of the Yankee, Twain was to create, as Defoe created in Crusoe, innovation incarnate.... The Yankee himself is aware of his kinship with Defoe's earlier prototype of modern man. 'I saw that I was just another Robinson Crusoe cast away on an uninhabited island,' he says, shortly after arriving in Camelot, 'with no society but some more or less tame animals, and if I wanted to make life bearable I must do as he did--invent, contrive, create, reorganize things; set brain and hand to work, and keep them busy. Well, that was my line.' " That Twain had reservations about the Whig hypothesis even as he advocated it is evident, however, and "by the end of the 1890's ..., under the impetus of personal tragedy, an increasing sense of guilt, and a larger awareness of the plutocratic and imperialistic drift of American society, Twain had brought the Whig hypothesis itself under direct attack and was moving toward a theory of historical cycles."

Schoenemann, F. "Mark Twain and Adolf Wilbrandt." *MLN*, 34 (1919), 372-74.

Though Wilbrandt's play is an attempt to "solve the main riddle of life," Twain saw it only as a " 'long, soulful, sardonic laugh at human life,' " an idea that he took with him into the composition of What Is Man? and The Mysterious Stranger.

In "Einige Bemerkungen zu Adolf Wilbrandts Der Meister Von Palmyra," MP, 61 (1946), 551-55, Max Lederer corrects Schoenemann in noting that the play is not about the meaning of life but rather about the Faustian desire for eternal life.

Schönemann, Friedrich. Mark Twain als Literarische Persönlichkeit. Jena: Verlag der Frommannschen Buchhandlung, 1925.
According to the author, Twain may have learned something about characterization from Dickens, and no doubt he acquired several of his pessimistic notions about human nature from Carlyle. But in discussing these and other possible influences, Schönemann occasionally assumes too much; for a corrective see Edgar H. Hemminghaus's commentary on Schönemann's findings in Mark Twain in Germany, New York: AMS Press, 1966, p. 109-11.

Taylor, Coley Banks. Mark Twain's Margins on Thackeray's "Swift." New York: Gotham House, 1935.
See the annotation of this item in Chapter 9, "The Eighteenth Century."

15. THE REALISTS

It is accurate to consider realism not a narrow school or a particular technique but a mode of writing that is present, to some degree, in the literature of every historical period--Homer, after all, tells us how to build a boat and slaughter a heifer. In the more specialized sense, however, Realism describes a literary mode prevalent in America, England, France, and Russia in the last half of the nineteenth century. The contemporary American critic George Parsons Lathrop defined it this way:

> Realism sets itself to work to consider characters and events which are apparently the most ordinary and uninteresting, in order to extract from these their full value and true meaning. It would apprehend in all particulars the connection between the familiar and the extraordinary, and the seen and unseen of human nature.... In short, realism reveals. Where we thought nothing worthy of notice, it shows everything to be rife with significance.

Realists believe in the significance of the insignificant, then; their goal is expressed in the maxim of Flaubert that Sarah Orne Jewett kept pinned to her writing desk: "To write everyday life as one writes history."

The dominant impetus toward realism in American literature comes as much, maybe more, from non-English-speaking countries as from England. In this respect the writings of the following authors, not all of them "pure" realists, are significant: Stendhal, Flaubert, and Balzac in France; Dostoevsky, Tolstoy, and Turgenev in Russia. What these writers had to offer is immediately apparent if one contrasts, say, the insubstantial fictional world of Cooper--whose characters, as Marcus Cunliffe suggests, live in a vaccuum--with the dense, richly populated one of Balzac. It was Balzac, according to James, who taught him that "the art of interesting us in things ... can only be the art of representing them." In James's own writings Balzac's solidity and specificity often complement the airy, otherworldly quality that derives from James's chief American influence, Hawthorne; the two influences together can be seen in such novels as Roderick Hudson. Later, Turgenev's realism had a similarly concrete influence on the writings of both James and Howells. It is interesting to note that Howells was so moved by the socialist example of another Russian, Tolstoy, that he thought at one point of imitating his life and living as a peasant. (Howells kept his creature comforts, of course, although Tolstoy's radicalism as well as his fearless style continued to exert considerable power over the American's thought and art.)

Of the single most influential Realist, Balzac, it must be said that he was, like all writers, a transitional figure. In The Wild Ass's Skin (La Peau de Chagrin) he acknowledges his debts to both Romanticism and Realism when he has his troubled main character follow fashion and seek solace, though skeptically, among the scientists. Raphael, having made a pact with the devil, whereby a talismanic ass's skin grants him his every wish as it shrinks in size and thus heralds the premature end of his days, wants to be told that the spell he is under is illusory. Thus he opines:

> In a century of enlightenment in which we have learnt that diamonds are carbon crystals, in an age when there is an explanation for everything, when the police would haul a new Messiah before the courts and refer his miracles to the Academy of Sciences, at a time when we require a notary's initials before trusting anything, why should I alone believe in a sort of Mene, Mene, Tekel, Upharsin? In God's name, no! I will not believe that the Supreme Being can take pleasure in tormenting one of his inoffensive creatures. Let us consult the scientists.

But Romanticism is not yet dead, and the scientists are unable to help Raphael. Yet he consults them anyway--he conducts himself as befits a dweller in an age of Realism. It is no wonder that James called the later naturalists who indeed thought themselves scientists "the grandsons of Balzac."

This preface draws on the following sources (see "List of Works Frequently Consulted" for full bibliographic information): Falk, p. 102, 72, 77, 105, 46-47; Wager, p. 159; Walker, p. 39; Cunliffe, p. 67-68; Matthiessen, p. 298; Lynn, p. 292. The Balzac quotation is from The Wild Ass's Skin, Harmondsworth: Penguin, 1977, p. 223. Students of Turgenev's influence may wish to see Royal A. Gettmann, Turgenev in England and America, Urbana: University of Illinois Press, 1941.

The following studies are grouped under the names, listed alphabetically, of major American fiction writers through James who were influenced by the British and Continental Realists.

Cooper

Palfrey, Thomas R. "Cooper and Balzac: 'The Headsman.' " MP, 29 (1932), 335-41.

Cooper's novel resembles in several respects Balzac's Jésus-Christ en Flandres, particularly in "the accounts of the two storms, which form the central episode in both stories."

Crane

Stallman, R. W. " 'Maggie.' " In Stephen Crane: A Biography. New York: George Braziller, 1968.

"The artistic source of Maggie would seem not to be Zola--although the thematic resemblances are strikingly close--but Flaubert's Madame Bovary. The two novels are alike in the way their respective romantic escapes from reality are rendered." Too, "Emma and Maggie live out lives of succession rather than sequence."

Hawthorne

Lundblad, Jane. "Hawthorne and Honoré de Balzac." In Nathaniel Hawthorne and European Literary Tradition. New York: Russell & Russell, 1965.

"Hawthorne's acquaintance with Balzac's work may have influenced his view of Old World art, that he had scanty means of studying in his own country. His conception of architecture may have received impulses from the reading of such works as La Recherche de l'Absolu and Le Cabinet des antiques, and his view of the relation between sculptor, work, and beholder, may have been influenced by the ideas expressed in Séraphita. Furthermore, the figures of the antiquarian in La Peau de chagrin, and Balthazar Claës in La Recherche de l'Absolu possess sufficiently many traits in common with Hawthorne's men guilty of cold-hearted pride in their own intellect, to warrant a surmise that they have contributed to the American writer's constant preoccupation with the type. Finally, Balzac's definite elevation of the Romantic genius may have accentuated Hawthorne's reaction against Romanticism in this respect, and sharpened the examination of conscience in himself and others that led to the ultimate formation of one of his major themes, that of the 'unpardonable sin.' "

Howells

Blankenship, Russell. "William Dean Howells." In American Literature as an Expression of the National Mind. Rev. ed. New York: Henry Holt, 1949.

"Next to his Italian residence the greatest single influence that ever touched Howells was the work of Tolstoy, the great Russian humanitarian novelist. So strong an artistic and ethical force was Tolstoy, that Howells wrote scarcely a book after 1886 that does not in some way exhibit this influence. Tolstoy brought to Howells an intimate knowledge of the depths of human nature and a contemplation of life's problems that is tempered by an intense feeling of moral earnestness and responsibility. The first visible fruits of the Tolstoy influence was A Hazard of New Fortunes.... About the same time that he became interested in social conditions the novelist left Boston and established his residence in

New York. In his new home he was brought into close contact with cosmopolitan thought, with a brutal and ruthless economics, and with distressing social conditions. In grappling with the questions raised by these conditions and with the issues created by the rapidly shifting current of thought during the nineties, the social theory and example of Tolstoy were a fixed influence with Howells just as the artistic methods of the Russian were a constant guide in the writing of novels. Other books written under the influence of Tolstoy and sociological thought are _A Traveler from Altruria_ and _Through the Eye of the Needle_."

James

Adams, Percy G. "Young Henry James and the Lesson of his Master Balzac." _RLC_, 35 (1961), 458-67.

Among James's early works that seem to have borrowed characters and incidents from Balzac are _Washington Square_ and a number of short stories.

Auchincloss, Louis. "_Washington Square_ and 'The Aspern Papers.' " In _Reading Henry James_. Minneapolis: University of Minnesota Press, 1975.

Auchincloss acknowledges that _Washington Square_ is based on an anecdote that the actress Fanny Kemble told James yet suggests that Balzac's _Eugênie Grandet_ is the novel's literary ancestor and speculates that James may also have been influenced by Trollope's _Sir Harry Hotspur of Humblethwaite_. All three novels depict a young woman's heartbreak at the hands of a mercenary suitor. James, however, achieves the highest drama by making his heroine's father as despicable as her lover. "The girl never fully recovers from the double blow to her heart and pride that her lover and father inflict. Between them, they destroy her life. But it takes both--that is the point. In Balzac and Trollope the lover alone is the villain."

Bowman, Sylvia E. "Les Hêroines d'Henry James dans _The Portrait of a Lady_ et d'Yvan Tourgueniev dans _A La Veille_." _EA_, 11 (1958), 136-49.

James's Isabel and Turgenev's Ellen have characteristics in common, their lives are similarly affected by other characters and by incidents, and so on. In his preface to the novel James describes _The Portrait_ as "one much-embracing echo" of Turgenev, and at least as much is embraced as is echoed, for situations and dialogues are much more complex than in the Russian novel (which is only about a third of the length of James's), and the evolution of Isabel takes place much more slowly and laboriously.

Cargill, Oscar. "_The Princess Casamassima_: A Critical Reappraisal." _PMLA_, 71 (1956), 97-117; this essay appears as

"The Princess Casamassima" in Cargill's The Novels of Henry James, New York: Macmillan, 1961.
See the annotation of this item in Chapter 7, "Shakespeare and the Renaissance."

Deakin, Motley F. "Daisy Miller, Tradition, and the European Heroine." CLS, 6 (1969), 45-69.
That All-American Girl Daisy Miller is actually quite like the heroines of some of James's favorite European novelists: Turgenev, Cherbuliez, George Sand, and Madame de Staël. These heroines, like Daisy, are affected to one degree or another by the struggle between the individual's desire for freedom and society's disapprobation.

Dunbar, Viola. "A Source for Roderick Hudson," MLN, 63 (1948), 303-10.
Dunbar finds similarities of "plot, character development, and prevailing ideas" between James's novel and L'Affaire Clemenceau of Dumas fils (eight years before he began Roderick Hudson, James reviewed the Dumas novel in The Nation, October 11, 1866, noting that "since the taste of the age is for realism, all thanks for such realism as this").

Edel, Leon. "The Architecture of Henry James's 'New York Edition.' " NEQ, 24 (1951), 169-78.
In planning for and corresponding about the definitive edition of his work published by Scribner in 1907-09 James was very insistent about having twenty-three volumes and seemed vexed when the total turned out to be twenty-four. This, says Edel, is because he wanted to pattern his collected works after the Comédie Humaine, which numbers twenty-three volumes altogether. An analysis of the way in which James grouped his tales thematically reveals that he followed Balzac's lead here as well.

Fay, Eliot G. "Balzac and Henry James." French Review, 24 (1951), 325-30.
This article is not concerned with James's specific debts to Balzac but may prove useful as a succinct introduction to the elements in Balzac that James admired (his portrayal of characters, his evocation of atmosphere, his grasp of facts) and deplored (his materialism, his gassy philosophizing, his ponderous style).

Grover, Philip. Henry James and the French Novel: A Study in Inspiration. New York: Barnes & Noble, 1973.
Throughout his career James analyzed and assimilated the lessons of the major French writers of the nineteenth century. He learned the most (1) from Balzac, who taught the rendering of

characters' inward and outward lives by the accumulation of detail, the use of antithesis and foreshortening (the representation of "all the sense without all the surface"); (2) from Flaubert, who used the _style indirect libre_ (which permits the author "to move from his own narrative voice to the reported speech and thoughts of his characters without too great a break in the phrasing and movement of the prose" and "to pass from the most diverse spoken idioms to ... musical and carefully composed narrative phrases"); and (3) from the school of Gautier, whence he acquired his devotion to form and style as ends in themselves.

Perhaps James's most important link with the French is seen in his embrace of the idea that the world of art and civilization belongs to everyone. The "grandeurs, splendours, treasures and felicities" of civilization are not the toys of the privileged; thus it is not surprising that a naive girl like Isabel Archer appreciates the wonders of the civilized world while a jaded aristocrat like the Princess Casamassima is just as happy without them. But whereas James's "contemplative, passive and absorptive characters" want to take the world by assimilation, the "pragmatic, active and assertive" characters of Balzac and Maupassant want to take it through the acquisition of power. In this sense, then, James can be said to out-French even the French.

Grover's book includes a useful chronology of James's life with special reference to his readings in French literature. Surprisingly, nowhere does Grover refer to another excellent (if narrower) study, Lyall H. Powers's _Henry James and the Naturalist Movement_, which is described in Chapter 16 of this book, "Scientific Thinkers and Naturalists."

Habegger, Alfred. " 'The Siege of London': Henry James and the _Pièce Bien Faite_." _MFS_, 15 (1969), 219-30.
James's story not only openly refers to but is also based on two "well-made plays": _L'Aventurière_, by Emile Augier, and _Le Demi-monde_, by Dumas _fils_. When one considers how static the story is in comparison to the plays whence it came, one sees clearly why James was not successful as a playwright.

Hamilton, Eunice C. "Henry James's _The Princess Casamassima_ and Ivan Turgenev's _Virgin Soil_." _SAQ_, 61 (1962), 354-64.
Hamilton locates numerous correspondences between James's novel and Turgenev's, which James had not only read but reviewed (in _The Nation_, April 1877), before writing his.

Kelley, Cornelia Pulsifer. _The Early Development of Henry James_. Rev. ed. Urbana: University of Illinois Press, 1965.
From his earliest writings it is clear that James wanted to be the American Balzac, to describe society as a whole and "catch the tone of his time." From an 1875 article on the French writer, however, it is easy to see that James had apprehended not

only Balzac's strengths but also his weaknesses, notably his failure to make his art serve a high purpose. In Washington Square (1880), a novel influenced by Balzac's Eugènie Grandet, James demonstrates that he has abandoned his desire to be the American Balzac, for "there are points of difference as well as those of likeness, and James is not just an imitator for he adapts and even improves upon the materials and treatments of his predecessor."

Specifically, the characters and plot outline of Washington Square are Balzacian, but the focusing of attention on a single character, Catherine, is pure James. Thus "unity, compactness, intensity result to a degree which is unknown in Balzac's novel where the interest frequently strays to Grandet and his money bags and business affairs."

Lerner, Daniel. "The Influence of Turgenev on Henry James." Slavonic and East European Review, 20 (1941), 28-54.

A thoroughgoing study of the two authors' personal relationship; their shared belief in the essential rightness of the "dramatic novel"; their use of such character types as the ficelle and the "central detached observer" as well as such patterns as the "eternal triangle"; and the specific influence of Turgenev on certain James tales as well as such novels as Roderick Hudson, The American, The Portrait of a Lady, and The Princess Casamassima.

But at bottom, writes Lerner, there is a big difference between the two authors: "despite [Turgenev's] sympathy for the Hamlets, he emphasized the crucial importance to the world of its Don Quixotes. James, devotee of the sensibility, had no concern for any but the Hamlets." (Lerner borrows these terms from Turgenev's "famous dichotomy of human natures, Hamlet and Don Quixote.") See Cargill on James in Chapter 7, "Shakespeare and the Renaissance."

Long, Robert Emmet. "James's Roderick Hudson: The End of the Apprenticeship--Hawthorne and Turgenev." AL, 48 (1976-77), 312-26.

According to Long, James was moving away from Hawthorne's influence as he wrote Roderick Hudson: "As a novel dealing with the colony of American artists in Rome, Roderick Hudson begins where The Marble Faun left off; but in doing so, James subjects Hawthorne to the correction and refocusing of a cosmopolitan intelligence," namely, Turgenev's. From the Russian James took the character of the young sculptor Shubin (from On the Eve), an artist who, like Roderick, "cannot escape from the charmed circle of [his] own egotism." Apparently James was also affected by Turgenev's limited belief in the power of free will.

Maguire, C. E. "James and Dumas, fils." Modern Drama, 10 (1967), 34-42.

James reviewed L'Etrangère of Dumas fils with seemingly unnecessary asperity. The reason, says Maguire, is that a Mr. Clarkson in the play is painfully close to Christopher Newman in The American, which novel James was working on when he wrote the review. Clarkson has "Newman's background, his shrewdness, his attitude toward work and honesty, his respect for the reputedly weaker sex, his refusal to be awed by externals."

Niess, R. J. "Henry James and Emile Zola: A Parallel." RLC, 30 (1956), 93-98.
When Zola's L'Oeuvre appeared, he was accused of having plagiarized Balzac's "Le Chef-d'oeuvre Inconnu," which accusation he denied. Actually, says Niess, he may have been influenced by James's "The Madonna of the Future"--which itself was almost certainly influenced by the Balzac tale.

Pacey, W. C. D. "Henry James and His French Contemporaries." AL, 13 (1941-42), 240-56.
"It was their rendering of sense-impressions and their technical dexterity which attracted him, their lack of moral and intellectual insight (as he saw it) which repelled him. That was his early attitude towards French novelists, and it remained his attitude, with only slight modifications, throughout his life." Pacey notes two general resemblances between the novels of James and those of the French realists: both have as their primary goal the representation of life rather than the elaboration of a highly contrived plot, and both exalt objectivity à la Balzac over authorial expressions of sympathy and disdain à la Thackeray.

Tintner, Adeline R. "Balzac's 'Madame Firmiani' and James's The Ambassadors." CL, 25 (1973), 128-35.
An early Balzac story, "Madame Firmiani," is like The Ambassadors in several ways, not the least of which is that both deal with an older man who travels to Paris to rescue a younger one from the clutches of a woman who is thought to be wicked but turns out to be the young man's salvation.

"For James there never was really a time when La Comédie Humaine was not in his bloodstream," notes Tintner, although "this lifelong indebtedness was fully acknowledged by James but never documented in detail." In this and the following items the author does her scholarly best to fill the gap.

________. "Balzac's Two Maries and James's The Ambassadors." ELN, 9 (1972), 284-87.
In the James novel Marie de Vionnet and Maria Gostrey have functions similar to those of two characters also named Marie in Balzac's Une Fille d'Eve.

________. "Henry James's Decadent Novel: The Bostonians and

Balzac's 'La Fille aux yeux d'or.' " CL, 29 (1977), 241-54.

"During a short period in the 1880s Henry James appears to have been influenced by the contemporaneous French decadent novel. This 'curious' strain surfaced most visibly in The Bostonians which is usually approached solely in terms of its political theme.... A close analysis of The Bostonians reveals how James appropriated one of the progenitors of the decadent movement, 'La Fille aux yeux d'or,' which enabled him both to combine his interest in 'the antagonism of the sexes' with exoticism and to 'correct' the excesses of the decadent movement proper by his characteristic technique of criticizing a work of literature by 'redoing' it."

________. " 'High Melancholy and Sweet': James and the Arcadian Tradition." CLQ, 12 (1976), 109-21.

See the annotation of this item in Chapter 2, "The Classics."

________. "The House of Atreus and Mme. de Bellegarde's Crime." N&Q, 20 (1973), 98-99.

There is reason to believe that James intended for the careful reader of The American to guess that Monsieur de Cintré was the lover of Madame de Bellegarde, who married off her daughter Claire to him in order to keep up appearances. This is suggested by Claire's brother, Valentin, who says: "We are very good friends; we are such a brother and sister as have not been seen since Orestes and Electra"--whose mother, Clytemnestra, was also an adultress and a murderer who did away with Agamemnon so that she could install her lover on his throne. But the clincher is that in the 1907 revision James put these words as well into Valentin's mouth: "We're fit for a museum or a Balzac novel." Added to the reference to the House of Atreus, the mention of Balzac convinces Tintner of Madame de Bellegarde's adultery, for in "one of the best known short stories in La Comédie Humaine, 'Les Secrets de la Princesse de Cadignan,' Diane de Maufrigneuse herself was also the victim of an adulterous mother who had married off her daughter to her lover." And "in Le Curé de Village Veronique Graslin, a character deeply loved by James, repents after having spent a life of concealed adultery, having collaborated in a murder with her lover."

________. "Hyacinth at the Play: The Play Within the Play as a Novelistic Device in James." The Journal of Narrative Technique, 2 (1972), 171-85.

"La Comédie Humaine contains at least a dozen rich episodes that take place at the theatre which James, in his profound absorption in Balzac, may have either consciously or unconsciously reused in his own theatre scenes." The James novels discussed are The American, The Princess Casamassima, and The Ambassadors.

———. "The Influence of Balzac's *L'Envers de L'Histoire Contemporaine* on James's 'The Great Good Place.' " *SSF*, 9 (1972), 343-51.

The James story appeared in 1898, by which time, in the opinion of many of his critics, the Balzac influence had waned. Not so, asserts Tintner: "Even at this late date he is still technically dependent on Balzac. He continues to find models for institutions and characters, for the atmosphere in which they exist, for the language by which he makes them live, in the rich, concretely documented storehouse of *La Comédie Humaine*. The difference lies in the fact that now the Balzacian substance is filtered through his increasingly idiosyncratic temperament."

———. "Isabel's Carriage-Image and Emma's Day Dream." *MFS*, 22 (1976), 227-31.

When Isabel Archer of *The Portrait of a Lady* says that her idea of happiness is "a swift carriage, of a dark night, rattling with four horses over roads that one can't see" and Henrietta Stackpole says that she sounds like "the heroine of an immoral novel," the reference is clearly to Emma Bovary's similar daydream in *Madame Bovary*. Yet James complained (in *Notes on Novelists*) that Emma was inadequate for the great role in which Flaubert cast her. We know that Isabel was James's favorite heroine; thus we must assume that she is Emma corrected--Emma as she should have been.

———. "James's Mock Epic: 'The Velvet Glove,' Edith Wharton, and Other Late Tales." *MFS*, 17 (1971-72), 483-99.

Not primarily a source study, this essay cites in passing Balzac's "La Paix du Ménage" as a possible source for "The Velvet Glove," noting that "the tone of romantic irony as well as the strategies of narration involving postponement of discovery are markedly similar in these two stories of almost equal length."

———. " 'The Old Things': Balzac's *Le Curé de Tours* and James's *The Spoils of Poynton*." *NCF*, 26 (1972), 436-55.

Tintner establishes beyond doubt the influence of *Le Curé de Tours*, Balzac's novel about "the struggle for the possession of fine furniture and *objets de vertu*," on James's *The Spoils of Poynton*. She notes that "the man who wrote [in *French Poets and Novelists*] 'there is nothing in all imaginative literature that in the least resembles his [Balzac's] mighty passion for *things*--for material objects, for furniture, upholstery, bricks and mortar' ... would surely look to Balzac's drama of things when he came to write his own."

Tribble, Joseph L. "Cherbuliez's *Le Roman d'une Honnête Femme*: Another Source of James's *The Portrait of a Lady*." *AL*, 40 (1968-69), 279-93.

Critics have already pointed out the influence on James's novel of George Eliot's Daniel Deronda and Middlemarch; too, James probably had in mind his dead cousin Minny Temple when he painted his portrait of Isabel Archer. Yet "Le Roman d'une Honnête Femme, written by the Swiss author Victor Cherbuliez and published in 1866 [and mentioned by James in an October 1873 review of another Cherbuliez novel], is so similar in a number of respects to The Portrait of a Lady that it seems impossible to deny that it had an influence on James." Tribble shows how James "took the ingredients of a minor novel and used them to fashion a major work of art."

Vidan, Ivo. "The Princess Casamassima between Balzac and Conrad." Studia Romanica et Anglica Zagrabiensia, nos. 21-22 (1966), 259-76.

This carefully developed essay transcends not only the notion of merely national literatures but also the conventional one-to-one formula of many source studies. In describing a larger tradition Vidan traces the development of certain themes (art and anarchism) as treated in Balzac's Les Illusions Perdues that influenced James's novel, which in turn influenced Conrad's The Secret Agent.

Willett, Maurita. "Henry James's Indebtedness to Balzac." RLC, 41 (1967), 204-27.

A thoroughgoing analysis of the influence of Père Goriot on The American as well as a briefer discussion of James's relation to Balzac. On the whole James found Balzac's view too amoral and material: Rastignac wants to bring Paris to its knees, whereas Newman's vision is of a heaven-on-earth constituted of intense experience. Still, "what James eventually learned from Balzac," writes Willett, "was how to convey the substantiality of such a vision through the dense texture of details."

Norris

Walker, Franklin. "The Dentist." In Frank Norris: A Biography. Garden City: Doubleday, Doran, 1932.

See the annotation of this item in Chapter 16, "Scientific Thinkers and Naturalists."

16. SCIENTIFIC THINKERS AND NATURALISTS

The phrase "seam of history" was used in the preface to the chapter on the Romantics to indicate a verifiable demarcation between one era and another. One such seam is clearly visible where the Victorian Era ends and what we might call the Age of Science begins. Two paramount factors account for the changes that resulted in the new period in human history. First is the weakening of the power of religion, itself a result of two causes: the dissolution of a few highly centralized and seemingly perdurable faiths into myriad small sects, and the rise of the Higher Criticism, a school that approached the Bible from a geographical and historical viewpoint rather than a theological one. The second and more important factor that resulted in the new age was the impact of evolutionary science. For to question the fine points of one's religion may be merely to enjoy a sort of highly intellectual pastime, whereas to admit that humanity's basis is purely physical rather than spiritual, that its presence on earth is due to a series of biological accidents, is to surrender almost every religious idea worth having.

Thus in this Age of Science, wrote the American man of letters E. C. Stedman in 1875, "our school girls and spinsters wander down the lanes with Darwin and Huxley and Spencer under their arms; or if they carry Tennyson, Longfellow, and Morris, read them in the light of spectrum analysis." In an overstatement that suggests the topsy-turvy outlook of the new age Huxley himself referred to poetry as "sensual caterwauling," and a character in Turgenev's Fathers and Sons suggested that "a good chemist is twenty-times as useful as any poet."

What makes the Age of Science distinct from any other "new" period is the way in which its discoveries were put to use. Whatever can be said on that subject is as true now as it was in 1875 and will continue to be true as long as human knowledge is fragmented and specialized; that makes this a logical point at which the present survey may conclude. What must be taken into account is that a given scientific fact, of which there is potentially an infinite number, may be put to a greater number of uses than a theological belief. Thus the Age of Science, for all its surety, is a less sure age, for there are more hard facts now but fewer guiding principles to tell us how the facts should be handled. It is up to people to decide for themselves how the facts should be used, which is another way of saying that the old alliances no longer hold. There will always be a squabble between Intellectual and Bourgeois, Idealist and Materialist, Us and Them, only now there is more infighting as well: even in the Us camp, it is Me versus You versus Him and Her.

Of course not everyone is willing to let a few comforting truths be replaced by an infinite number of seemingly unrelated facts. In 1883 Charles Dudley Warner (who was promptly dubbed "Charles Deadly Warning" in the media) inveighed against what he saw as the consequences in fiction of the new outlook: overanalysis, morbidity, pessimism, despondency, emphasis on sordid details, and neglect of the possibility of happy endings. He called for a return to the novel of entertainment as written by Sir Walter Scott. In his reply to Warner (in an essay on Alphonse Daudet in The Century) Henry James disputed the notion that a novel had to be "as comfortable as one's stockings or as pretty as a Christmas card." Rather, "the main object of the novel is to represent life." Fiction as entertainment, fiction as fact: these are the mottoes of the warring camps in the debate over literary scientism that closed the century.

This preface draws on the following sources (see "List of Works Frequently Consulted" for full bibliographic information): Falk, p. 25, 119-20; John T. Frederick, The Darkened Sky: Nineteenth-Century American Novelists and Religion, Notre Dame: University of Notre Dame Press, 1969, p. xi-xii. Those studying particular foreign influences of a scientific or naturalistic bent may wish to consult Marius Biencourt, Une Influence du Naturalisme Française en Amérique: Frank Norris, Paris: Giard, 1933; Albert J. Salvan, Zola aux Etats-Unis, Providence: Brown University, 1943; and Jeremiah Joseph Sullivan, "The Influence of Hippolyte Taine on the Theory and Practice of Major American Writers: 1865-1910," DAI, 31 (1971), 4181-A.

The following studies are grouped under the names, listed alphabetically, of major American fiction writers through James who were influenced by foreign scientific thinkers and naturalists.

Crane

Ahnebrink, Lars. "Zola and Crane." In The Beginnings of Naturalism in American Fiction. New York: Russell & Russell, 1961.

A comparative analysis of Maggie: A Girl of the Streets and L'Assommoir shows that Crane was indebted to Zola "as to plot, characterization, technique, episodes, and particulars." Additionally, Crane's George's Mother owes to the Zola novel its concern with the effect of strong drink ("when drunk, man as Zola and Crane saw him sloughed off the thin veneer of civilization and revealed his animal nature"). Finally, "it seems probable that La Débâcle served as a model for The Red Badge of Courage for some matters of structure and tone as well as for certain episodes." Ahnebrink is cautious to note that, influenced as they are by Zola's writings, these Crane novels bear the unmistakable stamp of their author's originality.

For another opinion on Zola's influence see the next item as well as Colvert's "The Origins of Stephen Crane's Literary Creed" (annotated in Chapter 14, "The Victorians").

Colvert, James B. "The Red Badge of Courage and a Review of Zola's La Débâcle." MLN, 71 (1956), 98-100.

Colvert sides with those who say that Crane probably never read Zola's novel. The reason why The Red Badge resembles the French novel, maintains Colvert, is that Crane read a review of a translation of La Débâcle (The Downfall is the English title) which appeared in the July 10, 1892, New York Tribune. Crane would have been very likely to read this review since that issue of the paper contained a sketch of his called "The Broken-Down Van."

Bryant Mangum, in "Crane's Red Badge and Zola's," ALR, 9 (1976), 279-80, agrees that Crane may have been influenced by the review but argues that he read the translated novel as well and took from it his central image: Zola's "courageous" litter-bearers wear "red badges" in their caps.

Fitelson, David. "Stephen Crane's Maggie and Darwinism." American Quarterly, 16 (1964), 182-94.

After two early warnings (that Crane may not have understood or even read Darwin, and that Darwinism is a doctrine too complicated to be treated with precision in so brief an essay), Fitelson discusses the impact on Maggie of Darwinism as popularly and generally understood. Both "the Darwinian Idea," as he is careful to call it, and Crane's novel suggest that life is a struggle and survival is its only goal.

Stone, Edward. "Crane and Zola." ELN, 1 (1963), 46-47.

Stone thinks "the macabre description of Jim Conklin's death [in The Red Badge of Courage] can be traced to the death of Zola's alcoholic tinsmith Coupeau [in L'Assommoir]." Part of his evidence is that both men are described as dancing as if on hot plowshares.

In "Crane, Zola, and the Hot Ploughshares," ELN, 7 (1970), 285-87, Marston LaFrance suggests that the plowshares image (which refers to a medieval test for guilt) may have been suggested to either Crane or Zola by Shelley, Wordsworth, or Browning, all of whom used it in their work.

Howells

Arms, George. "The Literary Background of Howells's Social Criticism." AL, 14 (1942-43), 260-76.

This article discusses the influence on Howells of the Marxist Laurence Gronlund, the Atlantic Monthly coterie of Howells's day, and the Norwegian novelist Björnstjerne Björnson. Björnson "not only provided a pattern which may have been that of several of Howells's novels but in striking fashion anticipated the pattern of his career" (that is, in his change "from a democrat to a social and economic radical").

Clark, Harry Hayden. "The Role of Science in the Thought of W. D. Howells." TWA, 42 (1953), 263-303.
In outlook Howells was a "soft" evolutionist: he accepted Darwin's theories and their social implications but looked forward to the day when people might cooperate in the replacement of their animal tendencies with more civilized modes of behavior.

In practice Howells shows the influence of scientific methodology: "Howells seldom intrudes on the factual development of his story. He projects several characters with definite backgrounds in particular conditions and, in calm and rational language, describes, rather than directs, the resultant action.... His familiarity with the principles of evolutionary science led him to question whether the world was not one of chance and moral relativism. In a world of natural selection and hereditary and environmental determinism, moral judgments are inconclusive, and it is this which explains in large measure Howells' tendency to withhold moral judgment in his novels. He seldom blames or praises; in general, he places his characters in definite conditions and lets them interact."

James

Clark, Harry Hayden. "Henry James and Science: The Wings of the Dove." TWA, 52 (1963), 1-15.
This well-argued essay shows how writers can reflect their times and yet remain true to their own vision. The Wings is shot through with Social Darwinism; in particular, the animal imagery reminds us of the savage materialism of the English upper classes, which, as James said in a letter, was "in many ways very much the same rotten and collapsible one as that of the French aristocracy before the revolution--minus cleverness and conversation." But the note of renunciation on which this and other James novels end is proof that ethics can triumph over grabbiness--it's a question, writes Clark, of "a free-willed renunciation of something of price for something priceless, especially for one's self-respect."

Cromer, Viris. "James and Ibsen." CL, 25 (1973), 114-25.
In his four published reviews of Ibsen plays as well as in his notebooks and letters James indicates a distaste for their content while acknowledging what he described as their "rare mastery of form." In an 1893 letter James wrote: "Yes, Ibsen is ugly, common, hard, prosaic, bottomlessly bourgeois.... And yet of his art he's a master." Ibsen confirmed James's resolve to employ, among other technical devices, the scenic method of narration.

Dietrichson, Jan W. "Henry James and Emile Zola." In Americana-Norvegica. Norwegian Contributions to American

Studies, ed. Sigmund Skard, vol. 2. Philadelphia: University of Pennsylvania Press, 1968.

After reviewing the known data concerning James's personal and professional knowledge of Zola and discussing the former's disapproval of the latter's intellectual and moral grossness (as well as his admiration of, among other things, the seriousness and honesty of the naturalists in general) Dietrichson concludes that Zola had little significant influence on James. In composing The Princess Casamassima and The Bostonians, however, James did adopt a couple of tricks that he could have learned from no one other than the French author, e.g., the habit of jotting down street expressions (such as "he cuts it very fine" or "that takes the gilt off, you know") that later found their way into The Princess.

Edwards, Herbert. "Henry James and Ibsen." AL, 24 (1952-53), 208-23.

James was familiar with two dramatic techniques in his late career, "the well-made technique of Dumas, Scribe, and Sardou" and "the naturalistic technique of Ibsen." In James's plays, most of which were written under the assumption that the drama was a second-rate form for undiscriminating audiences, we see the unmistakable mark of "Sardoudledom," with "its heavily plotted complexity, its marionette characters," and so on. Fortunately James took Ibsen for his model when it came to novel-writing: the "attainment of the Greek ideal of absolute unity and symmetry by Ibsen, frequently mentioned by critics, James was possibly the first critic, in English, to recognize, and he was likewise the first novelist to attain that ideal fully in the English novel." Edwards then briefly contrasts the structures of Rosmersholm and The Golden Bowl to make his point.

Egan, Michael. Henry James: The Ibsen Years. London: Vision Press, 1972.

As late as 1889 "the example of Sardoodledom, of the Scribean pièce bien faite, still reigned supreme" in the British theater. It was Ibsen who broke down the hold of the well-made play with its contrived plot and inevitable happy ending, and when he was denounced as "a corruptor of innocents and virgins, a purveyor of sex, socialism and feminine emancipation," James was one of the many who flocked to his support.

Actually James's attitude toward Ibsen wavered between admiration and hostility over the years, notes Egan (but is this not usually the case with an influence so strong that from time to time it must be resisted?). This is to say that Ibsen's influence can be seen to wax and wane in James's work. His impact on James is seen most obviously in The Other House, which is "pure Ibsen, unalloyed, undistilled and hawked directly from the pages of Hedda Gabler and Rosmersholm."

Ibsen's themes are put to a subtler and better use in The Turn of the Screw, which, like Ghosts, shows the terrible impact that adult lives can have on youthful ones. Although in the Ibsen play the corruption of the young is literal (little Oswald Alving dies of congenital syphilis), both works derive a major part of their horror from "the unnatural old age which besets the children as a consequence of their contact with the demons," a "perversion of nature" in the form of "premature old age which dehydrates youth and consumes its beauty."

Egan's final and most important point--a point that seems curious at first yet that proves to be extremely well taken--is that it was Ibsen who showed James how to be an American. *The Wings of the Dove*, like *Hedda Gabler* and *John Gabriel Borkman*, deals with "a sexual triangle composed of personalities in a situation not wholly of their own making." It is also James's finest novel and one in which he returns to the New England literary tradition to deal with something approaching "Hawthorne's sense of evil and moral transgression." But it is Ibsen who showed James how to avoid Hawthorne's allegorical rigidity and substitute in its place a vital dramatic quality (*The Wings* can even be broken down into a five-act dramatic structure complete with separate scenes).

So whereas source hunters unable to appreciate the full meaning of their discoveries might simply make James into warmed-over Ibsen, Egan demonstrates the subtle yet distinct way in which genius speaks to genius across the barriers of time, space, and language.

Powers, Lyall H. *Henry James and the Naturalist Movement.* East Lansing: Michigan State University Press, 1971.

Though James was never a naturalist per se, he was nonetheless highly influenced by the writers he called "the grandsons of Balzac": Flaubert, the Goncourts, Turgenev, Zola, Daudet, and Maupassant. Chapters I and II deal with James's first contact with the naturalists, his initial feeling of alienation from them, and, finally, his enthusiastic embrace of their principles. As Powers demonstrates, the most important aesthetic principle that James had in common with the naturalists was that of creating a faithful reproduction of life, or at least the illusion thereof--to try, as Maupassant put it, for "la vérité, rien que la vérité, toute la vérité."

Chapters III, IV, and V deal with *The Bostonians* ("James's initial attempt to write a novel in the naturalistic mode"), *The Princess Casamassima*, and *The Tragic Muse*. Powers concludes with a brief treatment of *The Ambassadors*, a novel that "to a considerable extent fulfilled the promise of development which Naturalism held," because it represents the trend away from the lives of common men and toward the more rarefied strata of humanity. "The success of realism lies there and there alone," wrote Edmond de Goncourt in 1879, "and no longer in the literary rabble."

Segnitz, T. M. "The Actual Genesis of Henry James's 'Paste.'" *AL*, 36 (1964-65), 216-19.

The supposed genesis of James's story is Maupassant's "La Parure," because that is the source that James himself cited. Evidently the Master was mistaken, however, because "Paste" is much closer in plot and specific details to another Maupassant story, "Les Bijoux."

Steegmuller, Francis. "Flaubert's Sundays: Maupassant and Henry James." Cornhill Magazine, 163 (1948), 124-30.

Not a source study per se, this essay will be of interest nonetheless to those concerned with the James-Maupassant connection. Steegmuller vividly recreates Flaubert's Sundays, which were attended by Turgenev, Taine, Daudet, Zola, Huysmans, Hérédia, and Edmond de Goncourt. Maupassant and James were decidedly lesser lights in such a company (they were twenty-five and thirty-two respectively) and frequently had only each other to talk to. The stage was thus set for a lifelong relationship, the fruits of which are indicated by, among other evidence, James's frequent references to Maupassant's work in his published notebooks.

Sullivan, Jeremiah J. "Henry James and Hippolyte Taine: The Historical and Scientific Method in Literature." CLS, 10 (1973), 25-50.

Probably Sullivan's most striking revelation is that "James's 1875 essay on Balzac followed Taine's 1858 essay point by point, idea for idea, generalization for generalization." According to Taine, Balzac produced representative characters via "the scientific and historical method of evolving types and general characteristics from an accumulation of data," a method James used in producing such representative types as Christopher Newman and Daisy Miller.

Frederick S. Frank's "The Two Taines of Henry James," RLC, 45 (1971), 350-65, does not deal with influence but does shed light on James's ambivalent attitude toward the French thinker.

Warren, Austin. "Henry James: Symbolic Imagery in the Late Novels." In Rage for Order. Chicago: University of Chicago Press, 1948.

"In poetic drama--The Tempest (on which he wrote an essay), the plays of Racine, Maeterlinck, and Ibsen--James came nearest to finding precedents for his later novels." James borrowed from these dramatists two devices: close conversation (his characters are given to "close, minute, unwearying analysis") and metaphor. These devices correspond to "two modes of knowing: dialectic and myth."

Melville

Foster, Elizabeth. "Melville and Geology." AL, 17 (1945-46), 50-65.

From Sir Charles Lyell's Elements of Geology and other works, Melville learned about "those discoveries of the new science which were proving most dangerous to religious faith in the nineteenth century: the vast antiquity of our planet; the gradual changes of the earth through the operation of natural causes; the rise and extinction of species in era after era; the appearance, in succeeding ages, of related forms and increasingly higher forms, which tended to discredit doctrines of special creation; and perhaps the theory that species were not fixed but were developed from common antecedent types."

The specific scientific works that Melville may have read are discussed in further detail in Tyrus Hillway, "Melville's Geological Knowledge," AL, 21 (1949-50), 232-37, and Foster's "Another Note on Melville and Geology," AL, 22 (1950-51), 479-87.

Mansfield, Luther S., and Howard P. Vincent. "Explanatory Notes" to Moby-Dick. New York: Hendricks House, 1952.

The authors attribute one of Melville's prefatory "Extracts" to Darwin's Voyage of the Beagle.

Norris

Ahnebrink, Lars. "Zola and Norris." In The Beginnings of Naturalism in American Fiction. New York: Russell & Russell, 1961.

"Norris, whose works reveal the greatest debt to Zola of the three writers concerned [the others are Crane and Hamlin Garland], was no doubt the one who was best acquainted with Zola's works, and the one who, temperamentally, was most akin to the French master. The familiar signs of Zola's influence are found in almost all of Norris's novels, but most notably in McTeague, Vandover and the Brute, The Octopus, and The Pit. The novels which seem to have appealed particularly to Norris are: Thérèse Raquin, L'Assommoir, Nana, Germinal, La Terre, La Bête humaine, and L'Argent. Norris's aim in McTeague was similar to Zola's in Thérèse Raquin: to study two different temperaments [those of a strong, slow man and a nervous woman] and to record the influence they exerted on each other. Norris's novel is also obviously indebted to L'Assommoir for matters of plot and episodes. The subplot seems to have been modeled on an episode in La Bête humaine. Vandover and the Brute presents similarities of method and character to Thérèse Raquin, La Bête humaine, and L'Assommoir. The Octopus is indebted to Germinal for certain ideas, part of the plot, and characterization, to La Bête humaine for episodes, and to La Terre for suggestions of the treatment of rural life. Finally, L'Argent suggested points of plot, descriptive technique, and some episodes in The Pit, in which there occur reminiscences from Nana and L'Assommoir."

Ahnebrink notes that Norris, like Crane and Garland, used

Zolaesque materials with moderation and restraint; in effect, he "toned down ... the extreme naturalism of Zola."

Lundy, Robert D. "Introduction" to The Octopus. New York: Sagamore Press, 1957.
Because Norris is indebted to Zola for scenes and techniques, critics have wrongly assumed that Norris borrowed as well "Zola's materialistic determinism, which asserts that man is the pawn of blind forces." Actually Norris believed in "evolutionary transcendentalism," which is quite opposed to Zola's belief since it posits that every evil leads to some higher good and that individuals are both free and responsible. Implicitly, Lundy reminds us that authors do not necessarily borrow the entire stock of those to whom they are obviously in debt.

Martin, Willard E., Jr. "Frank Norris's Reading at Harvard College." AL, 7 (1935-36), 203-04.
The record of books borrowed by Norris during his year at Harvard (1894-95) shows that he read Daudet, the Goncourt brothers, and Zola, among others, during the period when he was thought to have all but completed McTeague.

Pizer, Donald. "Introduction" to The Novels of Frank Norris. Bloomington: Indiana University Press, 1966.
Because it presented a disturbing picture of life ruled by chaos and chance the Darwinian hypothesis, though intellectually respectable, had to be reconciled with the basic tenets of established religion before it could be acceptable to the masses. One popularizer of Darwin was Norris's teacher Joseph LeConte, whose ideas may be reduced to a belief in God's existence, however harsh some of His laws, and the division of the human being into two selves, the animal one, which developed through evolution, and the spiritual one, which distinguishes humanity from the baser creatures. Norris used these ideas throughout his career: "In Vandover and McTeague he dramatized the fall of men who succumbed to bestiality, as natural laws destroy those men who have not kept pace with evolutionary progress, who are handicapped in the struggle for existence by their atavistic bestiality. In his 'middle trilogy' of popular novels--Moran of the Lady Letty, Blix, and A Man's Woman--he went on to develop a theme implicit in Vandover and McTeague, the ability of man to exploit for good his dual nature rather than be a victim of it--to use brute force, with the aid of 'a man's woman,' to invigorate moral strength and strength of purpose. In his incomplete trilogy of the wheat, and particularly in The Octopus, he described man's ability to perceive the cosmic processes and laws of nature and thereby ally himself with them and fully discover and obey God."

Taylor, Gordon O. "The Voice of Want: Norris and Dreiser."

In Passages of Thought: Psychological Representation in the American Novel, 1870-1900. New York: Oxford University Press, 1969.

Though an important factor in such novels as Roderick Hudson, The Portrait of a Lady, A Modern Instance, and Maggie: A Girl of the Streets, "sexuality never really emerges in the work of James or Howells or Crane as a subject of intrinsic psychological interest, as an aspect of real experience requiring (or allowed) careful psychological scrutiny." Norris's treatment of McTeague's confused yet powerful sexual yearnings for Trina Sieppe (in McTeague) is "as dependent on the popular Darwinism he learned from LeConte while a student at Berkeley as James's and Howells's portrayals of their earliest heroines' minds are dependent on the essentially Christian (if by then fully secularized) conventions of innocence."

Walcutt, Charles Child. "Frank Norris and the Search for Form." In American Literary Naturalism, A Divided Stream. Minneapolis: University of Minnesota Press, 1956.

Quoting Norris's biographer, Franklin Walker (see next three items), Walcutt establishes the novelist's youthful admiration for the works of Emile Zola. He then compares The Octopus with the Zola novel it most closely resembles, Germinal. Their common characteristics include (1) epic sweep, (2) the use of symbols to express vividly the forces that determine the characters' fates, and (3) the centrality of an economic institution that dominates the characters' lives. Walcutt cautions that "if these similarities represent an influence of Zola upon Norris it is a literary influence, a matter of method, of storytelling, that has no necessary relation to the philosophy of naturalism."

Indeed, The Octopus might have turned out the masterpiece it was clearly intended to be had Norris learned better the lesson of Zola, for when one begins to consider the dissimilarities between the two novels one apprehends the consistent and explicit yet unobtrusive nature of Zola's naturalism as opposed to Norris's muddle of naturalism, free will, and something Walcutt calls "natural dynamism" (according to which nature is seen as a conscious and benign force). Zola describes the clash between the mine owners and the miners in Germinal as inevitable and admitting of no possible outcome except a revolution that would create a system under which conflict is not possible. Norris's novel is more open-ended because more incoherent and, in places, merely orotund.

Walker, Franklin. "Blix." In Frank Norris: A Biography. Garden City: Doubleday, Doran, 1932.

Norris was a staff member of the San Francisco Wave, to which he contributed a number of stories. "Several times he apparently attempted to adapt Maupassant's studies of abnormal psychological types to his portrayal of degeneration, notably in A Case for Lombroso and His Single Blessedness. Admiration of Maupassant may also have led him to his use of mystery and horror in such stories as The Strangest Thing, The House with the Blinds, and The Third Circle."

________. "The Dentist." In Frank Norris: A Biography. Garden City: Doubleday, Doran, 1932.

Zola's L'Assommoir, Nana, and La Bête humaine guided Norris's writing of McTeague: "One need hardly point out that the detailed portrayal of the weakening of Gervaise Macquart had much to do with the treatment of McTeague and Trina. In addition, the Zolaesque multiplication of details, emphasis on strong sensory descriptions, particularly of smell, and use of contrast and symbolism are apparent."

There are also similarities between Norris's novel and Flaubert's Madame Bovary: "For instance, the mentalities and professions of McTeague and Charles Bovary, the argumentative natures of Marcus Schuler and Homais, and the descriptions of bourgeois festivals, such as the marriage of the principal characters, the theater performances, and the selling of the family furniture. Moreover, Norris is like Flaubert in his ability to focus on his major characters--dull people made miraculously interesting--to limit the milieu to its direct bearing on their action, and to build the plot organically about them."

________. "Naturalism." In Frank Norris: A Biography. Garden City: Doubleday, Doran, 1932.

"In Vandover and the Brute, Frank Norris followed the Zolaistic formula more closely than in any of his later novels. Impressed by Zola's portrayal of the degeneration of Gervaise and Jacques Coupeau in L'Assommoir, of Claude Lantier in L'Oeuvre, and of Jacques Lantier in La Bête humaine, he wrote a story which centered about a character from his own world, Vandover, telling his life from birth to disaster, picturing the gradual physical and moral decay of his too pliable, sensitive nature, subjecting him to misfortunes of circumstances which pile one upon another. In this book the conception of his principal character is much more imitative than is McTeague, for Vandover is the victim of inherent weakness of will and constant misfortune--a common naturalistic type--whereas the brutish McTeague in his rise and fall of fortune is original in conception and portrayal."

Ziff, Larzer. "Life Without Style: Frank Norris." In The American 1890s: Life and Times of a Lost Generation. New York: Viking, 1966.

At Berkeley, Norris was highly influenced by Joseph LeConte, geologist and popularizer of Darwin. LeConte wrote: "The stronger the lower is, the better, if only it be held in subjection. For the higher is nourished and strengthened by its connection with the more robust lower, and the lower is purified, refined, and glorified by its connection with the divine higher, and by this mutual action the whole plane of being is elevated."

By "lower" and "higher" LeConte meant humanity's sensual cravings and its reason, although it is easy to draw a parallel in the social structure and conclude, as many of LeConte's followers did, that the lower classes must be dominated of necessity by the upper. Since "a constant push and pull between upper and lower within man and between classes was a condition of health, moving both individuals and society to a higher plane," then "in the long run all conflict was for the best." Ziff says of Norris's adherence to LeConte's ideas: "Norris was the full beneficiary of both the literary merits and literary vices that were consequences of popular Darwinism. If his uncritical acceptance of it finally kept him from being a great writer, the genius which was released, once this handle to the world was grasped, brought into American literature not only a new cast of characters but a closer observation and shrewder delineation of the problems they shared with their fellows--not the least of which was sexuality."

Twain

Baender, Paul. "Alias Macfarlane: A Revision of Mark Twain Biography." AL, 38 (1966-67), 187-97.

In a manuscript Twain claims to have roomed in Cincinnati in 1856-57 with a pre-Darwinian pessimist named Macfarlane, whose conversation much influenced Twain's later views. Baender argues that the manuscript is largely rhetorical in nature (many students of Twain have accepted Macfarlane as real), even though it does contain autobiographical material.

Cummings, Sherwood. "Mark Twain's Social Darwinism." Huntington Library Quarterly, 20 (1957), 163-75.

Twain began his career as a social idealist. Later, depressed by business problems and personal tragedies, he developed a materialistic and pessimistic outlook shaped by his readings of Darwin and Huxley; "then it seemed to him that men were animals who lived by jungle law, that in society, business, and conquest they engaged in amoral competition in which the prize went to the strongest." Thus in Following the Equator (1897), he acquiesces in the rightness of imperialism as inevitable.

Later, however, Twain's social idealism asserted itself in a measure; through the periodicals he and Howells attacked imperialism in the Congo and elsewhere. As Cummings puts it, "from 1890 to 1900 he had been a social Darwinist most of the time; for the next ten years he would be one part of the time."

________. "Mark Twain's Acceptance of Science." Centennial Review, 6 (1962), 245-61.

A short yet comprehensive survey of Twain's alternate acceptance and rejection of findings during his lifetime in the fields of geology, astronomy, and evolutionary theory. "Accepting the conclusions of the scientists, he worked as best he could toward an understanding of the cosmos, except when now and then he was swamped by the nostalgic vision of a simple, common-sense world surrounded by 'the august secrets of the Deity.' Then it seemed to him that scientists were meddlers, destroyers, and dupes of theory."

________. "Science and Mark Twain's Theory of Fiction." PQ, 37 (1958), 26-33.

"From his reading in (among others) Darwin, who demonstrated the inexorable influence of environment on organic life, and Taine, who applied the Darwinian theory of environment to human society, Twain undoubtedly received instruction in the formulation of his own explicitly stated theory that fictional characters achieve reality only when depicted with reference to their formative environment. Furthermore, an examination of his most vivid novels--Tom Sawyer, Huckleberry Finn, and Pudd'nhead Wilson--shows how fully he implemented his theory."

Hill, Hamlin L., Jr. "Mark Twain's 'Brace of Brief Lectures on Science.' " NEQ, 34 (1961), 228-39.

Two spoofs on paleontology (herein reprinted) show that Twain "was aware of and to some extent sympathetic with the problems and methods of science even though he was also aware of the possibilities of their comic exploitation."

Krause, Sydney J. "Howe and Zola." In Mark Twain as Critic. Baltimore: Johns Hopkins Press, 1967.

Reading La Terre, Zola's novel of fraud, murder, and rape among members of a peasant family, may have helped Twain to get over his populist attitudes and could have affected the writing of A Connecticut Yankee. "There is at least an outside possibility," says Krause, "that his reading of La Terre was one of the factors that made Twain turn on his American democrat and brutalize him."

Rogers, Rodney O. "Twain, Taine, and Lecky: The Genesis of a Passage in A Connecticut Yankee." MLQ, 34 (1973), 436-47.

See the annotation of this item in Chapter 14, "The Victorians."

Waggoner, Hyatt. "Science in the Thought of Mark Twain." AL, 8 (1936-37), 357-70.

Twain had a "comparatively comprehensive" knowledge of science and was particularly influenced by two books, Darwin's Descent of Man and Huxley's Evolution and Ethics. It is widely known now that such influences confirmed Twain's fundamental pessimism, so perhaps Waggoner's most important contribution in this essay is his demonstration of the purpose to which Twain put his scientific reading--in Waggoner's words, Twain had the "habit of expressing his doctrines in semi-scientific terms, and then illustrating them with homely similes from experience."

Wilson, James D. "'The Monumental Sarcasm of the Ages': Science and Pseudoscience in the Thought of Mark Twain." South Atlantic Bulletin, 40 (1975), 72-82.

A consideration of Twain's contemptuous treatment of the pseudoscience of phrenology and faith healing is likely to open the reader's mind to Twain's disdain for much of authentic science. This is not to gainsay Waggoner's study (above); rather it is to emphasize Twain's ambivalence toward science, as pointed out by Hill (also above).

APPENDIX A: General Studies of the Influence of Foreign Cultures on American Fiction

---

Asselineau, Roger. "The French Stream in American Literature." Yearbook of Comparative and General Literature, 17 (1968), 29-39.

"During the first decade of the nineteenth century, the United States tried to shake off the influence of England in order to attain its intellectual independence. Throughout this transitional period French influences helped American writers to break from English thought and literature and to find themselves." Of particular importance in this respect, says Asselineau, is Emerson's debt to Montaigne.

Concerning novelists, Asselineau notes James's and Norris's predilection for the French Realists and Naturalists and Howells's aversion to them. Commenting on the present century, he disagrees with Philip Rahv and asserts that "there are no Red Indians in American literature. Even Whitman, Dreiser, and Hemingway have read French books and profited by them. They are Pale Faces disguised as Red Indians and all of them have French blood in their veins." (Rahv's distinction, of course, is between "Palefaces" and "Redskins.")

Denny, Margaret, and William H. Gilman, eds. The American Writer and European Tradition. Minneapolis: University of Minnesota Press, 1965.

Essays on various topics by such distinguished scholars as Robert E. Spiller, Henry Nash Smith, Alfred Kazin, Lionel Trilling and Harry Levin. In their introduction the editors observe that "if American scholars are to make full critical judgments of an American writer, they must always consider the extent to which the European tradition influenced him."

Horton, Rod W., and Herbert W. Edwards. Backgrounds of American Literary Thought. 3d ed. Englewood Cliffs: Prentice-Hall, 1974.

Although the emphasis in this comprehensive guide is on the domestic intellectual, social, political, and economic currents underlying American literature, attention is given to Puritanism, Enlightenment thought, Marxism, Naturalism, and so on.

Jones, Howard Mumford. American and French Culture. Chapel Hill: University of North Carolina Press, 1927.

Jones is perhaps our most accomplished interdisciplinary and cross-cultural scholar. Only a study as painstaking and as orderly as this one could permit the following conclusion, which, though anomalous, is convincing in light of the impressively solid scholarship that precedes it: "On the whole it is in the departments of manners and fashions that the French have exerted their most notable influence in shaping American culture. In intellectual matters they have had vogue rather than influence. The popular notion that the representative institutions of America owe much to Rousseau does not appear to be historically sound, and if Montesquieu played an important part in shaping the constitution, he yet derives from English thought and was useful largely because he so clearly represented the English idea at a time when hostility to England was great.... It does not appear that a knowledge of the French language was widely diffused except in upper social circles; nor has the total French immigration seriously colored the complexion of the American people. And yet, when all this is admitted, it yet remains true that no continental nation until the rise of German influence has possessed the social prestige of France."

Lombard, Charles. "The American Attitude Toward the French Romantics (1800-1861)." RLC, 39 (1965), 358-71.

"Several factors would explain the enthusiasm with which the French Romantics were often received. Much in their writing was marvelously suited to the literary and social outlook in America. Their revolt against classicism was appreciated in a country with fresh memories of a successful revolution. In the wilderness of the New World the praises of nature sung by Rousseau, Chateaubriand, Hugo, and Lamartine acquired new meaning. Adventurous spirits clamoring for social justice welcomed the liberal views of Mme de Staël and George Sand. Devout Americans distrustful of the Enlightenment and Jacobinism were once more favorably disposed towards French culture by the religious themes in Chateaubriand and Lamartine.... While often primarily concerned with England and Germany, American intellectuals in the first part of the nineteenth century still found time to study the implications of French Romanticism, a school they treated on the whole with considerable understanding, insight, and recognition of both its good and bad points."

Pochmann, Henry A. German Culture in America: Philosophical and Literary Influences, 1600-1900. Madison: University of Wisconsin Press, 1957.

This massive (nearly 900-page) text merits all of the praise that has been heaped upon it and then some. The title is self-explanatory; see annotations of individual sections in the preceding pages.

Wilkens, Frederick H. Early Influence of German Literature in America. New York: Macmillan, 1900.

Individual sections deal with the American reception of German drama, such German fictional forms as the tale of terror and the sentimental family novel (*Familienroman*), German poetry, and German philosophy, theology, and pedagogy. Wilkens's main concern is the interest German works had for the general public, though passing reference is made to such authors as Charles Brockden Brown and to such nonliterary figures as John Quincy Adams, here referred to, for reasons that are not quite clear, as "the father of German studies in America." There is a very useful appendix consisting of "A List of Translations of German Literature That Were Printed in the United States Before 1826."

Williams, Stanley T. *The Spanish Background of American Literature.* 2 vols. New Haven: Yale University Press, 1955.

The first volume of this exhaustive study deals with the origins of Spanish culture in America and its effect on nineteenth- and twentieth-century American authors. Mention is made of the Spanish-American influence on Melville's *Benito Cereno* and "The Encantadas"; the effect of *Don Quixote* on Twain's *Huckleberry Finn* and *Connecticut Yankee*; and tne impact of Cervantes and the picaresque novelists, as well as that of contemporary Spanish Realists, on the thought and writings of William Dean Howells. The second volume consists of eight essays on individual American interpreters of Spanish culture; expanding on his earlier remarks on Howells, Williams notes that both Cervantes and the picaresque novelists and the contemporary Realists influenced and supported Howells's fundamental belief in portraying the world as it is and in dealing with ordinary events.

Extended coverage is given in the second volume to Washington Irving. "Irving's seven years in Spain," writes Williams, "as well as his several thousand pages of history and fiction inspired by this country, make his interpretation peculiar to himself. No other major American writer of the nineteenth century became through residence and use of materials so deeply identified with any one Continental nation." Notable among Irving's Spanish-influenced writings are his semifictional *Conquest of Granada* ("a kind of freak romance with a disconcerting alloy of truth") and the more successful *Alhambra*, a collection of sketches and stories that Williams calls "the most distinguished literary work on Spain written by an American before 1850."

APPENDIX B: Studies of the Reading Habits of Individual Authors

---

Hawthorne

Kesselring, Marion L. Hawthorne's Reading, 1828-1850. New York: New York Public Library, 1949. Reprinted from BNYPL, 53 (1949), 55-71, 121-38, 173-94.

The records of the Salem Athenaeum reveal that Hawthorne read not only widely but also systematically; e.g., he checked out volume after volume of The Gentleman's Magazine in regular sequence and from 1829 through 1831 he planned a course in French literature that included Montaigne, Rousseau, Richelieu, Fénelon, Racine, Corneille, and Maintenon. He read the standard English authors of the eighteenth and nineteenth centuries; he used anthologies and encyclopedias "as a means of broadening his knowledge efficiently"; and he seemed to have had an especially strong penchant for books about travel to exotic lands. Kesselring's summary is followed by a compilation of individual books read by Hawthorne.

This study may be supplemented by the chapter entitled "Hawthorne: Life and Readings" in Jane Lundblad, Nathaniel Hawthorne and European Literary Tradition, New York: Russell & Russell, 1965.

Melville

Mansfield, Luther S. "Some Aspects of Melville's Reading." In Herman Melville: Author and New Yorker, 1844-1851. Chicago: University of Chicago Libraries, 1938.

Deals with books Melville was known to have reviewed, bought, or borrowed (largely from his friend Evert Duyckinck). Among the authors read who may also have influenced Melville's writings are Shakespeare, Sir Thomas Browne, Rabelais, and Esaias Tegner. Of the latter's Frithiof's Saga Mansfield notes: "Certainly the heroic style of parts of Mardi and of Moby Dick owed something to the bold measures of the Swedish poem."

Other authors listed by Mansfield whom Melville may have read but whose putative influence is not discussed here include Carlyle, Dickens, Goethe, the eighteenth-century English novelists, the Victorian poets, the Gothic writers, and the authors of the great picaresque novels.

Sealts, Merton M., Jr. Melville's Reading: A Check-List of Books

Owned and Borrowed. Madison: University of Wisconsin Press, 1966.

A revised and enlarged version of a study first published serially in the Harvard Library Bulletin, this compilation includes 567 separate entries, a number of which consist of more than one item (e.g., the thirty-seven-volume Harper's Classical Library). Perhaps despairing of an attempt at systematically analyzing the tastes of a reader as eclectic as Melville, Sealts instead discusses briefly what the author of Moby-Dick read during the different periods of his life. (However, one cannot but note that one of the first books Melville encountered in his father's library was Burton's Anatomy of Melancholy and that he was reading Schopenhauer during his final illness--fit choices for this somberest of authors.)

Poe

Campbell, Killis. "Poe's Reading." Studies in English (University of Texas), no. 5 (1925), 166-96.

According to Campbell, Poe knew the following authors fairly well: Shakespeare, Milton, Byron, Coleridge, Moore, Bulwer, Dickens, Disraeli, Tennyson, William Harrison Ainsworth, and E. B. Browning. He was at least acquainted with the chief Greek and Latin writers, Dante, Cervantes, the great French playwrights, the German transcendental philosophers, and such English essayists as Macaulay, Hazlitt, and Lamb. Campbell says Poe knew nothing of Jane Austen, Thackeray, and Robert Browning, but in "Poe's Reading: Addenda and Corrigenda," Studies in English, no. 7 (1927), 175-80, he notes that Poe owned a copy of Browning's Strafford, which had apparently been presented to him by its author.

Twain

Gribben, Alan. " 'Good Books and A Sleepy Conscience': Mark Twain's Reading Habits." ALR, 9 (1965), 295-306.

Of marginal value as a source study, this essay nonetheless gives the lie to Twain's reputation as an unlettered funny man and dispels whatever doubt may remain about his being a reader of "finical thoroughness" who used his own system of annotation and frequently noted, next to offensive passages, the reasons for his disapprobation.

________. " 'I Kind of Love Small Game': Mark Twain's Library of Literary Hogwash." ALR, 9 (1965), 65-76.

A discussion of Twain's "affection for bad writing" followed by an annotated bibliography of his especial favorites, including, typically, The Sentimental Song Book, by Julia A. Moore (Gribben notes that "it is generally agreed that the didactic doggerel of this farmer's wife inspired Emmeline Grangerford's lugubrious elegies in Huckleberry Finn"). Later, Twain decided that the Irish poet Emanda M'Kittrick Ros had succeeded Moore as "Empress of the Hogwash Guild."

Hemminghaus, Edgar H. "Mark Twain's German Provenience." MLQ, 6 (1945), 459-78.
It is clear that "Mark Twain's approach to the Germans, their language, and their literature was unquestionably one of great amicability and affectionate admiration. Through personal observations, contacts, and extensive reading he attained a comprehensive understanding of the German soul." Twain read Heine in the original, he knew something of Goethe's works, and he was an enthusiastic admirer of Schiller, Martin Luther, and Nietzsche, among others.

INDEX

This index covers the sixteen chapters of the text plus the appendixes. It includes the names of all authors of primary and secondary works and the titles of all primary works. The page numbers of the main entries for individual authors are underlined.